PRO BONO *in* PRINCIPLE *and in* PRACTICE

Pro Bono

in

Principle

and in

Practice

Public Service and the Professions

Deborah L. Rhode

STANFORD LAW AND POLITICS
An imprint of Stanford University Press
Stanford, California 2005

Stanford University Press
Stanford, California

Printed in the United States of America on acid-free,
archival-quality paper.

Library of Congress Cataloging-in-Publication Data

Rhode, Deborah L.
    Pro bono in principle and in practice : public service and the professions /
Deborah L. Rhode.
        p.   cm.
    Includes bibliographical references and index.
    ISBN 0-8047-5106-4 (cloth : acid-free paper)—
ISBN 0-8047-5107-2 (pbk. : acid-free paper)
    1. Legal assistance to the poor—United States.   I. Title.
KF336.R486   2005
347.73'17—dc22   2005004365

Original Printing 2005
Last figure below indicates year of this printing:
14   13   12   11   10   09   08   07   06   05

Designed by James P. Brommer
Typeset in 10.5/15 Minion

Contents

Acknowledgments

This book owes many debts. Crucial support and insights came from Amanda Moran, my editor at Stanford University Press, who saw from the outset what the study could and should be. Generous funding for the empirical survey came through the efforts of my Stanford colleagues Joseph Grundfest and David Mills, and from the Roberts Program in Law and Corporate Governance at Stanford Law School. Assistance with the empirical design and analysis was provided by Barbara Curran of the American Bar Foundation, by Stanford colleagues John Donohue and Deborah Hensler, and by statistician Elizabeth Cameron. Stanford librarians Paul Lomio, Sonia Moss, and Erika Wayne gave invaluable reference assistance. I am grateful to all the Stanford students who helped in compiling survey data and preparing the manuscript, particularly Nathan Doty, Carolyn Janiak, Jonathan Sanders, Angie Schwartz, and Christopher Walker. The book also benefitted greatly from colleagues who commented on earlier drafts: Cindy Adcock, John Donohue, Lawrence Friedman, Esther Lardent, and Alan Morrison. My deep appreciation goes as well to my Stanford assistant Mary Tye, who helped prepare the manuscript with exceptional skill, judgment, and good humor. Yet in this, as in all of my work, I owe my greatest debt to my husband, Ralph Cavanagh. His support and insight are what make every publication possible. And his commitment and achievements as a public interest lawyer reflect all that this book hopes to inspire.

PRO BONO *in* PRINCIPLE *and in* PRACTICE

Chapter One

The Bar's
Pro Bono Responsibilities

INTRODUCTION

The American bar's contributions of unpaid service "pro bono publico" (for the public good) often express what is most admirable in the legal profession. But not often enough. Over the course of their careers, many lawyers give generously of their time and talents to causes that would otherwise be priced out of the justice system. Some lawyers also provide significant financial support to legal aid organizations. Yet the majority do not. Most lawyers make no contributions, and the average for the bar as a whole is less than half an hour a week and fifty cents a day.[1] Moreover, much of what passes for "pro bono" is not aid to the poor or to public interest causes, but either favors for friends, family, or clients, or cases where fees turn out to be uncollectible.[2] The bar's pro bono activities are, in short, a reflection of both the profession's highest ideals and its most grating hypocrisies.

At many bar association meetings, both pro bono traditions are on display. A case in point occurred at a recent southern bar convention. Its program included a presentation of pro bono awards for exceptional service that truly was exceptional. These lawyers had made great personal sacrifices to give hundreds of hours annually in assisting impoverished clients and communities. But the ceremony also featured lavish praise for lawyers who had volunteered during the meeting for a brief community service project. Their efforts were presented as emblematic of the selfless public spirit that defines our profession. In fact, the service project involved fewer than a sixth of the lawyers present, who had sacrificed a few hours of golf or shopping in order to pick up trash in a local riverside park. The project reflected no ongoing commitment to environmental causes; the cleanup occurred only every other year when the bar met at that location. In alternate years, when the convention took place at an ocean resort, the community service project involved a sandcastle contest, with entrance fees donated to legal aid organizations. During the previous summer, the contest had reportedly raised several hundred dollars. If these efforts reflected all that is best in the legal profession, the public might draw a conclusion quite different from the one that bar leaders intended.

This book explores the aspirational principles and actual practices concerning lawyers' pro bono service. It begins with the premise that both the profession and the public have much to gain from reducing the gap between charitable ideals and practices. To that end, the book offers the first broadscale study of the factors that influence pro bono work. It includes both a comprehensive review of prior research and findings from an empirical survey drawn from some 3000 lawyers.

The book is organized to situate the bar's public service within a broader context. This opening chapter traces the evolution of attorneys' pro bono responsibilities. It reviews the history of the American bar's charitable assistance and the profession's current ethical rules and contribution levels. Chapter 2 summarizes the justifications and critiques of pro bono mandates for lawyers and law students. Chapter 3 explores the literature on altruistic commitments. It surveys the frequency and benefits of charitable involvement, as well as the individual motivations, educational experiences, and situational factors that encourage it. Discussion then turns to comparative perspectives. Chapter 4 examines public service traditions in other professions; Chapter 5 explores lawyers' pro bono work in other nations. A final section presents findings of the empirical survey and an agenda for reform. Chapter 6 focuses on the workplace and Chapter 7 on law schools. Both summarize questionnaire and interview responses from three groups: lawyers who graduated from six schools that had different approaches to pro bono work; recent individual and law firm winners of the American Bar Association's (ABA) annual Pro Bono Publico Award; and large law firms for which annual pro bono data are publicly available. The survey findings include information on the backgrounds and pro bono activities of the responding lawyers, their workplace and law school experiences, and their perceptions concerning influences on charitable involvement. Chapter 8 concludes the book by drawing on these findings, together with previous research, to propose strategies for reform. The objective is to identify changes in workplace and law school cultures that can more effectively translate public service principles into professional practices.

Society's stakes in this effort are substantial. It is a shameful irony that the country with the world's greatest concentration of lawyers has one of the least adequate systems of legal assistance. Over four-fifths of the estimated legal needs of the poor remain unmet, and the proportion of the nation's legal expenditures that goes to legal aid and public interest legal organizations is less than 1%.[3] Recent federal and state restrictions have prevented government-funded programs from assisting large categories of socially unpopular and legally vulnerable clients such as prisoners, undocumented aliens, and plaintiffs in civil rights and class action lawsuits.[4]

Without private lawyers willing to fill more of these gaps, millions of critical legal needs will go unaddressed, and urgent public interest causes will go undefended. A nation and a profession that consider themselves global leaders in human rights can and must do better. This book reminds us of those aspirations and identifies strategies for realizing them in practice.

HISTORICAL BACKGROUND: COURT-APPOINTED COUNSEL FOR THE POOR

European Traditions

The tradition of pro bono service has extended historical roots, although what exactly it has entailed remains subject to dispute. The duty to represent indigents without a fee in the Anglo-American system has been traced to practices in early Roman tribunals, medieval ecclesiastical courts, and thirteenth- to fifteenth-century Scottish and English legal proceedings. Under the Roman patron system, patrician heads of extended households assumed obligations to represent their dependents without payment.[5] Historians, however, disagree about whether this practice was truly analogous to modern pro bono work, which is intended to benefit primarily clients with whom the lawyer has no personal relationship. According to most scholars, Rome had no tradition of providing free legal assistance to the poor; rather, their plight was regarded with "some indifference" within the culture generally.[6]

A closer historical parallel to contemporary pro bono practice emerged in Great Britain. In medieval ecclesiastical courts, clerical advocates could be appointed to represent the poor, and some evidence from the ninth, tenth, and eleventh centuries suggests that they occasionally appeared in secular courts as well.[7] As the legal profession evolved in both England and Scotland during the thirteenth and fourteenth centuries, private practitioners became subject to similar obligations. Serjeants, the most elite branch of the early English legal profession, served as officers of the court in a more than nominal sense and could be denied the right of practice for refusing a court's appointment to represent an indigent litigant.[8] A more widely applicable obligation was codified in a 1495 English civil law statute, which provided for the appointment of "learned Councell" to represent paupers, and in a corresponding Scottish law of 1424.[9] It is unclear, however, how often courts actually made such appointments, and equally unclear how often appointed attorneys had to serve without compensation.[10] For its first three centuries, the English statute was highly limited in application. It covered only those whose assets totaled less than 5 pounds and who could obtain, at their own expense, an opinion by counsel that the cause was meritorious. Moreover, in some courts, only indigent plaintiffs, not defendants, were entitled to assistance.[11]

Although the power of judicial appointment was not confined to criminal cases, it was most commonly exercised in that context through a ritual known as dock briefs.[12] By payment of a token fee, indigent defendants could enlist the service of any barrister who happened to be in court while they were in the prisoner's dock for indictment, and who did not disappear before the court could make the appointment. The practice persisted because some barristers were willing to take these cases in order to gain experience and enhance their reputation.[13] Although counsel who refused to serve could in theory be held in contempt, the most systematic research available has disclosed no cases of discipline for their evasion of uncompensated appointments.[14]

Nineteenth- and Twentieth-Century American Practices

Evidence concerning the evolution of pro bono service in this country is also somewhat sketchy. Little systematic information is available about how often lawyers provided uncompensated representation, either voluntarily or as a result of court orders. Although some commentators assert that such representation was common in small-town nineteenth-century America, they generally cite no supporting research.[15] Early state and national bar ethical codes recognized no obligation to provide pro bono assistance to the poor. Until the 1970s, the closest the profession came were two exhortatory provisions in the ABA's 1908 nonbinding Canons of Professional Ethics. Canon 4 advised that "A lawyer assigned as counsel for an indigent prisoner ought not to ask to be excused for any nontrivial reason." Canon 12 suggested that "a client's poverty" might require a reduced fee or "even none at all," and that "[t]he reasonable requests [for assistance] of brother lawyers, and of their widows and orphans without ample means should receive special and kindly consideration."[16] However generous their response to widows and orphans of colleagues, lawyers' solicitude for indigent prisoners and poverty communities was generally noticeable for its absence.

The limited information available indicates that American judges have exercised authority to appoint pro bono counsel intermittently in criminal cases and infrequently in civil matters.[17] Until the mid-twentieth century, although most criminal defendants could not afford lawyers, only about a dozen states required courts to appoint counsel in all felony cases or to advise defendants of their right to request such assistance. A smaller number required appointments only in capital cases. The rest of the states gave courts discretion to appoint a lawyer or authorized them to do so when defendants affirmatively requested one. No state granted a right to counsel for appeals or for habeas corpus proceedings seeking federal review of a state conviction. Although courts occasionally exercised their inherent authority to appoint a lawyer if there appeared to be strong grounds for an appeal, unassisted defendants were seldom able to make such a showing.[18] In civil cases, courts had to determine that fundamental fairness required an attorney's assistance before appointing uncompensated counsel. Rarely was that standard met.[19]

A primary reason for the infrequency of judicial appointments was financial. As late as 1950, over half the states made no provision for paying court-appointed attorneys in non-capital cases. States that did authorize compensation set rates far below prevailing fees. In some jurisdictions, payments remained at little more than token levels, such as $5 or $10 for a felony matter. Only two states provided reimbursement for expenses such as investigation or expert witnesses. Unsurprisingly, the lawyers willing to accept court assignments under such circumstances were among the least qualified members of the bar: new entrants seeking experience or more senior attorneys who could not attract paying clients.[20] Also unsurprisingly, the adequacy of representation available under this system left much to be desired. When courts resorted to a variation of the English practice of dock briefs, the process was often as one appellate judge described it:

> [T]he [trial] judge usually picks out some lawyer who happens to be in the court. . . . The lawyer then spends a few minutes with his new client at the side of the courtroom or perhaps in an anteroom. . . . In most of such assignments, after a few minutes of conference, the defendant is advised to plead guilty and he feels he has no choice but to do so. This mock assignment of counsel and the cursory hurry-up job of a busy uncompensated lawyer makes a farce of due process of law.[21]

Not only was this system ill designed to secure competent representation, its burdens fell unequally among attorneys. Most of those drafted were criminal defense lawyers who sought paid appointments and were not the group that could most readily afford to provide uncompensated service.[22] In counties with small numbers of lawyers and inadequate indigent defense systems, the burdens on trial attorneys could be substantial, although it is doubtful that they often reached the "staggering proportions" of "slave labor" that some bar leaders denounced.[23]

CONSTITUTIONAL CHALLENGES
TO COURT APPOINTMENTS

The deficiencies of this assignment process did not escape attention. Although reported cases disclose no disciplinary actions for lawyers' failure to accept uncompensated matters, the record reveals repeated challenges to courts' appointment power.[24] Indeed, one long-standing and still common reaction to mandatory service has been a "Pavlovian [response that] it must be unconstitutional."[25] Attorneys have raised challenges to unpaid or inadequately paid appointments on several grounds:

- They constitute a "taking" of property without just compensation in violation of the Fifth Amendment to the United States Constitution and analogous provisions in state constitutions.
- They subject lawyers to "involuntary servitude" in violation of the Thirteenth Amendment.
- They force lawyers to represent positions and individuals that they find objectionable in violation of their First Amendment rights to freedom of speech and association.
- They impose special obligations on lawyers, or particular groups of lawyers, that are not shared by other professionals in violation of Fourteenth Amendment requirements of equal protection of the laws.

Just Compensation Claims

The most common, and occasionally successful, claims have been based on just compensation clauses. Although most courts have rejected such claims, a few have interpreted takings clauses in state constitutions to prevent uncompensated court appointments.[26] The United States Supreme Court has never spoken directly to the issue. But in dicta and in one summary ruling, it has implied that uncompensated state court appointments are permissible, at least for criminal cases. In *Ex Parte Sparks*, the Court summarily dismissed an appeal from an Alabama supreme court decision upholding the state's mandatory assignment system for indigent criminal defense.[27] The rationale for permitting such a system seems clear from earlier just compensation rulings. In those prior cases, the Court had reasoned that "[t]he Fifth Amendment does not require that the Government pay for the performance of a public duty it is already owed," and that attorneys, as "officers of the court," are "bound to render service when required."[28] One influential federal appellate court decision offered an alternative ground for rejecting just compensation claims. In this court's view,

> an applicant for admission to practice law may justly be deemed to be aware of the traditions of the profession which he is joining, and to know that one of these traditions is that a lawyer is an officer of the court obligated to represent indigents for little or no compensation upon court order. Thus, the lawyer has consented to, and assumed, this obligation.[29]

With respect to appointments in civil cases, the United States Supreme Court has avoided squarely resolving the issue of judicial power. In the only case on point, *Mallard v. United States District Court for Southern District of Iowa*, a majority of Justices concluded that a statute authorizing the federal judiciary to "request an attorney to represent" indigents does not grant judges the power to compel such representation. However, a closely divided Court expressly reserved the question of whether the judiciary has authority to compel indigent representation as part of its "inherent power" to regulate matters pertaining to the justice system. A majority of justices wrote or joined separate opinions confirming that authority.[30]

Most lower state and federal courts that have addressed the question have agreed that they have discretion to appoint counsel, although some have strained to find a basis for awarding compensation in appropriate cases.[31] In one leading decision, *Family Division Trial Lawyers v. Moultrie*, the circuit court of appeals for the District of Columbia considered constitutional challenges to a pro bono plan involving lawyers who sought statutorily compensated work in juvenile delinquency cases. Attorneys were informed that if they declined pro bono appointments for indigent parents in other juvenile matters, they would no longer receive assignments for compensated cases. The lawyers contended that the system violated both the Thirteenth Amendment ban on involuntary servitude and the takings clause of the Fifth Amendment. In rejecting the first claim, the court noted that no attorneys were subject to "forced labor"; they could simply stop requesting compensated appointments. With respect to the just compensation argument, the court of appeals rejected the argument that *any* uncompensated services constituted a "taking." However, it remanded for a determination of whether the amount of work demanded was so "unreasonable" that it effectively denied lawyers "the opportunity to maintain a remunerative practice" in the D.C. system and therefore violated their constitutional rights.[32]

The *Moultrie* court's analysis is consistent with other judicial decisions on pro bono requirements, as well as with a prior line of Supreme Court takings cases. According to a leading opinion by Justice Oliver Wendell Holmes, once the diminution of property value reaches "a certain magnitude," the government must provide just compensation.[33] In subsequent decisions, the Court has suggested that this "certain magnitude" is reached when the exercise of state power will "frustrate distinct investment-backed expectations." It is not reached if the owner is still capable of realizing a reasonable profit on the investment.[34] In another line of cases involving regulatory schemes, the Court has reasoned that where the state has provided a "reciprocity" of burdens and benefits, there is no taking because the economic harm is linked to an economic advantage.[35] Such reasoning underlies state court decisions finding that pro bono requirements are a reasonable condition of the privileges of legal practice as long as the required service is not unreasonable, but that compensation is necessary if the service is substantial and imposes considerable hardship.[36]

Involuntary Servitude Claims

Lawyers' second constitutional claim is that coerced representation constitutes a form of involuntary servitude in violation of the Thirteenth Amendment. Although a few courts have agreed, almost never do they or the plaintiffs making that claim engage in any serious analysis of the history of this post–Civil War amendment or the decisions interpreting it.[37] Judges who have engaged in such analysis have consistently rejected attorneys' involuntary servitude challenges. As a well-established line of Supreme Court precedents makes clear, the "term involuntary servitude was intended to cover those forms of compulsory labor akin to African slavery."[38] In effect, the amendment encompasses only service enforced by physical restraint.[39] As long as failure to provide the required labor does not result in loss of liberty, no constitutional violation has occurred. Accordingly, most lower courts have reasoned that if the sanctions for noncompliance with pro bono obligations involve only fines or loss of the license to practice, lawyers are not subject to involuntary servitude; they can "choose freedom."[40]

An alternative basis for rejecting Thirteenth Amendment challenges lies in another line of legal precedents upholding reasonable mandatory service to fulfill a public duty or to meet a public need. On this reasoning, courts have sustained a wide variety of work requirements, including everything from military service and highway construction labor to student community service and cafeteria duties.[41] According to most courts and commentators, because representation of indigents has long been viewed as a public need and professional responsibility and is recognized as such in the bar's own ethical codes, involuntary servitude challenges are unconvincing.[42]

Equal Protection Claims

A further constitutional claim is that requirements of pro bono representation violate the Fourteenth Amendment requirement of "equal protection of the laws" by imposing an obligation on lawyers that is not shared by other professionals. If that obligation falls disproportionately on certain groups of lawyers, it raises additional equal protection concerns.[43] Although such objections have generally been unsuccessful in the courts, they have been effective in campaigns to block adoption of proposed pro bono requirements. For example, critics raised strong equal protection concerns about a mandatory New York plan that would have allowed lawyers to substitute cash contributions for personal service, and would have permitted law firms to satisfy their members' obligations collectively, by designating a few attorneys to fulfill their colleagues' responsibilities.[44] In opponents' view, any proposal mandating cash contributions from lawyers was objectionable because many nonlawyers were equally well situated to provide financial assistance that would expand legal representation of the poor. Moreover, the proposed plan would have imposed special hardships on the solo practitioners and small-firm lawyers who would not have been able either to buy their way out of service obligations or to pass them on to others.

Similar equal protection challenges have been raised against mandatory court-appointment systems that draft only practitioners in certain specialties or attorneys who seek paid assignments.[45]

Some of those equity concerns may be convincing on policy grounds, as Chapter 2 suggests, but they are unpersuasive as constitutional claims. Courts have consistently held that a requirement imposed only on certain professionals is permissible as long as it is rationally related to a legitimate state objective.[46] Because professionals are not a suspect class, and because reasonable regulatory obligations do not infringe any fundamental interest, they need not satisfy more demanding strict scrutiny standards. Under the rational relationship test, wide latitude is available for professional regulatory structures. Decision makers may "deal with the different professions according to the needs of the public in relation to each."[47] Given the strong public need for legal services, courts and commentators have generally concluded that reasonable pro bono requirements are rationally related to legitimate state objectives and raise no valid equal protection concerns.

First Amendment Claims

First Amendment claims have fared no better. In essence, critics of pro bono obligations have argued that requiring attorneys to represent a client whom they find objectionable violates their rights to freedom of speech and association. The primary doctrinal basis for this claim is the Supreme Court's decision in *Keller v. State Bar Association of California*, which held that mandatory bar dues cannot be used to support political or ideological positions.[48] Generalizing from this decision, opponents of pro bono argue that lawyers cannot be compelled to support specified clients or causes as a condition of practicing law.[49]

The main problem with such arguments is that they fundamentally misrepresent the nature of the lawyer's role and the degree of coercion in pro bono service. As bar ethical codes have long maintained, "a lawyer's representation of a client, including representation by appointment, does not constitute an endorsement of the client's political, economic, social or moral views or activities."[50] Moreover, the proposed pro bono plans to which critics have objected have offered a range of service options and an opportunity to provide cash assistance as an alternative to direct representation. Such plans are readily distinguishable from the bar dues requirement in *Keller,* which gave lawyers no choice in the causes that their funds would support. Accordingly, most experts have agreed that well-designed pro bono obligations pose no serious threat to First Amendment interests.[51]

Although none of the constitutional challenges to pro bono requirements seems well founded, their frequency over the past century reflects a level of opposition that has undermined public service initiatives. The prevailing view within the profession has been that unmet legal needs should be addressed through voluntary efforts and government-subsidized programs. Yet as the following discussion makes clear, only in recent years has the organized bar provided significant support for either approach, and current contribution levels leave much to be desired.

The Evolution of Voluntary Pro Bono Contributions and Bar Ethical Rules

Bar leaders have long maintained that assistance to those who cannot afford it is a basic responsibility of all lawyers and a central feature of professional identity. However, that view has not been widely shared among the rank and file.[52] For most of its history, the legal profession has neither provided a substantial amount of voluntary pro bono service to the poor nor supported organizations that have done so.

Legal Aid Contributions

The first American legal aid societies were founded in the late nineteenth century with support from local charities and municipal governments— and with little assistance from the profession.[53] In 1919, Reginald Heber Smith published a landmark study, *Justice and the Poor,* which reported a total of only about 40 legal aid organizations with some 60 full-time attorneys and a combined budget of about $200,000 for the entire country. Little of this money came from the bar. Fewer than 10% of the lawyers in any surveyed city contributed support, and in some metropolitan areas, the proportion was only 2% or 3%.[54] A representative Chicago campaign in 1913 found only twenty firms willing to donate at least $250 for legal services; the New York Legal Aid Society's 1934 effort yielded support from only 229 of the city's some 17,000 attorneys. In other metropolitan areas, after much debate and dispute, bar associations contributed only token amounts, on the order of $100. As late as 1950, only about 9% of legal aid funding came from the profession. The majority was from local charities, supplemented by private donors.[55] Most attorneys were no more generous with their time than with their funds. Although the National Bar Association, founded in 1925 by African-American attorneys, made efforts to enlist pro bono assistance for free legal clinics in the early part of the twentieth century, few other bar organizations made promoting such public service a priority.[56] As Smith noted with frustration, "the majority of our judges and lawyers view the situation with indifference. They fail to see behind the denial of justice the suffering and tragedy which it causes."[57]

During the mid-twentieth century, the bar sought to encourage greater pro bono involvement. Part of the motivation was to prevent the government from responding to pervasive unmet needs by loosening the rules against practice by nonlawyers or by significantly increasing public funding for civil legal aid. Initially, the organized bar opposed such funding out of concern that government subsidies would lead to government control and result in the functional equivalent of socialized medicine.[58] By the mid-1960s, a growing concern about poverty within the culture generally and the profession in particular increased support both for government-subsidized aid and lawyer pro bono assistance. The value of such assistance in turn increased as the poor acquired more legal entitlements. And as the profession became more diverse and socially conscious, more lawyers and law students demanded public service opportunities.[59]

The Code of Professional Responsibility

This growing support for pro bono initiatives found recognition in the ABA's new Code of Professional Responsibility, adopted in the 1970s. Several of its aspirational Ethical Considerations address lawyers' obligations to broaden access to the legal system. Most explicitly, Ethical Consideration 2-25 provides:

Historically, the need for legal services of those unable to pay reasonable fees has been met in part by lawyers who donated their services or accepted court appointments on behalf of such individuals. The basic responsibility for providing legal services for those unable to pay ultimately rests upon the individual lawyer, and personal involvement in the problems of the disadvantaged can be one of the most rewarding experiences in the life of a lawyer. Every lawyer, regardless of professional prominence or professional workload, should find time to participate in serving the disadvantaged. . . . [It has also] been necessary for the profession to institute additional programs to provide legal services. . . . Every lawyer should support all proper efforts to meet this need for legal services.

No disciplinary rule reinforces this "basic responsibility," and the rewards of aiding the disadvantaged have proven inadequate to the occasion. Ironically enough, the growth in government-subsidized legal aid during the 1970s removed some of the impetus for assistance from the private bar.[60] Although systematic information on pro bono contributions is lacking, one representative study found that lawyers from the most generous firms provided only about five hours a year.[61] In another mid-1970s survey, the average investment was only about 6% of billable hours, and only about 5% of this work went to legal aid and indigent criminal defense.[62] Few lawyers reported any involvement in law reform; most pro bono service benefitted friends, relatives, and employees of lawyers and their clients, or bar associations and middle- and upper-middle-class organizations such as Jaycees, Little Leagues, garden clubs, and symphonies.[63]

The inadequacy of the bar's response did not escape notice, particularly in light of growing evidence about the scope of unmet legal needs. Those needs escalated during the 1980s, after the Republican administration's cutbacks in federal funding for legal aid. State and national surveys consistently found that about four-fifths of the civil legal problems of the poor remained unaddressed, and that many of the near poor were also priced out of the justice system.[64] Although such evidence helped convince the profession to intensify its lobbying for government-funded legal aid offices, it was also apparent that they could address only a small part of the need. To help fill the gap, the organized bar dramatically expanded its voluntary pro bono programs. Between 1980 and 1990, the number of such programs grew from 50 to over 600.[65]

Bar leaders also began to call for more demanding ethical rules governing pro bono service. In 1977, a Special ABA Committee on Public Interest Practice issued a report calling on state and local bar associations to take an active role in supporting pro bono work. The report also endorsed the concept of a quantifiable, although still aspirational, minimum obligation. Partly in response to the ABA initiative, bar leaders in California and New York issued proposals calling for modest levels of required public service, on the order of 30 to 50 hours per year. These proposals met with overwhelming opposition and were unceremoniously withdrawn.[66]

The Model Rules of Professional Conduct

Controversy continued at the national level during the early 1980s in debates over the ABA's new Model Rules of Professional Conduct, which were intended to replace the outdated Code of Professional Responsibility. The commission charged with drafting the Model Rules initially proposed a requirement that lawyers provide a minimum of 40 hours of work per year at no fee or reduced fee, or the financial equivalent, to persons of limited means or to organizations assisting them.[67] Outraged opposition prompted the commission to propose instead that lawyers simply make an annual report of pro bono work, and that the rule leave unspecified what would qualify as "pro bono."[68] Even this minimal obligation proved unacceptable.[69] Opinion polls found that about four-fifths of the bar opposed any pro bono requirement.[70] As originally adopted, Rule 6.1 simply provided that "A lawyer should render public interest legal service. A lawyer may discharge this responsibility by providing professional services at no fee or a reduced fee to persons of limited means or to public service or charitable groups or organizations, or by service in activities for improving the law, the legal system or the legal profession."[71] Over the past two decades, efforts to strengthen pro bono ethical standards have come and gone, but mainly gone. In 1993, the ABA again rejected the possibility of mandatory service, but it did amend Rule 6.1 to quantify an aspirational contribution of 50 hours per year. In 2002, the ABA further emphasized that every lawyer has pro bono obligations and a professional responsibility to provide legal services to those who cannot afford them. As modified, Rule 6.1 provides that:

> Every lawyer has a professional responsibility to provide legal services to those unable to pay. A lawyer should aspire to render at least (50) hours of pro bono publico legal services per year. In fulfilling this responsibility, the lawyer should:
>
> (a) provide a substantial majority of the (50) hours of legal services without fee or expectation of fee to:
>
> (1) persons of limited means or
>
> (2) charitable, religious, civic, community, governmental and educational organizations in matters which are designed primarily to address the needs of persons of limited means; and
>
> (b) provide any additional services through:
>
> (1) delivery of legal services at no fee or substantially reduced fee to individuals, groups or organizations seeking to secure or protect civil rights, civil liberties or public rights, or charitable, religious, civic, community, governmental and educational organizations in matters in furtherance of their organizational purposes, where the payment of standard legal fees would significantly deplete the organization's economic resources or would be otherwise inappropriate;
>
> (2) delivery of legal services at a substantially reduced fee to persons of limited means; or
>
> (3) participation in activities for improving the law, the legal system or the legal profession.
>
> In addition, a lawyer should voluntarily contribute financial support to organizations that provide legal services to persons of limited means.

The Comment to the Rule adds that "when it is not feasible for a lawyer to engage in pro bono services," the lawyer may instead contribute "financial support to organizations providing free legal services to persons of limited means" or may "satisfy the pro bono responsibility collectively, as by a firm's aggregate pro bono activities." The financial support should be "reasonably equivalent to the value of the hours of service that would have otherwise been provided." To underscore the purely aspirational nature of the Rule, the ABA added the term "voluntary" to its title and language to its Comment, emphasizing that the "responsibility set forth in this Rule is not intended to be enforced through [the] disciplinary process."[72]

Again in 2001, the ABA's Ethics 2000 Commission rejected proposals for mandatory pro bono service or an annual reporting requirement. The only changes ultimately adopted were the addition of a sentence to the Rule emphasizing that "every lawyer has a professional responsibility to provide legal services to those unable to pay" and a sentence to the Comment indicating that "law firms should act reasonably to enable all lawyers in the firm to provide the pro bono services called for in this Rule."[73]

Reform efforts at the state level have paralleled the national experience. Over the last decade, almost half the states have amended their pro bono rules.[74] Many jurisdictions have considered mandatory responsibilities but only four have adopted any. Florida, Maryland, and Nevada require lawyers to report their voluntary pro bono contributions.[75] New Jersey requires lawyers to accept court appointments in cases involving indigents, but it exempts practitioners in specified categories such as prosecutors, public defenders, legal aid attorneys, and individuals who have contributed 25 hours a year of pro bono legal assistance to the poor through qualifying legal aid organizations.[76]

Other states vary in their approaches, although it is by no means clear whether the differences in aspirational rules make for differences in actual practices. Two states (California and Oregon) have no pro bono provisions in their ethical codes, and two others (Illinois and Massachusetts) recognize the obligation only in their code preambles.[77] About half of all jurisdictions have a rule similar to the 1983 version of Model Rule 6.1, which provides a highly elastic definition of pro bono work and specifies no quantifiable level of contribution; these jurisdictions count reduced-fee assistance to any client as well as services to improve the law, the legal system, or the legal profession.[78] States that establish more specific standards generally suggest between 20 and 50 hours of aid, or a minimum number of cases; the average recommended commitment is 43 hours.[79] Only one state limits the definition of pro bono work to legal services for the poor; other jurisdictions have more inclusive definitions, typically along the lines of the 1993 Model Rule version, which encompasses almost any public service.[80] About a quarter of the states permit financial contributions to a legal aid organization as a full or partial alternative to personal assistance.[81]

Despite the absence of ethical rules requiring pro bono service, local courts have occasionally exercised their inherent power to appoint uncompensated counsel, generally in criminal cases where a funding appropriation runs out or where fees are set too low to attract enough volunteers.[82] A few county courts also have established mandatory programs, either for the entire local bar or for lawyers in a particular field such as family law.[83] Such programs have attracted little sustained opposition, which may be attributable to the minimal number of hours or practitioners involved and the absence of any sanction process. As the preceding discussion noted, the scope of judicial authority to compel service remains unsettled, but most courts and commentators agree that a reasonable level of mandatory assistance is constitutionally permissible. The primary constraint on judicial initiatives has been political rather than doctrinal. Particularly at the state level, where judges are elected, few have been willing to antagonize lawyers who provide crucial campaign support.

The Extent of Pro Bono Work

Bar Initiatives

Over the past decade, many courts and bar associations, along with private and public sector employers, have made increasing efforts to institutionalize voluntary pro bono service. It is now the dominant method of assisting underserved groups.[84] All but a few states have some statewide pro bono agency, and many state supreme courts have established structures to identify and address unmet legal needs.[85] An executive order issued under the Clinton administration has directed federal agencies to "develop appropriate programs to encourage and facilitate pro bono legal and other volunteer services."[86] So too, many state governors, attorneys general, and agency heads have established policies encouraging and identifying pro bono service opportunities.[87] Both national and local organizations such as the Pro Bono

Institute at Georgetown University Law Center and the New York Volunteers of Legal Service recruit law firms and corporate employers to pledge a specified number of hours of pro bono work. The Institute's Pro Bono Challenge requires law firms to contribute an amount of time equivalent to 3% or 5% of firm revenues to causes and clients that meet the Model Rule's definition; the New York Volunteers of Legal Service requires 30 hours per lawyer.[88] A number of Web sites, including one cosponsored by the Pro Bono Institute and the American Corporate Counsel Association, match lawyers with organizations needing volunteers.[89] Virtually all bar associations give annual awards that recognize pro bono work, at least one voluntary association (Orange County, Florida) mandates a contribution of time or money, and the ABA's Pro Bono Center provides assistance to more than 1000 programs.[90] Major lawyers' periodicals like the *American Lawyer* and the *National Law Journal* also publish law firm rankings and profiles of outstanding contributors.[91] And the National Association for Law Placement Directory of Legal Employers now includes comprehensive information about pro bono programs.

Participation Rates

Yet despite such initiatives, a wide gap remains between pro bono aspirations and practices. No comprehensive national data exist on the extent of lawyers' pro bono contributions. Full information is difficult to come by because only three states mandate reporting of contribution levels, and other states with voluntary reporting systems have low response rates ranging between 3% and 33%.[92] Moreover, the definition of pro bono in both required and voluntary systems is generally expansive and ambiguous, and lawyers often stretch its scope to include work for which they expected to be paid but which turned out to be uncompensated or undercompensated.[93] Many attorneys also count services for friends, family members, bar associations, and organizations that could afford to pay for services.[94] For example, New York lawyers claim among the highest participation rates in the country. Almost half (47%) report engaging in pro bono work, but three-quarters include assisting a close friend or relative.[95] An Oklahoma questionnaire on volunteer activity that asked for average weekly hours spent on civic/community/pro bono/charitable work would include teaching Sunday school, coaching soccer, and serving on opera boards.[96]

In most jurisdictions, participation rates in pro bono activity, variously defined, range between 15% to 18%, and of those who participate, contributions range from an average of 42 hours per year in New York to a median of 20 hours in Texas.[97] The highest participation rate, 52%, is in Florida, the only state that both requires reporting of contributions and makes the information publicly available.[98] When adjusted for the number of lawyers who make no contributions, hourly assistance ranges from an average of 20 hours in New York and 18 hours in Florida to a median of 5 in Texas. Less than 10% of practitioners accept referrals from federally funded legal aid offices or bar-sponsored poverty-related programs.[99] Only two-fifths of surveyed in-house legal departments participate in pro bono work, and the average yearly commitment is less than 8 hours per legal department employee.[100] Most lawyers are no more charitable with their money than their time. Reported financial contributions range from an average of $82 per year in New York to $34 per year in Florida.[101] In short, the best available research finds that American lawyers average less than half an hour of work per week and under half a dollar per day in support of pro bono legal assistance.

Public service programs involving the profession's most affluent members reflect a particularly dispiriting distance between the bar's idealized image and actual practices. In Silicon Valley, during a period of rapid revenue growth, almost no firms managed to meet the modest 30 annual-hours-per-lawyer average that used to be the accepted minimum.[102] Only a third of the nation's large law firms have accepted the Pro Bono Challenge, and only about 60% have met its standard, which requires contributions equivalent to 3% to 5% of gross revenues.[103] Fewer than 30 firms have achieved the New York Volunteers' goal of 30 hours.[104] And only 18 of the nation's 100 most financially successful firms meet the Model Rules' standard of 50 hours per year of pro bono service.[105] The approximately 50,000 lawyers at these firms averaged less than 10 minutes per day on pro bono activities.[106] At many of those firms, the vast majority of charitable assistance comes from associates; few partners set an example by providing or supervising pro bono service.[107]

Influences on Participation

What is equally dispiriting is that pro bono participation bears little relation to the ability to afford it. Rates do not necessarily improve in times of greatest prosperity. During a decade when the average revenues of the 100 most profitable firms increased by over 50%, their average pro bono hours dropped by a third.[108] Although pro bono contributions by these firms increased slightly after the 9/11 terrorist attack, the growth has been modest.[109] Clearly, market forces have some effect on volunteer activity, but the relationship is more complicated than is often assumed. Neither a good economy nor a bad economy is necessarily better for pro bono. When demand for legal services is strong, many lawyers believe that they or their firms are too busy with paying work to take time for volunteer activity. Conversely, when times are hard, many view pro bono service as a luxury they cannot afford.[110]

As law firm surveys reflect, pro bono work is determined less by economic imperatives than institutional priorities. A strong commitment is clearly not inconsistent with commercial success. A significant number of the nation's most profitable firms have high participation levels.[111] Some evidence suggests that, at least for large firms, pro bono participation is positively correlated with financial success.[112] Indeed, as Chapter 2 makes clear, public service often yields long-term economic benefits to those who provide it. Yet neither self-interest nor societal interests have appeared sufficient to motivate most lawyers to make substantial pro bono contributions. To encourage greater involvement, bar leaders and legal educators have called on law schools to play a greater role in socializing students to view public service as a professional responsibility.

The Development of Law School Pro Bono Programs

Historical Background

Pro bono programs in law schools are a relatively recent development. Before the last two decades, students interested in law-related volunteer work generally had to identify service opportunities themselves.[113] Schools provided little administrative support, and most exposure to public interest causes and low-income clients occurred in clinical courses, externships, or summer jobs. In the late 1980s, a growing number of faculty, administrators, and students, as well as bar leaders, began encouraging law schools to do more to promote public service. Tulane instituted the first law school pro bono requirement in 1987.[114] Over the next 15 years, most schools developed formal pro bono programs.

Several initiatives encouraged that trend. In 1990, an association that later became Pro Bono Students America created a clearinghouse that began matching students with volunteer opportunities in public interest organizations. The association initially targeted students at its host institution, New York University School of Law, and then expanded to include students and organizations throughout the state, the nation, and the international community.[115] In 1996, the ABA amended its accreditation standards to provide that every law school "should encourage its students to participate in pro bono activities and provide opportunities for them to do so."[116] The revised standards also encouraged schools to address the obligations of faculty to the public, including participation in pro bono activities.[117] In 1997, the Association of American Law Schools (AALS) appointed a Commission on Pro Bono and Public Service Opportunities in Law Schools. The Commission's Report and Recommendations helped lead to the creation of an AALS Section on Pro Bono and Public Service, and a follow-up AALS Pro Bono Project that provided technical support to individual schools.[118] The section now has over 400 members.[119]

Law School Programs

These initiatives were partly responsible for a dramatic increase in law school pro bono programs. Fifteen years after the first requirement was instituted, a survey of 147 ABA-accredited schools found that about a fifth of responding schools had instituted pro bono/public service requirements; about half (83 of 147) had developed formal, administratively supported voluntary programs, and about a quarter were relying on student groups to provide opportunities.[120] Only about 10% of schools had no organized pro bono programs.

The scope and content of current programs vary considerably. Of schools that require service (30 of 147), about half have an hourly minimum, ranging from 20 to 70 hours, in placements for which students receive no academic credit or pay, or limited credit. A few of these requirements count nonlegal community service as well as legal work. Another half of the schools that mandate pro bono participation include internships, externships, and courses bearing credit. Some of these programs require that the work occur only in for-credit clinics. A few schools count classes in poverty law or independent study, and one includes nonlegal community service. Two schools that have a mandatory program, Tulane and the University of Pennsylvania, were part of the empirical survey described in Chapter 6.[121]

Among the schools with formal voluntary pro bono programs (83 of 147), four-fifths have a referral system with a coordinator or group of coordinators. These coordinators or advisors are responsible for developing, promoting, and monitoring pro bono placements. Some of these coordinators provide individual counseling. Others maintain lists of opportunities, and many offer administrative support. This category includes Yale, another of the participants in the empirical survey.[122] The remaining schools have an alternative voluntary approach, which is to provide substantial administrative support for student-run programs. These programs often work in partnership with outside organizations. The support provided by the schools ranges from full-time staffing of a center to substantial administrative assistance. Fordham, another survey participant, has such an approach.[123] A third model, which a quarter of schools follow (34 of 147), relies on student-run associations. Most of these associations have a faculty supervisor or a partnership with an outside organization, and some raise their own funds.[124] A final group of schools lacks an organized pro bono program. Two schools in this survey, Chicago and Northwestern, fell into this category during the time period the survey covered. Chicago subsequently began relying on independent student groups, and Northwestern has developed a referral system with a coordinator.

Student and Faculty Participation

Comprehensive recent data on voluntary student involvement are lacking. However, pro bono administrators interviewed for the AALS Commission Report estimated that only about a quarter to a third of the students at their schools participated, and that average time commitments were quite limited.[125] Some student involvement was at token levels and seemed intended primarily as résumé padding.[126] Accordingly, the Commission concluded that the majority of students graduated without pro bono legal work as part of their educational experience.[127] Although some schools have strengthened their pro bono programs and a few have instituted requirements since the Commission issued its report, no evidence suggests that voluntary student involvement rates have changed dramatically. Most schools remain a considerable distance from meeting the Commission recommendation that every institution "make available to all students at least once during their law school careers a well-supervised law-related pro bono opportunity and either require the students' participation or find ways to attract the great majority of students to volunteer."[128]

Quantitative information on faculty pro bono service is unavailable, but impressionistic accounts suggest room for improvement here as well. Few schools require contributions by faculty, and fewer still impose substantial or specific levels.[129] Even policies that mandate faculty participation do not specify sanctions for noncompliance, which often leads professors to view the requirements as "aspirational."[130] In the AALS Commission survey, only half of administrators agreed that "many" faculty at their schools were providing "good role models to the students by engaging in uncompensated pro bono service themselves."[131] And those administrators often added that many other faculty were not.[132]

Yet improving pro bono programs does not appear to be a priority at most schools. About two-thirds of deans responding to the AALS Commission survey expressed satisfaction with the level of pro bono participation by students and faculty at their law schools.[133] Given the limited number of students involved at most institutions, the inadequate role of faculty, and the strong justifications for broad pro bono involvement, so much satisfaction is itself unsatisfying.

For most of its history, the American bar has resisted seeing pro bono service as a professional obligation. Until relatively recently, organized pro bono programs were generally noticeable for their absence in legal education and legal workplaces. Although support for public service has grown dramatically over the last two decades, most practitioners have yet to embrace the view, set forth in bar ethical codes, that "every lawyer has a professional responsibility to provide legal services to those unable to pay."[134] Why lawyers should assume that responsibility, in practice as well as in principle, is the subject of this book.

Chapter Two

The Rationale for
Pro Bono Responsibilities

The rationale for pro bono work rests on two central claims. One involves the value to society of addressing unmet legal needs and the profession's responsibility to contribute to that effort. A second justification involves the value to lawyers, individually and collectively, of such pro bono contributions. Both have proven controversial. Critics first question why law, and why lawyers. Why should legal needs assume priority over other social welfare concerns in allocating charitable assistance? Why should lawyers bear distinctive burdens that other occupations do not share? If access to law is a societal interest, why shouldn't society pay its cost? Critics also question the value to lawyers of a public service responsibility that they are unwilling or incompetent to assume. These challenges take on additional force if the responsibility is mandatory rather than aspirational. No significant increase in pro bono work is likely to occur without effective responses to these concerns.

Society's Justifications for Pro Bono Service

Access to Law

Society's justification for pro bono assistance starts from the premise that access to law is a fundamental interest and that the legal profession has some obligation to help make law available. As the Supreme Court has recognized in other contexts, the right to sue and defend is the right that protects all other rights.[1] Access to law is particularly critical for the poor, who often depend on legal entitlements for basic goods and services, such as food, housing, education, and medical care. Yet a wide gap remains between the rights available in theory and those available in practice. An estimated four-fifths of the individual civil legal needs of the poor remain unmet.[2] Moreover, these estimates do not include many collective interests for which attorneys' services are often crucial, such as environmental quality, voting rights, or educational opportunities. Nor do these assessments count post-conviction criminal proceedings, in which government-subsidized lawyers are frequently unavailable.[3]

Existing legal services and public interest organizations can address only a fraction of these concerns. Fewer than 1% of lawyers are in legal aid practice, which works out to about one lawyer for every 1400 poor or near-poor persons in the United States. The United States spends only about $2.25 per capita on legal assistance, a ludicrously inadequate amount for the seventh of the population that is eligible for assistance.[4] Organizations that receive federal funding are barred from representing entire categories of the most politically unpopular and legally vulnerable causes, such as those involving prisoners, undocumented aliens, abortions, and welfare reform.[5] And public interest legal organizations lack the staff and resources to handle more than a small fraction of unrepresented public interests.[6] The result is that millions of Americans suffer untold misery because legal protections that are available in principle are inaccessible in practice. Domestic violence victims cannot obtain protective orders, elderly medical patients cannot collect health benefits, disabled children are denied educational services, defrauded consumers lack affordable remedies . . . The list is long, and the costs are incalculable.

Moreover, those costs involve not just injuries to individuals; the lack of legal assistance also threatens broader values. In a democratic society, equality before the law is central to the rule of law and to the legitimacy of the state. Social science research confirms what political theorists have long argued: public confidence in legal processes depends heavily on opportunities for direct participation.[7] So too the legitimacy of American adversarial processes depends on some measure of representation for both sides to a controversy. As a Joint Conference of the Association of American Law Schools and the American Bar Association put it,

> The moral position of the advocate is here at stake. Partisan advocacy finds its justification in the contribution it makes to a sound and informed disposition of controversies. Where this contribution is lacking, the partisan position permitted to the advocate loses its reason for being. The profession has therefore a clear moral obligation to see to it that those already handicapped do not suffer the cumulative disadvantage of being without proper legal representation, for it is obvious that adjudication can neither be effective nor fair where only one side is represented by counsel.[8]

Access to Lawyers

In most circumstances, access to law is meaningless without access to lawyers. The American justice system has been designed by and for the legal profession, and individuals who attempt to navigate without counsel are generally at a disadvantage. That disadvantage is particularly great among the poor, who typically lack the skills and information necessary for effective self-representation. Researchers consistently find that "pro se" litigants (parties who represent themselves without counsel) on average do substantially less well than those with attorneys.[9] Inequalities in legal representation compound other social inequalities and undermine commitments to procedural fairness and social justice. A prominent New York report on pro bono put it bluntly: "we cannot promise due process but raise insurmountable obstacles to those who seek it."[10]

Because access to law so often requires access to lawyers, they bear a particular responsibility for helping to make legal services available. As courts and commentators have long noted, the state grants lawyers special privileges that entail special obligations. In the United States, attorneys have a much more extensive monopoly over the provision of most legal assistance than attorneys in other countries.[11] The American legal profession is responsible for creating and guarding that prerogative, and its success in restricting lay competition has helped to price services beyond the reach of millions of consumers.[12] Some pro bono contribution is not unreasonable in return for lawyers' privileged status.[13]

An alternative rationale for imposing special obligations on lawyers stems from their historic role as officers of the court and their unique contribution to our governance structure.[14] What exactly the "officer of the court" designation entails is subject to dispute. However, many courts and commentators have viewed public service in general, and representation of indigents in particular, as central to professional identity.[15] As a prominent New York bar report explained, much of what lawyers do "is about providing *justice*, [which is] . . . nearer to the heart of our way of life . . . than services provided by other professionals. The legal profession serves as [an] indispensable guardian of our lives, liberties and governing principles. . . . Like no other professionals, lawyers are charged with the responsibility for systemic improvement of not only their own profession, but of the law and society itself."[16]

Because lawyers occupy such a crucial role in our governance system, there is also particular value in exposing them to how that system functions, or fails to function, for the have-nots. Pro bono work offers many attorneys their only direct contact with what passes for justice among the poor. Giving broad segments of the bar some experience with poverty-related problems and public interest causes can lay crucial foundations for change. Pro bono programs have often launched social reform initiatives and strengthened support for government subsidies of legal aid.[17] Because the private bar often has greater independence than public sector lawyers, and greater resources for large-scale litigation than financially strapped public interest organizations, it serves a crucial role in promoting otherwise underrepresented social concerns.

THE PROFESSION'S JUSTIFICATIONS FOR PRO BONO SERVICE

Benefits to Lawyers

A further rationale for pro bono work rests on benefits to lawyers individually and collectively. As with the other forms of volunteer activity noted earlier, pro bono participation brings a range of professional and personal rewards. Particularly for young attorneys, such work can provide valuable training, contacts, trial experience, and leadership opportunities.[18] Through pro bono assistance, lawyers can develop new areas of expertise and demonstrate marketable skills. Involvement in community groups, charitable organizations, high-visibility litigation, and other public interest activities is a way for attorneys to expand their perspectives, enhance their reputations, and attract paying clients.[19]

Lawyers also report the same kinds of psychological rewards from service that motivate other volunteer activities. Pro bono work can be a way to "give back," to promote social justice, and to make an immediate positive difference in someone's life.[20] For many private practitioners, whose paid work is predominantly commercial, pro bono work can express the values that directed them to legal careers in the first instance. When such public service options are lacking, lawyers pay a price, both personally and professionally. American Bar Association (ABA) surveys consistently find that lawyers' greatest dissatisfaction with their practice is a lack of "contribution to the social good."[21] Pro bono work can provide that contribution. As the pro bono director of one Wall Street firm noted, "lawyers talk about their [pro bono] work in a way they've never done before. People say, 'This is the best day of my life.'"[22]

Benefits to Legal Employers

By promoting the professional growth, reputation, and satisfaction of individual lawyers, participation in public service also serves the interests of their employers. Lack of career development opportunities is one of the main reasons that lawyers change jobs.[23] Although relatively few surveyed lawyers cite inadequate support for pro bono work as a major explanation for leaving a position, the opportunity for such work may be an important part of why other lawyers stay; it can significantly enhance the quality of their professional lives.[24] Some lawyers and law students also consider pro bono opportunities in the choice of employment settings; as Chapter 6 suggests, more might do so if reliable comparative information about workplace practices were readily available. Strong public service programs can produce tangible, although hard to quantify, employer benefits in terms of retention, recruitment, and job performance.[25] As one winner of a bar pro bono award noted, such activity is an "enormous morale booster for the entire firm," including staff as well as attorneys.[26] "Everyone feels that they touched a life. . . . No office picnics or parties can give you that."[27]

Benefits to the Profession

Pro bono activity is also a way to enhance the reputation of lawyers as a group. In one representative survey, which asked what could improve the image of lawyers, the response most often chosen was their provision of free legal services to the needy; two-thirds of Americans indicated that it would improve their opinion of the profession.[28] In another survey, almost half of those responding thought that lawyers did not contribute enough to their communities through donations of time, legal services, or money. Only a quarter disagreed.[29]

For all these reasons, the vast majority of surveyed lawyers believe that the bar should provide pro bono services.[30] However, as noted earlier, only a minority in fact provide significant assistance, few of their efforts aid low-income clients, and the vast majority oppose mandatory service requirements that would improve that record.[31]

OPPOSITION TO PRO BONO SERVICE

The gap between aspirational principles and actual practice reflects a number of factors. One is willful ignorance. Some lawyers simply deny the data. Unburdened by factual support, they insist that "no worthy cause" goes unassisted, thanks to voluntary pro bono efforts, legal aid programs, and contingent fee representation.[32] Other attorneys point with pride to their workplace policies and ignore the distance between rhetorical support and institutional norms that discourage nonbillable activities.[33] A final, more common approach is to acknowledge the problem of unmet needs but to deny that pro bono service is the solution. In one representative survey, about 60% of California attorneys believed that poor people's access to legal assistance would continue to decline, but an equal number opposed minimum pro bono requirements.[34]

Opposition to pro bono responsibilities takes a variety of forms. Some question the social value of pro bono work, whether voluntary or mandatory. Others acknowledge its social value but believe that if society benefits, society should pay; the responsibility is not one that individual lawyers or their employers should have to assume. A third group of critics objects only to mandatory pro bono programs, which raise distinctive moral and practical concerns.

Why Legal Assistance?

The first and most sweeping challenge to pro bono work is that it is ineffective or inefficient in promoting societal values. For example, in a prominent *Yale Law Journal* article, Professors Charles Silver and Frank Cross criticize pro bono legal programs for the poor on the ground that they encourage contributions of law-related services rather than other forms of assistance that would be more effective in alleviating poverty.[35] In their view, "[p]ro bono efforts divert legal services . . . to consumers who are unable or unwilling to pay market rates. . . . It would be more efficient to transfer cash from lawyers to the poor while leaving the market for legal services undisturbed."[36] Silver and Cross point out that the "average poor person spends a minuscule portion of his or her budget on legal services. . . . [I]t [therefore] seems odd to suggest that lawyers should be required, or even encouraged to donate legal services when poor persons would rather have other things."[37] Other commentators agree and argue that neither the poor nor their elected representatives place the same priority on law as does the legal profession.[38]

There are a number of difficulties with this analysis. First, it seems "odder" still to suggest that the value of legal assistance can be accurately gauged by what the poor currently pay for it. The poor also pay very little for quality private education for their children, but that hardly demonstrates that they do not value first-rate schools. Individuals who cannot meet their most basic subsistence needs are often unable to make purchases that would prove cost-effective in the long term; that is part of what traps them in poverty. Moreover, law is a public good. Many of the claims that lawyers assert on behalf of the poor have benefits beyond those realized by any individual client. Holding employers or landlords accountable for unsafe conditions, requiring government officials to comply with due process procedures, or making merchants liable for fraudulent consumer practices can help deter future abuse.

It is also odd to assume that pro bono assistance has lower value than cash transfers. In fact, such assistance is often necessary for poor people to obtain cash transfers to which they are entitled; a few hours of legal work may obtain a lifetime of Social Security disability payments for an impoverished claimant whose benefits were improperly terminated. For many other forms of legal assistance, it would be difficult, if not impossible, to attach a precise dollar value, but most individuals would doubtless put the value higher than the cost of assistance. Obvious examples include pro bono programs that make it possible for the poor to divorce and remarry, to assert a political asylum claim, or to unearth exculpating DNA evidence. Here again, legal enforcement cannot be measured solely by individuals' ability or willingness to pay. The benefits often extend to third parties and to society as a whole. And it is by no means self-evident that equivalent cash contributions would have a greater effect on poverty. Even if every lawyer gave the equivalent of 50 hours a year, the net transfer would amount to less than \$4 per poor person per week.[39]

Yet the limited impact of lawyer charity, whether of time or money, gives rise to a related objection to pro bono initiatives. Even if all lawyers could be persuaded to contribute a reasonable amount of competent service, critics note that it would "hardly make a dent" in unmet legal needs.[40] And at existing contribution levels, pro bono work is even less adequate to address the problem of unequal legal access, "except on a randomly individualized basis that makes getting a free lawyer something akin to winning the lottery."[41] Moreover, most lawyers refuse pro bono cases that involve unpopular clients or positions contrary to paying clients' interests, which often leaves the most vulnerable groups unrepresented.[42] The risk is that modest but highly visible public service will serve largely as window dressing; it may enhance lawyers' image and give them a "public relations shield against critics of the current system" while deflecting attention from the substantial inequalities that remain.[43]

Although this concern is not without force, neither is it compelling in the contemporary political climate. Popular opinion polls do not suggest that the public is deluded about the extent of lawyers' charity.[44] Nor is it likely that contributions are diverting attention from the problem of unmet needs. Whose attention? Politicians who have succeeded in curtailing legal aid funding do not appear much interested in increasing access to justice, whether through pro bono service or government-subsidized programs.[45]

Indeed, those politicians typically oppose the reformist agenda of much pro bono work. Their concerns build on long-standing objections to public interest and legal aid litigation. A widely circulated article published by the Manhattan Institute claims that much pro bono service is in fact neither free nor for the public's good. It is rather a strategy of "millionaire attorneys for forcing their charitable preferences on middle class taxpayers."[46] For example, suits by affluent lawyers from large New York firms assertedly have forced the city to spend "billions" in "irrational" ways on the homeless and have squandered scarce resources on welfare recipients, HIV-infected victims, and sex discrimination claimants.[47] Another commonly cited example involves representation of "deadbeat" tenants or consumers. Landlords and merchants forced to litigate such matters allegedly pass on their costs in rents or prices to other, equally impoverished but more deserving tenants and customers who honor their financial obligations.[48] From critics' perspective, decisions about how to balance competing demands on taxpayer dollars should remain with publicly accountable officials, not with "elite lawyers to make an end run around the political process."[49]

Of course, what counts as "pro bono" is always open to dispute. But the real target of this line of criticism is the reform litigation itself, not its pro bono status. Liberal activism by a countermajoritarian judiciary is objectionable to most conservatives, whether or not a client is paying for it.[50] Moreover, as legal scholars have often pointed out, it is not inconsistent with democratic principles for the public to delegate some social reform functions to nonmajoritarian processes. Such a delegation is particularly appropriate to protect the needs of "discrete and insular minorities," or diffuse majorities that lack resources to organize in a political system increasingly captive to well-financed interests.[51] Pro bono representation can play a critical role in enforcing legal rights and principles that other branches of government fail to vindicate.

Such representation does not necessarily circumvent democratic processes; it often seeks to realize the legislative intent underlying statutory guarantees. In many contexts, pro bono initiatives increase accountability in governmental policymaking. For example, such efforts can provide a crucial check against the capture of agencies by the groups to be regulated, or can supplement the limited resources of enforcement officials. Elected representatives often lack the time, information, incentives, and technical expertise to supervise implementation of statutory mandates. So too, pro bono lawsuits frequently serve as a catalyst for political action; in purpose and effect, their primary role may be to galvanize communities, organize client groups, increase public awareness, and strengthen demands for reform.[52] Contrary to critics' assertions, it is by no means clear that the costs of defending such lawsuits are all passed on to other poor people, or that those costs are excessive in light of the deterrent value that they serve. A case in point is the frequently cited concern that landlords will raise the rent to cover the expense of litigating frivolous claims by deadbeat tenants. Yet understaffed legal services offices have little reason to spend scarce resources litigating the meritless cases that critics endlessly invoke. Indeed, the little systematic research available finds that the great majority of unrepresented tenants have valid legal claims that they are unable to assert without free assistance.[53] Moreover, in many low-income housing markets, tenants' inability to afford rent increases will force landlords to absorb the costs associated with more equal representation.[54] This is not to suggest that society in general or the poor in particular would benefit if every potential claim were fully litigated. But neither is ability to pay an effective way of screening out frivolous claims

Why Lawyers?

A second line of criticism acknowledges the value of such legal assistance but maintains that if access to law is a societal value, society as a whole should bear its cost. The poor have fundamental needs for housing and medical care, but we do not require landlords or physicians to donate their help in meeting those needs.[55] Why should the responsibilities of lawyers be greater? As one California appellate court put it, "No crystal ball is necessary to foresee the public outrage which would erupt if we ordered grocery store owners to give indigents two months of free groceries or automobile dealers to give them two months of free cars. Lawyers in our society are entitled to no greater privileges than the butcher, the baker and the candlestick maker, but they certainly are entitled to no less."[56] Other opponents of pro bono requirements similarly argue that attorneys face increasing competition from within and outside the profession and do not enjoy a monopoly position that justifies special obligations.[57] After all, individuals can represent themselves and have access to a growing range of self-help publications and services.[58] According to Harvard Law Professor David Shapiro, "to say lawyers have a monopoly or even a powerful cartel is to misrepresent the dynamics of the present day practice of law."[59]

Yet to ignore the extent of lawyers' protected status is to misrepresent those practice dynamics in even more profound ways. Butchers, bakers, and candlestick makers enjoy far less protection from competition than attorneys. Every state makes it a criminal offense for nonlawyers to engage in the "practice of law."[60] Unlike the vast majority of other nations, the United States grants lawyers the exclusive authority to give legal advice except in certain limited areas. The organized bar has waged long-standing and often highly successful campaigns to protect its turf from competitors, and has itself presented pro bono assistance as a preferable alternative to nonlawyer services.[61]

Moreover, contrary to critics' claims, it is by no means unprecedented for society or for a professional group to mandate reasonable charitable contributions in exchange for special occupational privileges. One obvious example is the requirement of a minimum level of unpaid public service programing by those who receive exclusive broadcast licenses.[62] A still closer analogy is doctors, who are often inaccurately presented as a group unburdened by service obligations. In fact, some federal and state statutes require hospitals and the physicians who staff them to provide urgent medical assistance to indigents.[63] Doctors' aspirational ethical code, as currently interpreted, makes clear that they bear partial "responsibility for the medical care of those who cannot afford essential health care."[64] And as Chapter 4 notes, a much higher percentage of doctors than lawyers provide unpaid services, and at more substantial levels.

In any event, there are alternative justifications for imposing special service obligations on lawyers. As earlier discussion indicated, one rationale turns on the centrality of law in American life and the importance of legal representation in maintaining the legitimacy of the justice system. Another rationale is that part of what lawyers sell are "public assets" in the sense that they are created by the state.[65] For example, the protection of the attorney-client privilege is a marketable commodity, but not one that is attributable to individual lawyers' talents or labor. As professor David Luban explains, "This is the difference between the lawyer and the grocer: the lawyer's lucrative monopoly would not exist without the community and its state; the monopoly and indeed the product it monopolizes is an artifact of the community."[66] The community may justifiably expect some public service contribution from attorneys in exchange for the privileges that it provides.

MORAL OBJECTIONS TO MANDATORY PRO BONO SERVICE

Unlike the preceding critics, most lawyers acknowledge some professional responsibility to provide pro bono service. What they reject, as Chapter 1 noted, is any effort to make that responsibility mandatory. As a matter of principle, many lawyers insist that "compulsory charity" is a contradiction in terms. From their perspective, requiring pro bono work would undermine its moral significance and compromise altruistic commitments.[67] Critics of mandatory service believe that it would discourage attorneys from providing assistance over the prescribed minimum, that both the quantity and quality of aid would suffer, and that the experience would lose its meaning.[68] As Shapiro predicts, "To turn an aspiration of public service into an enforceable obligation, then, would be to deprive the professional of an element of choice that may be an important part of self-fulfillment. Compelled altruism is not much of a virtue."[69] Nor would it serve the same purpose in enhancing volunteer attorneys' individual reputations and the legal profession's public image.[70] Many lawyers also view mandatory service as a morally unjustifiable infringement of their own rights, a form of "involuntary servitude," and a violation of their freedom of speech and association.[71]

There are problems with each of these claims, beginning with the assumption that pro bono service is "charity." Rather, as the preceding discussion suggested, pro bono work is not simply a philanthropic exercise; it is also a professional responsibility. The effect that some minimum service requirement would have on overall pro bono patterns is difficult to gauge. No evidence indicates that voluntary assistance has declined in the small number of jurisdictions where courts now appoint lawyers to provide uncompensated representation.[72] Nor is it self-evident that most lawyers who already make public service contributions would cease to do so simply because others were required to join them. As to the large numbers of lawyers who do not voluntarily contribute pro bono assistance but claim that required service would lack moral significance, Professor Luban has it right: "One hesitates to state the obvious, but here it is: You can't appeal to the moral significance of a gift you have no intention of giving."[73]

Finally, claims about "involuntary servitude" and infringement of speech and association are unconvincing as a matter of constitutional law for reasons noted in Chapter 1, and their moral status is no stronger. Asking lawyers to meet the Model Rules' pro bono standard, less than an hour a week of uncompensated assistance or the financial equivalent, is hardly servitude. As law professor Michael Millemann notes, "It is surprising—surprising is a polite word—to hear some of the most wealthy, unregulated and successful entrepreneurs in the modern economic world invoke the amendment that abolished slavery to justify their refusal to provide a little legal help to those, who in today's society, are most like the freed slaves."[74] And lawyers who find even minimal assistance unduly burdensome could substitute a financial contribution.

So too, as long as pro bono requirements allow a reasonable range of choice in the activities that qualify, claims of compelled speech and association are unconvincing.[75] Lawyers have long insisted, and the ABA Model Rules of Professional Conduct affirm, that the "representation of a client, including representation by appointment, does not constitute an endorsement of the client's political, economic, social, or moral views or activities."[76] Indeed, attorneys' defense of that principle, and their willingness to assist unpopular causes on a pro bono basis, has been crucial in safeguarding First Amendment protections for all citizens, including members of the legal profession.

PRACTICAL OBJECTIONS TO MANDATORY PRO BONO SERVICE

The stronger arguments against pro bono obligations involve pragmatic rather than moral concerns. Many opponents who support such obligations in principle worry that they would not prove efficient, effective, or equitable in practice.

Problems of Definition

A threshold problem involves defining the services that would satisfy a pro bono requirement. If the definition is broad and encompasses any charitable work for a nonprofit organization or needy individual, then experience suggests that poor people will not be the major beneficiaries. Lawyers traditionally have targeted most of their pro bono efforts to friends, relatives, or representation designed to attract or accommodate paying clients.[77] Under a loosely defined requirement, predominately middle-class individuals and organizations such as hospitals, museums, schools, and churches are likely to benefit most. Other favored groups would undoubtedly include conservative legal foundations, which typically represent causes that do not lack for funding, and which often oppose the work of legal services organizations.[78] By contrast, if a pro bono requirement is limited to the low-income clients given preferred status in the ABA's current aspirational rule, then that definition would exclude many crucial public interest organizations, such as those focusing on civil rights, civil liberties, and environmental issues. Any compromise effort to permit some but not all charitable groups to qualify for pro bono credit would raise concerns of political bias.

Related problems would arise in determining who would be subject to pro bono requirements and whether they would permit any exceptions or alternatives to direct personal service. For example, should exemptions be

allowed for lawyers suffering temporary hardships, and if so, what circumstances should qualify? Should all attorneys be covered, even those who
work for legal aid, public interest, and public defender offices that serve
low-income individuals? These attorneys, who generally face crushing work-
loads and receive far lower pay than lawyers in private practice, are likely to
feel that they already have "given at the office."[79] Yet if unpaid service is a
professional responsibility, then any exemptions raise obvious equity concerns and may seem arbitrary to other relatively low-paid attorneys who
work for government agencies or serve clients of limited means.

Similar difficulties in designing mandatory pro bono programs involve
whether to permit obligations to be satisfied collectively, and whether to allow cash contributions in lieu of service. Supporters of such options argue
that it is efficient for law firms to allocate all of their members' public service
responsibilities to designated attorneys who are interested and competent to
assume them. It also makes economic sense to permit buyouts for lawyers
who are unwilling or unqualified to provide direct services to clients most in
need of assistance. Yet such buyout options seem unfair to many solo practitioners and small-firm lawyers who cannot readily pass on the costs of these
buyouts to affluent clients or offload their own obligations onto other colleagues.[80] Further difficulties arise in specifying appropriate cash contributions. A flat hourly rate compounds the hardships for the profession's lowest
earners; a progressive rate is unacceptable to many highly paid large-firm attorneys who have led the campaign for mandatory service.[81]

Problems of Quality

A further objection to mandatory pro bono requirements is that many lawyers lack expertise or motivation to serve underrepresented groups, and not
all of these attorneys would exercise buyout options.[82] In opponents' view,
corporate lawyers who dabble in poverty cases are unlikely to provide cost-
effective services. The performance of many court-appointed attorneys in
defending indigent criminal cases does not inspire confidence that con-
scripted practitioners would provide acceptable representation.[83] Critics also
worry that some lawyers' inexperience and insensitivity in dealing with low-
income clients will compromise the objectives that pro bono requirements

seek to advance.[84] The basis for such concerns is often apparent even in voluntary pro bono programs. Some attorneys object to spending time on "piddling matters" or representing individuals who have "messed up their lives" and who, even after receiving assistance, "do something to botch it up even more."[85]

Mandatory programs are likely to provoke far greater backlash. Such concerns are part of what drives opposition to pro bono requirements, even among many of the nation's strongest advocates of increased access to justice. For example, the ABA's Standing Committee on Legal Aid and Indigent Defendants testified against a proposed ABA ethical rule mandating pro bono assistance on the ground that "poor clients . . . deserve lawyers who want to represent them and will do it with vigor."[86] The Association's Standing Committee on Pro Bono and Public Service took a similar view.[87]

Problems of Enforcement

From critics' perspective, requiring attorneys to contribute minimal services of largely unverifiable quality cannot solve the problem of unequal access to justice. Worse still, the costs of administering mandatory programs and of establishing referral, training, and oversight structures will divert resources from more efficient forms of legal assistance.[88] Opponents often worry about the "burgeoning bureaucratic boondoggle" that they assume would be necessary to monitor compliance.[89] Even with substantial expenditures, it would be extremely difficult to verify the amount of time that practitioners allocated to pro bono work or the quality of assistance that they provided. A further risk is that minimal mandatory service requirements would reduce pressure for more fundamental reforms that are necessary to address unmet needs. Such strategies include simplification of legal procedures, expanded subsidies for poverty law programs, greater assistance for pro se litigants, and fewer restrictions on provision of routine legal services by nonlawyers.[90]

Addressing the Objectives

Supporters of pro bono requirements make several responses. It is certainly true that some practitioners lack the skills and motivation to serve those most in need of assistance. But as Millemann notes, the current alternative is scarcely preferable: "Assume that after four years in college, three years of law school, and varying periods of law practice some lawyers are 'incompetent' to help the poor. . . . All this despairing assumption tells us is that the poor are far less competent to represent themselves, and do not have the readily available access to attaining competency that lawyers have."[91] To be sure, subsidizing additional poverty law specialists would be a more efficient way of expanding assistance than relying on reluctant dilettantes. But an adequate increase in government support does not seem plausible in this political climate; nor does a major increase in voluntary contributions from the bar. A pro bono requirement that permitted financial buyouts could dramatically expand the resources available to poverty law offices, which opponents view as the most cost-effective way to provide service.

Other strategies are also available to reduce the likelihood of incompetent and unmotivated assistance under a mandatory public service program. One option is to allow lawyers in organizations to satisfy their obligations collectively through contributions from their most qualified and committed colleagues. Another possibility is to give continuing legal education credit for time spent in training for pro bono work and to offer bar-supported malpractice coverage for lawyers who meet competence standards. Many voluntary programs now equip participants through relatively brief educational workshops, coupled with well-designed manuals and accessible backup assistance.[92] It is by no means clear that mandatory programs would be less effective.

Although opponents of a pro bono requirement assume that it would result in higher levels of incompetence than the current voluntary system, they offer no factual basis for that assumption. Indeed, one of the weaknesses of the bar's voluntary structure is that it rarely includes performance evaluations, let alone ones that include client assessments.[93] The reasons are obvious. Pro bono programs generally have resources that are far too limited to meet the need for assistance, and participants are often understandably reluctant to divert scarce time and funding to evaluation rather than direct service. Moreover, many administrators have relatively little incentive to expose negative client experiences. Because the beneficiaries are not paying for assistance and the demand for representation vastly exceeds the supply, providers need not be especially concerned about encouraging repeat use or ensuring favorable recommendations to other potential clients. And to the extent that pro bono programs are aimed at improving the public image of lawyers or the sponsoring organization, bar leaders may see little reason to collect potentially unflattering information.

As a consequence, we have no systematic evidence about lawyers' performance under voluntary pro bono systems. Nor do we have comparable data about their performance in the few court systems that require service. What little information is available indicates that after some initial resistance, such systems experience few problems of noncompliance and few client complaints about the quality of assistance.[94] Of course, the absence of complaints cannot be taken as an assurance of quality. Even if recipients of assistance are aware of substandard performance, they may see little to be gained from complaining. Impressionistic accounts suggest that quality varies, but that concerns can be mitigated by an option to contribute money rather than time.[95] In any event, administration does not appear to pose undue difficulties or expense. The same is true of continuing legal education requirements, which state bars enforce without the massive monitoring costs or "bureaucratic boondoggles" that critics of mandatory pro bono programs have predicted.[96]

In the absence of more research and experience with such programs, their effectiveness is difficult to assess. But even without such experience, a threshold question is worth considering. Suppose critics are correct that attempts to ensure full compliance with pro bono requirements would be inadequate or prohibitively expensive. Would a mandatory program still provide sufficient benefits to clients and lawyers to justify its costs? Opponents of pro bono requirements generally discount those benefits, particularly the ones to lawyers. Given the controversial nature of much high visibility pro bono litigation, critics doubt that expanding the resources available for such lawsuits would enhance the bar's image. For example, opponents note that lawyers' unpaid service is responsible for dissolving antigang injunctions in violent urban areas, asserting felons' rights to vote, defending racial preferences in educational admission policies, and challenging the Boy Scouts' exclusion of gay scoutmasters.[97] More of same is not likely to do much for a profession that most Americans believe is already responsible for bringing too many unmerited lawsuits.[98]

Nor, according to critics, would pro bono requirements deliver all the benefits to individual lawyers that supporters claim, such as improvements in skills, reputation, or understanding of what passes for justice among the have-nots. Silver and Cross point out that if pro bono work was in fact sufficiently valuable, "lawyers would be tripping over each other in a mad rush to do it."[99] Because bar participation rates reflect no such enthusiasm, "the natural inference is that lawyers do not find this work particularly rewarding."[100] To suggest that they should nonetheless be required to participate in public service in the hope that it will "transform their values and political beliefs . . . seems condescending and authoritarian."[101]

Yet the claim that there is value in exposing lawyers to the legal problems of the underrepresented poor is not qualitatively different from the claims supporting other educational requirements, such as professional responsibility courses in law school or in continuing legal education programs. The aim is to make better lawyers. No one is telling lawyers what they should value or believe, what lessons to draw from their pro bono experiences, or even which underrepresented clients to serve. This is hardly a call for "authoritarian" manipulation.

Moreover, the fact that most lawyers do not provide substantial pro bono assistance does not establish that they find it unrewarding. On the contrary, as the survey data summarized in Chapter 6 indicate, many lawyers would like to participate in such activities but are in institutions with reward structures that push powerfully in other directions. Most law firms neither give adequate credit for pro bono work in meeting billable hour quotas nor value it in promotion and bonus decisions.[102] Because so few institutions fully support public service, a large proportion of the profession never has significant involvement. And practitioners who do not know what they are missing do not demand the structural reforms necessary to provide it. One benefit of a pro bono requirement would be to support lawyers who want to participate in legal aid and public interest projects but work in organizations with different priorities. Many of the nation's highly profitable law firms and corporate employers fall into that category.[103] They could readily afford a greater pro bono commitment, and a formal requirement could nudge them in that direction.

Compromise Proposals

As the preceding discussion makes clear, most of the bar's objections to pro bono requirements are unconvincing in principle or unsubstantiated in practice. Only through greater experience with such requirements will it be possible to gauge their relative costs and benefits. However, given widespread opposition to mandatory service, few judges or bar leaders appear willing to risk the political backlash and negative publicity that would result from attempts to impose minimum obligations.[104] The most realistic reform options are likely to rest on systematic evaluations of the few existing requirements, together with mandatory pilot programs and reporting requirements for voluntary contributions.

The limited information available concerning mandatory reporting systems suggests that they could produce modest gains in bar participation rates at reasonable cost, but would still provoke intense opposition.[105] Until recently, Florida was the only state with a reporting requirement, and it remains the only one that releases public data on compliance and participation rates. Maryland adopted a requirement in 2002 and Nevada did so in 2003, but their reports remain confidential and no aggregate statewide data are available. Florida's system costs approximately $10,000 a year and has about a 90% compliance rate.[106] In the first decade after its adoption in 1993, Florida lawyers' pro bono hours increased by 63%, from 806,874 to 1,313,950, and their financial contributions grew by 67%, from $1,518,781 to $2,531,445.[107] How much of that increase was due to reporting and how much to the judiciary's proactive support of pro bono initiatives remains open to dispute.[108] In any case, Florida attorneys' average annual contribution still leaves much to be desired: about 18 hours and $34.[109]

Recent campaigns for similar reporting systems in other jurisdictions have been unsuccessful. The ABA Ethics 2000 Commission rejected mandatory reporting, as have at least eight states. Opposition has often been vitriolic, in part because many attorneys view mandatory reporting as the first step toward mandatory service. Indeed, critics have denounced reporting in much the same terms as service itself: as "coerced counsel," "involuntary servitude," and an infringement of lawyers' individual rights.[110] In a compromise effort, a dozen states have adopted voluntary reporting systems. However, these generate relatively low response rates, ranging from 3% to 35%, and their impact on participation rates is unclear.[111]

On balance, as discussion in Chapter 8 suggests, mandatory reporting systems are a small step in the right direction. Requiring lawyers to disclose their assistance to individuals of limited means or organizations that serve them would at least increase pressure to provide such aid, and at relatively little administrative cost. That pressure could intensify if prospective employees and clients were encouraged to pay attention to pro bono performance records.

In any event, with or without mandatory pro bono initiatives, it makes sense to encourage greater voluntary contributions. Lawyers who want to participate in pro bono service are likely to be its most effective supporters and providers. How best to encourage a voluntary commitment to charitable work, and what role law schools can play in that effort, demand closer scrutiny.

The Rationale for Law School Pro Bono Programs

Public Service Justifications

The most commonly cited justifications for pro bono service by law students and professors parallel the justifications for pro bono service by lawyers. Leaders in legal education generally agree that such service benefits participants and the public, that it is a professional responsibility, and that schools should prepare future practitioners to assume it. In a survey by the Association of American Law Schools (AALS) Commission on Pro Bono and Public Service in Law Schools, 95% of deans agreed that "an important goal" of legal education is "to instill in students a sense of obligation to perform pro bono work during their later careers."[112] During the formative stages of their professional identity, future lawyers need to develop the skills and values that will sustain commitments to public service.[113] To that end, law schools need to offer effective pro bono programs, and faculty need to model such commitments themselves.

This rationale for pro bono programs assumes that positive service experiences in law school will encourage involvement after graduation. The assumption is that students will discover the rewards of altruism and experiential learning noted in Chapter 3. Involvement in pro bono activities may also break down the rigid distinctions that prevail in many law schools between students who are preparing for public interest careers and those who are not. These "on the boat or off the boat" dichotomies send the wrong message about integrating private practice and public service.

Evidence for this link between law school pro bono work and subsequent participation comes from student surveys. At Tulane, which was the first law school to impose pro bono requirements, two-thirds of graduating students reported that participation in community service had increased their willingness to participate in the future, and about three-quarters agreed that they had gained confidence in their ability to represent indigent clients.[114] Three-fourths of the students at Columbia and over four-fifths of those at Louisville who participated in a mandatory pro bono program also indicated that their experience had increased the likelihood that they would engage in similar work as practicing attorneys.[115] However, before this study, no systematic research attempted to corroborate such claims by comparing the amount of pro bono work done by graduates who were subject to law school requirements and graduates who were not.[116] And as noted below, this study's findings provide no such corroboration. To be sure, the research on altruism and service learning discussed in Chapter 3 indicates that a positive experience working on public interest causes can encourage future involvement. However, that experience need not occur in a mandatory pro bono program.

Educational Justifications

Yet the rationale for public service programs in law school does not rest solely on their capacity to promote subsequent volunteer service. Pro bono placements have independent educational value. Like other forms of experiential learning, participation in public service helps bridge the gap between theory and practice and enriches understanding of how law relates to life. Individuals tend to be especially motivated to learn when information and skills are offered in a context that they care about.[117] For law students as well as lawyers, pro bono work can provide valuable training in interviewing, negotiating, drafting, problem solving, and working with individuals from diverse racial, ethnic, and socioeconomic backgrounds.[118] Aid to clients of limited means exposes both students and faculty to the urgency of unmet needs and to the capacities and constraints of law in addressing social problems. As former Tulane Law School Dean John Kramer notes, pro bono work can help sensitize many individuals "to worlds they usually ignore."[119] For other individuals, it is a way to help sustain the commitments to social justice that led them to a legal career in the first instance.[120] Pro bono work also can increase awareness of ethical issues and the human costs of professional inattention or incompetence.[121] Involvement in public service can, in short, give students a sense of the good that legal assistance can do in the world and the personal satisfactions of providing it.

So too, pro bono programs can provide other practical benefits such as career information, contacts, and job references.[122] Students can get a better sense of their interests and talents, as well as a focus for further academic and placement choices. Pro bono work in law school also may encourage more participants to press potential employers for information about their policies toward such work. Too many students who report interest in public service now lack this information, and the absence of comparative data reduces the pressure on employers to develop adequate policies.[123]

Institutional and Societal Justifications

For law schools, pro bono programs can prove beneficial in several respects apart from their educational value for students. Most obviously, such programs demonstrate a tangible commitment to the community. Pro bono placements offer opportunities for cooperation with local bar organizations and for outreach to alumni who can serve as sources, sponsors, and supervisors for student projects. Successful projects can contribute to law school efforts in recruitment, public relations, and development. Over 90%

of surveyed deans agreed that pro bono activities had provided valuable goodwill in the community, and two-thirds felt that such work had also proven valuable with alumni.[124] Other survey data report similar benefits.[125] Individual faculty can profit from community contacts and from opportunities to enrich their research and teaching through direct service. Some pro bono initiatives, in cooperation with clinics, can play a significant role in public education and public policy. Notable cases are the Innocence Projects, pioneered at Cardozo and Northwestern Law Schools, which have relied on law and journalism students to investigate criminal cases and which have found evidence exonerating wrongfully convicted defendants. Those exonerations have, in turn, profoundly affected public views about capital punishment and contributed to Illinois' widely publicized moratorium on the death penalty.[126]

MANDATORY PRO BONO SERVICE IN LAW SCHOOLS

Given this range of benefits, it is hard to find anyone who opposes law school pro bono programs, at least in principle. But in practice, considerable disagreement centers on the form that these programs should take and the priority that they should assume in a world of scarce institutional resources. Many students and faculty oppose mandatory service, and many administrators are unwilling to provide the support necessary for effective voluntary initiatives.

Moral Objections and Responses

The opposition to required participation by students or faculty again parallels the opposition to required participation by lawyers. In a widely circulated statement opposing Harvard Law School's pro bono obligation, Professor Charles Fried voiced the moral objection to coerced charity, which he equated with "compulsory chapel": "I agree with the premise that public service is an important part of a lawyer's professional life but we have no right to compel our students to conform to our idea of law. . . . Although significant public service is the right choice, it must be a free choice. Volunteerism under the lash is 'voluntary' only in the Orwellian sense that it is unpaid. This is the volunteerism of the Cuban cane fields."[127] To anyone familiar with the actual conditions of Cuban field work, this analogy may seem less than compelling, particularly given the modest hourly commitments expected under most mandatory pro bono programs. And given the educational value of pro bono placements, a service obligation seems no less justifiable than other law school requirements.

Nor are faculty members' moral objections more convincing. Most track the arguments raised by practitioners and are vulnerable on similar grounds. It also bears note that the bar's own ethical codes include no exemption for academics. Accordingly, law schools have ample reason to mandate that those who teach the law abide by its codes of professional conduct, including its aspirational standards. Many faculty, however, seem to have internalized Mark Twain's insight that while it is noble to do good, it is also noble to teach others to do good—"and much less trouble."[128] But students notice the difference, and hypocrisy is not a powerful teaching tool.

Professors' startlingly frequent response, that almost everything they do outside the classroom is "pro bono," is likely to meet with considerable skepticism outside academic circles.[129] The same is true of faculty members' equally common assertions that they are providing the equivalent of charitable service by accepting a lower salary than they could obtain in private practice.[130] As Luban notes, professors receive ample nonfinancial forms of compensation in exchange for their foregone income: "shorter and more flexible hours, greater personal autonomy, tenure, leisurely summers, the luxury of thinking and writing whatever [they] want, freedom from the anxiety [and pressure of contemporary practice]. . . . [T]he lifestyle choice of comfortably compensated professordom over stress-ridden riches" hardly qualifies as charitable service.[131]

In any event, the burdens of satisfying more conventional definitions of pro bono work should not be overstated. Faculty have a wide range of opportunities to assist public interest and legal aid causes. If, as many professors assert, they lack expertise to provide direct legal representation to low-income clients, they can help underrepresented groups in other ways: writing briefs, conducting research, advising nonprofit organizations, supervising student pro bono work, and so forth. For academics who lack the time, skills, or motivation for any of this work, an equivalent financial contribution remains an option.

Practical Objections and Responses

As is true with debates over mandatory service by lawyers, the most serious objections to service by law faculty and students are practical rather than moral. Critics raise concerns about the effectiveness of both mandatory and voluntary programs in enhancing professional skills and responsibilities. One objection is that a service obligation for which no compensation or credit is available devalues the importance of public interest work and imposes disproportionate hardships on certain groups, particularly students with substantial family obligations or financial needs that force them to add part-time jobs to already demanding schedules. The burdens are likely to be greatest for students from economically disadvantaged backgrounds, the very group that pro bono responsibilities are intended to assist.[132] Disproportionate supervisory burdens may also fall on clinical faculty, who already have longer classroom hours and generally provide more unpaid service than other colleagues.[133] To address such concerns by minimizing the amount of pro bono work expected creates other problems. Harvard Professor Lucie White argues that current public service programs too often offer only a brief experience of providing routine services to low-income clients. Such services do not address the root causes of poverty and can encourage a kind of minimal noblesse oblige paternalism that often leaves both providers and recipients unsatisfied.[134]

Differences in racial, ethnic, socioeconomic, and educational backgrounds exacerbate the problem, particularly if students lack "cross-cultural competence" and are not in classroom or workplace settings that foster it.[135] The risk is that pro bono participants may wield their expertise "in a way that affronts their clients' intelligence and life experience."[136] Clients may resent the seeming arrogance and insensitivity of students; students may resent the seeming ingratitude and unworthiness of clients.[137] In describing this risk, White invokes a scene from *Praying for Sheetrock*, Melissa Faye Greene's prize-winning history of a Georgia voting rights case. The scene involves the first meeting between the African American plaintiffs and their white lawyers:

> The amazing thing, to Thurnell Alson, was how quickly and easily the young white lawyers had named the ill health of the country; how they had listened as the three McIntosh men tumbled out their tales of poverty, underemployment, and a sense of being the untouchables in McIntosh's caste system; how the lawyers had nodded, made notes on their yellow pads, exchanged glances with one another over the heads of the black men, and . . . how —when the McIntosh men had finished speaking—the lawyers had pronounced the recent events to be the results of discrimination and a "violation of due process" as proudly as a toddler shown a picture of a cow says "Moo." Then they planned to affix *his* name to their cleverness. The whole process amazed him.[138]

As White notes, students often have to "work hard to learn to use the skills that they are learning as lawyers without insulting or infuriating their clients."[139] Those skills can be hard to acquire in pro bono settings that lack active supervision and opportunities for guided reflection.

A related concern, particularly with mandatory programs, is that not all participants will have the time or motivation to provide quality assistance. Some law graduates who complete mandatory pro bono service, including a significant number in my own survey, are quite critical of their experience. They feel bored and unchallenged by routine tasks.[140] For these reluctant students, client contact may confirm adverse stereotypes of poverty communities. Program participants are often put off by claimants who appear ungrateful or undeserving of the remedies that they seek.[141] Many students lack understanding of the stresses of poverty that can cause clients to miss appointments, to misunderstand instructions, or to mistrust lawyers. Experience with disaffected students can, in turn, discourage overburdened field supervisors from spending the time necessary to make mandatory placements more effective. They prefer working with motivated students in externships, clinical courses, or voluntary pro bono programs.[142]

Such reactions compound the challenges of finding appropriate placements for required service. Some administrators have difficulties identifying sufficient positions to accommodate students' time constraints, academic schedules, and skill levels. When schools expand placement options by paying for supervisors, it adds significantly to program costs.[143] Other schools minimize these difficulties by adopting highly expansive definitions of pro bono work, which are not limited to legal services for clients of limited means. Although such definitions pose fewer problems in accommodating participant needs and interests, they also offer fewer opportunities for exposing students to the legal needs of underserved communities. Restrictive definitions that serve the latter goal bump up against shortages in supervised positions and claims of ideological bias. Groups such as the Washington Legal Foundation and the American Enterprise Institute have criticized law schools' public service placements for being skewed in support of "legal activism of a distinctly left-wing variety."[144]

Defenders of pro bono programs make several responses. Although acknowledging the limitations of brief routine service, they note that the alternative is always, "compared to what?" Not all students will have the interest in, or opportunity for, more sustained involvement through clinics and externships. And not all schools are willing or able to invest the resources necessary to provide such opportunities for the entire student body throughout their law school education. Pro bono placements are not a substitute for faculty-supervised course work, but they can be a less costly supplement. Many provide unique opportunities for work on public interest issues beyond the scope of even the best financed clinics. Well-designed pro bono programs can offer an array of nonroutine placements, along with training that sensitizes students to the dynamics of poverty and effective client relationships.[145]

As the AALS Commission noted, mandatory programs also "are the strongest possible way" to convey the message that public service is a professional responsibility.[146] They reach the large group of students who would not take advantage of voluntary pro bono programs, externships, or clinical courses. By their own accounts, some of these individuals become converts to public interest causes, and most students have a sufficiently positive experience that they report increased interest in future pro bono service.[147] Many participants work more than the required hours; at Harvard, Columbia, and Pennsylvania, for example, most students exceed the minimum.[148]

Surveyed administrators of mandatory programs do not report significant difficulties of the sort triggering critics' concerns. Neither student resistance nor poor-quality service has been a major problem; participants' own internalized standards, peer pressure, or desire for a favorable job reference supply the necessary motivation for competent assistance.[149] The response from organizations where students work has been "overwhelmingly positive"; almost never do schools lose placements because of performance concerns.[150]

Virtually all administrators also report memorable success stories. A telling example was a Loyola student specializing in corporate tax who believed that he had no skills relevant to poverty communities and who strongly objected to compulsory service. But after gaining a tax refund for his first impoverished client, the student became one of the pro bono program's strongest supporters.[151] Like a substantial number of other converts, he continued involvement after graduation by supervising students and providing financial support.[152] A participant in Columbia's required program had a similar experience. On his program evaluation form he wrote, "I still think mandatory public service is communism, fascism and slavery. But I never would have done a minute without it and it is the most valuable thing I have done in law school and probably in my life."[153]

Voluntary pro bono programs also have distinctive benefits, such as the reinforcement of individual initiative and altruistic commitment. At schools like Fordham and Yale, many students do not simply participate in public service; they also learn how to run a public service program. Participants develop the fund-raising, recruitment, and community outreach skills necessary to sustain pro bono involvement throughout their careers.[154]

As this overview makes clear, pro bono programs have multiple objectives, and no single model is most effective in realizing all of them. Different approaches involve different trade-offs, and little research has been available to compare their contributions. The research survey findings summarized in the chapters to follow are a step toward determining what law school and workplace strategies are most likely to promote valuable pro bono experiences.

Chapter Three

ALTRUISTIC BEHAVIOR

Although the concept of altruism has generated a rich body of research, that work rarely figures in discussions of lawyers' pro bono activities.[1] Part of the reason may be the daunting scope of relevant material across multiple disciplines, including philosophy, psychology, economics, sociology, religion, and political science, as well as applied work on philanthropy and community service. Generalizing insights to the legal profession is a challenge, given not only the volume of related research, but also the diversity in definitions of altruistic behavior and the range of methodologies for assessing it. The challenge is further complicated by dissimilarities in factual settings between most of the empirical and clinical studies of altruism and lawyers' pro bono activities.[2]

Yet despite these complications, many of the research findings on altruism are sufficiently consistent across widely varying contexts to yield insights for the legal profession. Accordingly, the following analysis begins by surveying the definition, benefits, and frequency of altruism, with particular attention to charitable contributions of time and money. Subsequent discussion focuses on the individual motivations and situational factors that influence altruistic activity in general and charitable involvement in particular. Of particular relevance for the legal profession are the effects of education and workplace culture. A final section explores strategies that are most likely to prove useful in encouraging lawyers' pro bono service.

Definitions of Altruism

Sociologist Auguste Comte coined the term *altruism*, derived from the Italian, *altrui*, which means "other."[3] Under Comte's definition, altruism signified an unselfish regard for the welfare of others.[4] In contemporary usage, most theorists apply the term to voluntary actions that promote the interest of others, primarily for reasons other than self-interest.[5] Some theorists add the requirement of significant self-sacrifice, in order to distinguish altruistic acts from other forms of helping behavior.[6]

Whether pure altruism is possible has been a matter of long-standing dispute. The egoistic branch of moral philosophy, joined by the rational choice school of economics, generally denies the possibility of wholly disinterested actions.[7] These frameworks assume that all reasoned action is motivated by some self-interest; after all, why else would someone act?[8] In this view, when people act to benefit another, it is because they derive personal satisfaction from doing so. Yet this approach verges on tautology and ignores a relevant moral distinction. As many theorists note, an action taken because benefitting others feels intrinsically rewarding stands on different ethical footing than an action taken because it will bring extrinsic rewards.[9] Unpaid legal work designed to attract favorable publicity or to accommodate a paying client does not carry the same moral significance as the less self-serving support of a poverty law program. Both contributions are charitable, but only the latter seems genuinely altruistic.

As that last example suggests, and subsequent discussion confirms, much of lawyers' pro bono work is not purely altruistic. Although pro bono services, by definition, are provided for reasons other than payment from the client, they are often partly motivated by individual and collective self-interest. Attorneys may be acting partly out of personal desires for recognition, contacts, experience, and goodwill, or in response to shared concerns about their employer's reputation and public relations. Yet a similar point could be made about many actions that are commonly labeled "altruistic." As a wide range of data makes clear, motivations for assisting others usually are mixed, and a degree of self-interest is typically present.[10] For that reason, some theorists avoid the term *altruism* and refer instead to *prosocial* behavior.[11] However, the more common practice, and the one followed here, is to use altruism in the broadest sense, to encompass any charitable actions, including pro bono legal work. This definition includes unpaid assistance to benefit others even if some personal satisfaction or rewards are also expected.

Whether motives matter in assessing charitable contributions is of obvious relevance to debates over pro bono legal work. For example, if law firms give full billable hour credit for unpaid public service, or law schools give academic credit for such work, does that undercut its moral foundations? If so, should we care? Or, to borrow philosopher Bernard Williams's example, when a man gives money to famine relief, does it matter whether his motive is to enhance his standing with the Rotary Club?[12] Some argue that it makes no difference why individuals provide assistance; the point is to get them to do so. An alternative view, and the one developed here, is that it is desirable to encourage actions taken primarily out of concern for others, but that pure selflessness is an unrealistic ideal. Our Rotary Club member is no moral hero, but he has helped to save lives instead of buying a more expensive television set. As a practical matter, some positive reinforcement is necessary for most individuals most of the time.[13] Lawyers are no exception. Altruistic motivations should be nurtured because, as subsequent discussion suggests, they are more likely to promote effective and sustained service. But as this survey makes clear, purely selfless intentions are neither necessary nor sufficient to sustain all pro bono activity.

THE BENEFITS OF ALTRUISM

Benefits to Society

Encouraging individuals to engage in public service for intrinsic reasons rather than extrinsic rewards serves multiple objectives. From a societal perspective, it is generally less expensive and more effective to rely on internal motivations than on external incentives and sanctions to ensure quality assistance.[14] That is particularly true in contexts like pro bono legal work, where recipients generally are not in a position to evaluate or challenge the adequacy of aid. Those who provide legal services on the basis of deeply felt values or empathy with the client are more likely to do their best than those who are merely fulfilling academic requirements or hourly quotas. Of course, these motivations are not mutually exclusive, and external credit can ensure that individuals have sufficient time to offer the quality of assistance that they are intrinsically motivated to provide. The point is simply that encouraging individuals to view pro bono contributions as an integral and satisfying part of their professional identity, rather than just another educational or workplace obligation, is likely to enhance their performance.

Fostering individuals' sense of social responsibility and concern for others serves multiple public and private sector interests. In addition to the tangible services provided, charitable involvement strengthens cultural cohesion. As political theorists such as Robert Putnam put it, volunteer activity develops "social capital"—the "trust, norms, and networks" that facilitate cooperation and civic engagement.[15] Participation in activities that bridge the distance between different class, ethnic, and racial groups also helps to build the sense of shared purpose and mutual respect that is critical to a well-functioning society.[16] So too, the benefits to legal employers described in Chapter 2 also occur in other workplace settings. Over the last decade, a growing number of American corporations have integrated community service into their business plans in order to improve community relations, enhance recruitment and retention, and build employee skills.[17]

Benefits to Individuals

Charitable activity serves individual interests as well. A wide array of studies finds that volunteering is correlated with both physical and mental health. Compared with the population generally, people who regularly assist others besides family and friends live longer, experience less pain, stress, and depression, and have greater self-esteem.[18] Volunteers also report a sense of physical well-being, both immediately after helping and when the service is remembered, and are more likely to be happy with their lives.[19] One of the most commonly cited benefits of assistance is that it makes individuals "feel better" about themselves; other frequently noted rewards include opportu-

nities to "broaden horizons," "do something worthwhile," build social relationships, and gain educational or employment-related experience.[20] Some
evidence suggests that significantly greater physical and psychological benefits accompany volunteer work that involves personal contact and that occurs on a regular basis (at least two hours a week).[21]

Although the correlation between volunteer activities and well-being does
not establish a causal relationship, the evidence available suggests that such a
relationship exists and that selfless action is good for the self. That evidence
includes the high frequency of individuals' subjective experience of benefits,
the consistent association of volunteering with objective measures of health,
and the biological indications of a "helper's high."[22] Although the neurolog-
ical basis for heightened physiological well-being is not well understood,
some research suggests that caregiving activities reduce stress, which im-
proves the functioning of the immune system and triggers the release of en-
dorphins that produce pleasurable physical sensations.[23] So too, volunteer
work, like other forms of organizational activity, tends to reduce individuals'
sense of isolation and increases their sense of efficacy and self-esteem.[24]

THE FREQUENCY OF
CHARITABLE BEHAVIOR

Given all these positive effects, it is somewhat surprising that most Americans do not participate in volunteer activities. According to recent comprehensive surveys, fewer than half (44%) of adults in the United States contribute time to charitable or nonprofit organizations. The average is about
three and a half hours per week.[25] Such contribution levels appear modest
considering the broad definitions of service considered: assisting church
bingo games or coaching school soccer teams would count.[26] Although a
much larger proportion of Americans make financial contributions (89% of
families), the average amounts are small, and relatively little supports services for the poor or public interest and social justice causes.[27] About three-
quarters of charitable donations go to religious institutions and activities.[28]
Individuals with the greatest amount of time or financial resources available
for charitable contributions are not necessarily the most generous. For example, in one large-scale national study, only about half of retired individu-

als reported volunteering, either by assisting an organization or by informally "helping [someone] out."[29] In terms of financial contributions, the wealthy sacrifice a smaller portion of their income than less well-off groups.[30]

Evidence on the links between personal characteristics and charitable involvement is mixed. Some research finds that volunteering is highest among adults who are white, married, well educated, middle-aged, employed, and in households with above-average incomes.[31] Other studies find that the amount of time that individuals volunteer does not vary substantially by race, ethnicity, religion, or sex, although women are slightly more likely to contribute time than men and to target their activities and financial assistance to the poor.[32] As earlier discussion noted, the number of attorneys who provide legal assistance to nonprofit organizations or to low-income individuals is probably under one-quarter of the bar, which is only about half the level of volunteer activity among the general public.[33]

The relationship between personal characteristics and financial contributions is somewhat different. Religious affiliation is the strongest factor driving charitable donations. Education also matters; college graduates give two to three times as much to charity as other Americans, even after controlling for income.[34] Blacks give significantly more of their discretionary income than whites, especially to religious institutions. Married couples and single women are more generous than single men, and at upper-income levels (those making over $50,000) the differences are especially pronounced; single men give a fifth of what single mothers contribute.[35] Regional differences also matter, and anecdotal evidence suggests that giving rates are higher in communities with strong traditions of philanthropy by large individual donors or local companies.[36]

No data are available on lawyers' overall charitable activity compared with the general population. However, pro bono legal contributions do not appear impressive in comparison either to general American giving patterns or to lawyers' own capacity to give. Attorneys' average financial contributions to legal aid organizations are modest, particularly when considered in relation to their total income (under one-tenth of 1%).[37] In short, the bar is no exception to the truism that generosity is not determined by capacity. What does drive charitable assistance merits closer scrutiny.

THE INFLUENCES ON
CHARITABLE BEHAVIOR

Research on the factors influencing altruistic activities includes a broad array of data and methodological approaches. Some information is available from large-scale studies comparing Americans who make a significant charitable contribution with those who do not.[38] Other insights emerge from smaller, qualitative studies of volunteers and "moral heroes."[39] Psychological research drawing on experimental circumstances also helps identify the situational factors that influence voluntary assistance.[40] Finally, child development studies trace the origins of personal traits that affect giving behavior.[41]

In describing the influences on altruism, researchers generally distinguish between intrinsic and extrinsic factors. Intrinsic factors include the personal characteristics, values, and attitudes that motivate decisions to help others. Extrinsic factors involve the social rewards, reinforcement, costs, and other contextual dynamics that affect charitable assistance. These factors are, of course, related. Individual motivations can only be understood in the context of larger forces that shape personal commitments and group identity. A full exploration of the roots of giving behavior also requires attention to biological predispositions that interact with social learning patterns.[42]

Personal Characteristics

Of the intrinsic factors linked to volunteer activity, two personal characteristics appear most significant: a capacity for empathy and a sense of human or group solidarity.[43] Volunteers generally seem able to identify with others and to see themselves and those whom they help as part of a common social condition. Such feelings of responsibility and empathy are strongest among members of individuals' immediate community or groups with whom they share some key characteristic, such as race, ethnicity, religion, or sex.[44] Lawyers who assist public-interest organizations often report a feeling of responsibility to give something back to others, especially those united by some common bond or history of subordination.[45]

So too, a sense of civic or religious obligation, or a symbolic link between a particular needy group and a broader national cause, may widen individuals' sense of moral community. For example, in Holland and Denmark during World War II, efforts to rescue the Jews from Nazi persecution came to seem emblematic of national resistance; many rescuers were motivated by a sense of patriotic duty and the need to protect national integrity from fascist oppression.[46] Similarly, in the United States, in the aftermath of the 9/11 terrorist attacks, the outpouring of assistance for victims and their families was fueled partly by a desire to demonstrate national strength and solidarity.[47]

For many individuals, charitable assistance is thus a way to express deeply felt values. Volunteers often attribute their contributions to desires to create a better society and to express religious beliefs or ethical principles such as commitment to civil liberties or racial equality.[48] These volunteers' self-esteem and moral identity become bound up in helping others.[49] Yet ethical or religious convictions are neither necessary nor sufficient to inspire altruistic acts. Many individuals who engage in extraordinarily courageous forms of assistance report little moral reflection; their participation appears spontaneous, not a matter of ethical deliberation or principled decision making.[50] And, as noted earlier, religious affiliation does not predict helping behavior.[51] Even seminary students en route from a lecture on the Good Samaritan are not likely to act like one and to aid someone in apparent distress if they are late for their next appointment.[52]

In short, personal characteristics are part, but only part, of what explains altruistic activity. However, if the goal is encouraging such activity, then it is useful to foster those characteristics and to understand the factors that nurture them. Social science research suggests a number of strategies, although it yields no clear consensus about their relative importance. Some evidence suggests that all humans have an innate capacity for empathy. Sociobiologists theorize that basic altruistic responses have evolved through natural selection.[53] A predisposition to help others who would be in a position to reciprocate has obvious adaptive benefits.[54] Such sociobiological theories are consistent with psychological research indicating that even infants and toddlers respond empathetically to others' distress or need.[55]

Social Influences

It is, however, clear that adults vary in their ability to empathize, and that whatever their innate predispositions, socialization has a significant influence on voluntary service.[56] Experiences in childhood and early adulthood are often critical. Direct exposure to injustices, and to social activism that addresses them, can leave a lasting imprint.[57] Those who participate in volunteer activities during their formative years, and who observe parents' participation, are much more likely to volunteer later in life than those who lack such experiences.[58] Charitable conduct is also greater among children and adults who observe such conduct by someone outside the family who is powerful or admired.[59] In this case, as in other contexts, actions speak louder than words, and example works better than exhortation.[60] Charitable inclinations can also be strengthened by teaching methods that build students' awareness of others' needs and that provide constructive channels for assistance.[61]

Social networks are also important in shaping values and in encouraging or discouraging individuals to act on altruistic impulses. People pick up cues about appropriate behavior from moral reference groups in schools, workplaces, churches, communities, professional associations, and volunteer organizations.[62] Individuals vary considerably in terms of which groups are most critical and how much their approval matters. But as a general matter, giving behavior is influenced by a desire to meet social expectations and to conform to surrounding norms.[63] Such norms and expectations also shape understandings of occupational role. For many individuals, including lawyers, helping others is integrally bound up in a sense of professional as well as personal identity.[64]

Observation of social norms not only affects internalization of altruistic values, it also affects responsiveness to opportunities for assistance. Individuals are much more likely to provide help or financial contributions if others do so first.[65] Conversely, cultural norms that place preeminent value on financial success will inhibit altruism. As economist Robert Kuttner notes, "when everything is for sale, the person who volunteers time . . . who foregoes an opportunity to free-ride, begins to feel like a sucker."[66] So too, in the classic bystander intervention studies, individuals are less likely to assist someone in peril or distress if others are present and fail to volunteer aid.[67] Such indifference serves both to diffuse responsibility for the failure to intervene and to suggest that intervention may not be necessary or appropriate. However, some evidence suggests that a legal requirement to provide assistance may diminish the influence of bystanders' inaction; individuals perceive a failure to help as more reprehensible if it is also illegal.[68]

Extrinsic factors apart from legal requirements also influence the likelihood of volunteer assistance. The rewards and costs of such conduct play the most obvious role. As noted earlier, volunteer work often provides tangible personal benefits. It can present opportunities to gain transferable knowledge, skills, and personal contacts. It may also enhance an individual's reputation with peers, employers, and community members, as well as confer social status.[69] Such possibilities can substantially increase the attractiveness of volunteering.[70] Conversely, participation is likely to decrease where costs are high in relation to benefits because of the time required to gain expertise or provide service, the controversial nature of the activity, and related risks or opportunity costs of involvement.[71]

Other situational factors similarly affect volunteer assistance. Individuals are more likely to contribute if they feel competent to help, if they have sufficient time and resources, if the beneficiaries' need is urgent, and if a group that they are assisting seems effective in its efforts.[72] Those who receive a specific request for aid have much higher rates of participation than those who do not.[73] The chances of involvement similarly increase when individuals are asked to focus on unmet needs and on their own ethical obligations, or when they are given some direct personal exposure to the misery of others.[74] Face-to-face experience with poverty-related problems is generally more effective than abstract appeals in inspiring service. As novelist Arthur Koestler put it: "Statistics don't bleed."[75]

How these factors interact to affect voluntary assistance is, however, more complex than simple cost-benefit analysis might suggest. In many contexts, offering external rewards for helping others will encourage such behavior in the short term, but in the long term will backfire and diminish assistance.[76] When people view their aid instrumentally, as a means to achieving extrinsic benefits, rather than valuable in itself, their willingness to provide such assistance in the future declines if the benefits are discontinued.[77] So too, external coercion, such as surveillance, deadlines, or sanctions, can also undermine intrinsic motivation.[78] One of the few efforts to explore lawyers' motivations found that civil rights activists who were motivated by internalized values were more likely to make substantial and sustained contributions than individuals responding to extrinsic rewards.[79]

Yet much of the research finding "backfire" effects involves token benefits for one-time activities that hold limited interest.[80] Rewards that are related to merit or that involve praise rather than material incentives do not seem to undermine intrinsic interest and can enhance motivations for involvement.[81] Sustained volunteer work that reflects preexisting moral commitments may not be adversely affected by modest benefits or pressures such as academic requirements or workplace credit toward hourly quotas. As the following discussion notes, well-designed educational programs involving service opportunities may enhance future interest in altruistic activity.

COMMUNITY SERVICE
AND SERVICE LEARNING

Over the past quarter century, a growing number of high schools and colleges have increased support for community service. Drawing on a longstanding tradition of experiential learning and a series of influential foundation reports in the 1980s, many educational leaders have looked to school-based service programs as a way to prepare students for the responsibilities of citizenship.[82] Recent declines in political participation and civic engagement among young adults have focused growing interest on educational initiatives that might counteract such trends.[83] Federal funding through the National and Community Service Act of 1990 has reflected and reinforced this interest by supporting public service programs for high school and college students.[84]

In response to these developments, schools have added extracurricular service opportunities, courses with community placements, and "study-serve" positions that pay students with federal work-study funds for assisting nonprofit organizations.[85] A growing number of schools also have instituted mandatory community service programs, sometimes in response to state or municipal requirements.[86] By the early part of the twenty-first century, about four-fifths of incoming college freshmen had done some volunteer work during the preceding year in high school. Over 900 higher educational institutions were members of the Campus Compact, a consortium dedicated to promoting public service. On average, about a third of the students at member schools participated in service activities.[87] Among educational experts, the approach that commands greatest support is "service learning," which integrates community placements with academic course work.[88] This approach is generally preferable because it maximizes the likelihood of adequate supervision and structured reflection.

Service Learning Objectives

Such service learning has multiple objectives, most of which parallel the goals of law school pro bono programs. One objective is to enhance students' ethical commitment and social responsibility. As Thomas Ehrlich of the Carnegie Foundation puts it, the aim is to increase students' capacities "to make reasoned judgments infused with moral and civic concerns."[89] Community service, coupled with opportunity for guided reflection, is a way to improve ethical reasoning and foster empathic responses. It can enable individuals to "analyze complex issues where competing values are at stake and develop judgments . . . in respectful dialogue with others."[90] By increasing understanding of the direct human consequences of social injustice, such programs can assist students in finding constructive channels for altruistic commitments.[91] When participants begin to see "their problems" as "our problems," the foundations for civic engagement grow stronger.[92] The hope is that these learning experiences may inspire future public service and help individuals "shape their lives and work in civic and morally committed directions."[93]

A second goal is to enrich students' education by enhancing their motivations to learn and by increasing their analytic, problem solving, and collaborative skills.[94] A wide variety of research indicates that individuals benefit from teaching methods that actively engage them in the learning process, and that provide opportunities for interaction with peers in addressing real-world concerns.[95] Community service placements, by broadening the array of skills and tasks required, increase the likelihood that students with different capabilities will connect productively with their course work.[96] When such placements expose participants to individuals of different class, racial, and ethnic backgrounds, the experience can develop tolerance, respect, and cross-cultural competencies that are essential in an increasingly diverse society.[97]

A final objective of service learning is to enrich understanding of social problems and to build academic/community partnerships in developing appropriate responses.[98] The key component of service learning is guided reflection: out-of-class assignments and in-class discussions that enable the students to link their service with their academic study. By bridging the gap between theory and practice, such courses enable current and future generations of scholars to bring their skills to bear on central personal and policy challenges.

Critiques of Service Learning

The capacity of community service programs to accomplish these objectives has been subject to considerable debate. The strongest criticism centers on mandatory programs, particularly those that are not integrated with academic curricula. Some concerns focus on the increased costs and administrative burdens of overseeing placements, which divert scarce resources from schools' core academic mission.[99] Many school administrators resist the concept of "mandatory altruism" and view "fluffy feel good stuff" as competing with efforts to provide "good grounding in the basics."[100] A widely circulated critique of mandatory service learning in public education concluded that "Schools that can barely teach the fundamental skills and information needed by every citizen are now being used by government and adult activists to shape students' attitudes and assumptions about citizenship itself. This is arguably the last thing that should be tampered with by a government that is supposed to be the creation of its citizens, not the other way around."[101]

A related concern is that the civic and ethical dimensions of community service programs are either "frustratingly ill defined" or inappropriately partisan.[102] Prominent theorists like Stanley Fish argue that the role of educators is "not to change the world, but to interpret it."[103] To the extent that service programs have an explicit or implicit social agenda, they may compromise principles of academic freedom and blur the boundaries between education and politics.

Other critics support community service in principle but question its effectiveness in practice. As they note, some placements are inadequately structured and supervised, and some students respond poorly in even the best-designed programs.[104] If the amount of time participants spend on site is too brief, or if they lack sufficient opportunities for guided reflection, the experience may have little educational value. And if students are insufficiently motivated, their participation may be counterproductive for all concerned.[105] Some critics believe that communities too often have been seen simply as "subjects to be studied" and have gained little from academic collaboration.[106] Particularly where service requirements are not well integrated into the curricula, the result may be to foster a superficial noblesse oblige approach to social problems. The emphasis on volunteering may encourage students to see direct service to needy individuals as a substitute for political activism and policy initiatives that address the sources of need.[107]

The Effectiveness of Service Learning

The claims of both supporters and critics rest on limited evidence, often on small-scale qualitative analysis or anecdotal experience. Adequate measurements and longitudinal data do not exist on many key issues, such as the extent to which service programs foster civic engagement, social responsibility, effective collaborative strategies, and long-term contributions to public interest and charitable causes.[108] Nor is reliable research available comparing different program structures.

However, the limited evidence available suggests that both service learning and voluntary community placements have positive effects on students' academic performance, sensitivity to social problems, and support of altruistic activity. The most systematic large-scale study, involving some 22,000 college students, found that those who engaged in both community service programs and service learning courses had higher grade-point averages and stronger critical thinking and writing skills than those who did not, controlling for relevant factors such as high school grades and predispositions toward service.[109] Students in service learning courses also reported substantially higher commitments to "activism," to "promoting racial understanding," and to pursuing a "service-related career" than other students.[110] Further studies have found that community service participants, compared with individuals in control groups, improve more in problem-solving and leadership skills, and attach greater importance to "working toward equal opportunity" and "volunteering to help people in need."[111] Participation is also associated with gains in academic aspirations and a sense of civic responsibility (including a willingness to participate in community projects).[112]

However, some of these gains, although statistically significant, are relatively small, and whether they translate into long-term behavior remains an open question.[113] It is equally unclear how required service programs compare to those that are voluntary. One of the few studies on point found that students with an inclination to volunteer indicated a greater willingness to volunteer in the future after their experience in a mandatory college service program, but that students who were not so inclined reported less willingness to volunteer after being required to do so.[114] In another large-scale survey of some 12,000 alumni of college service programs, volunteer experiences had a positive influence on a range of behaviors related to academic achievement and altruistic contributions, such as helping others in difficulty and participating in community action programs.[115]

Taken together, these findings suggest that well-designed opportunities for public service advance justifiable educational goals. Contrary to critics' claims, it does not appear that community work competes with other academic objectives; rather, it builds capacities and strengthens commitments in ways that conventional classroom learning cannot. Nor do carefully structured service programs compromise academic freedom or pose some distinctive threat of partisan proselytizing. Teachers in many educational settings can abuse their authority and use their podiums as bully pulpits; the risks are not inherently greater in service learning, where faculty generally share an explicit goal of building students' own capacities for independent moral judgment and respect for competing views. So too, critics' assumption that higher education should be value-free and should seek only to understand the world, not change it for the better, ignores the history of American academic institutions. Most were founded with the explicit goal of building character as well as advancing knowledge.[116] And most of their current leaders share the conviction that by fostering a deeper understanding of social problems, higher education can appropriately help to address them.[117]

Yet although academic institutions generally acknowledge the value of supporting public service, they vary considerably in their effectiveness in doing so. A growing body of research, however, is available to help structure successful programs. As this research makes clear, a critical first step is to make community service an educational priority, and to recognize its significance in budgets, curricula, and extracurricular activities. Resources must be sufficient for course development and volunteer placements, and efforts should be made to link public interest and academic work. The goal should be to maximize students' sense of choice and control over service placements and to ensure adequate supervision and guided reflection.[118] Participants should have meaningful assignments, frequent on-site visits, sustained client relationships, institutional support and feedback, and opportunities to develop transferrable skills, including leadership and decision-making capabilities.[119] A mandatory program that involves participants in the design of their own service can help reduce resistance and encourage them to see involvement as a reflection of personal values rather than simply as compliance with a requirement.[120] Institutions should also offer career counseling to help students make service opportunities part of their postcollege plans and to provide information about how well various employers, graduate programs, and professional schools support such opportunities.[121] Finally, more systematic research is needed to evaluate service programs and to identify concrete strategies for improvement.

Implications of Altruism Research for Pro Bono Programs

Taken together, these research findings offer useful insights about pro bono programs for lawyers and law students. As a threshold matter, the capacities of even the best-designed programs should not be overstated. By the time individuals launch a legal career, it is too late to alter certain personal traits and experiences that influence public service motivations. Such factors include a willingness to empathize, a sense of civic or group responsibility, and early positive exposure to volunteers and volunteer work. If these formative influences are lacking, pro bono programs may hold little appeal.

Promoting Effective Programs

Yet the preceding research also suggests that well-designed strategies by law schools, bar associations, and legal employers can increase the quality and attractiveness of pro bono service. Requests for involvement, coupled with an array of choices that match participants' interests with unmet needs, are likely to expand participation. Providing direct exposure to the human costs of social problems can also prove important. Pro bono commitments can be further reinforced by educational efforts that focus attention on the urgency of unmet needs, the profession's obligation to respond, and the personal benefits of doing so. Enlisting well-respected practitioners and faculty as mentors and role models could assist those efforts. Adequate training can help ensure that individuals feel competent to offer services; it can also encourage participation by developing skills that are valuable in other practice settings. Additional strategies include public recognition, awards, and credit toward academic or billable hour requirements. The point of all these efforts should be to help participants see pro bono service as a rewarding and rewarded part of their professional identity.

Mandatory or Voluntary Service

A more complicated question is whether a mandatory or voluntary program would better serve this goal. On this point, social science research yields no clear answers, although it clarifies trade-offs. Requiring pro bono service offers several advantages. Most obviously, such a requirement makes failure to contribute assistance morally illegitimate and reinforces the message that such contributions are a professional obligation. Institutionalizing that obligation could diminish the number of apathetic bystanders who are now free riders on the bar's reputation for public service and whose nonparticipation discourages participation by others. And at least some individuals who would be involved in mandatory but not voluntary programs would likely become converts to the cause and provide assistance beyond what a minimum requirement would demand. The potential disadvantages of compelling service are equally clear. By diminishing participants' sense that they are acting for altruistic reasons, a pro bono requirement could erode commitment and discourage contributions above the prescribed minimum. If adequate programs are not in place to train participants, accommodate their interests, and monitor their performance, the results will be unsatisfying for all concerned.

Similar trade-offs are likely under voluntary pro bono initiatives. Their advantages are readily apparent. By reinforcing participants' sense that they are acting out of principle rather than obligation, such programs may foster deeper commitments than mandatory approaches. Those who volunteer also are likely to pick an area of practice where they are competent or wish to become so; those compelled to serve may lack adequate choices or motivation. Yet if purely elective programs cannot attract widespread participation, they undermine the message that pro bono service is a professional responsibility. Without a formal requirement, law schools and employers will face less pressure to provide appropriate support for pro bono programs. And individuals who might learn most from direct exposure to unmet needs may be least inclined to volunteer.

How these trade-offs balance out in particular contexts is difficult to assess. Any adequate analysis requires much more comparative data about mandatory and voluntary programs. The findings reported in Chapters 6 and 7 concerning law firm and law school approaches are a step toward providing that information, as well as identifying the most significant influences on pro bono service.

Chapter Four

PUBLIC SERVICE IN
COMPARATIVE PERSPECTIVE

Although the American bar has long viewed itself as the world's leader in pro bono service, it is not unique in this tradition—indeed, it has much to teach and learn from other professions. Yet surprisingly little comparative information is available. This chapter provides the first systematic survey of the evolution of pro bono responsibilities across disciplinary boundaries. By focusing on public service in medicine, engineering, and business, the following overview seeks both to synthesize information from widely disparate sources and to chart a common agenda for reform.

MEDICINE

The Evolution of Charity Care

The profession most analogous to law in its service tradition is medicine. Doctors' responsibility to treat those unable to pay is deeply rooted in medical ethics. By the early Middle Ages, caring for the poor was considered the hallmark of the virtuous physician.[1] In this country, the profession's first code of ethics, adopted by the American Medical Association (AMA) in 1847, advised that "Poverty . . . should always be recognized as presenting valid claims for gratuitous services. . . . [T]o individuals in indigent circumstances, professional services should be cheerfully and freely accorded."[2]

No systematic data are available on how many physicians actually (or cheerfully) assumed this obligation. However, historical records suggest that most charitable health care occurred in teaching hospitals owned or controlled by universities. For example, in the 1930s and 1940s, Johns Hopkins Hospital served nearly half of the indigent population in Baltimore and provided more free treatment than the city's entire municipal hospital system.[3] Such levels of charity were not unique. Throughout the twentieth century, academic medical centers bore a disproportionate share of the profession's obligation to the poor, largely as a result of their status as a public trust.[4] In exchange for generous government subsidies, the privileges of self-regulation, and protection from lay competition, academic medical centers assumed major societal responsibilities, including indigent care and research on public health. The profession's leadership was conscious of this implicit social contract. In 1919, the head of Columbia University Medical School advised his faculty always to "keep in mind that we are a public service institution."[5]

No comprehensive national data are available on the extent of charitable care by the profession as a whole. However, regional records indicate that large municipal hospitals affiliated with public medical schools made impressive contributions. By the end of World War I, nearly all of their patients were charity cases.[6] Urban private teaching hospitals typically reserved 60% to 80% of their beds for free care, and they reportedly considered it an embarrassment to drop below 50%.[7] Although local governments provided partial reimbursements for indigent care, most of the funding came from gifts and physicians' donations of time. One 1953 study estimated that foregone professional fees exceeded $100,000,000 a year.[8] This level of service was possible because academic institutions, medical societies, and hospitals actively pressured private physicians to contribute charity care. In the early 1960s, the expectation was for these doctors to donate a half a day per week of unpaid service in hospital clinics, and to charge other patients according to their ability to pay.[9] How many physicians met this expectation remains unclear, but because peer pressure was the only enforcement mechanism, the gap between principle and practice was undoubtedly substantial. Still, such informal pressure appears to have been more influential in the medical than in the legal profession, partly because of the dominant role that academics played in both charitable and regulatory contexts. The same faculty who solicited volunteers for teaching hospitals constituted the majority on accrediting bodies and certifying boards, so their requests could not be readily disregarded.[10]

By the mid-twentieth century, however, it had become increasingly apparent that charitable contributions could not keep pace with the needs of the poor. To address the gap, the federal government began to assume greater responsibility for indigent medical services.[11] Yet ironically enough, the 1965 Medicare and Medicaid legislation, which dramatically expanded health care funding for elderly and low-income groups, had an unintended adverse effect on the medical profession's charitable contributions. Once the government began reimbursing academic medical centers for nearly all of the indigent services formerly provided free of charge, teaching hospitals lost their identity as primarily charitable institutions. This transformation, together with the establishment of government-funded community health centers and other public health clinics, relieved much of the pressure on private physicians to provide free or reduced-fee care.[12] Moreover, as the possibility of reimbursement through federal funds and private insurance coverage increased, so too did the opportunity costs of providing unpaid services. Before the mid-1960s, many doctors were unable to fill their schedules with patients who could afford full fees; charity care was a way of productively using their time and building relationships that might yield profitable referrals.[13] The growing availability of third-party payments allowed more physicians to develop full-time practices with compensated services. Moreover, because public and private funders often forced physicians to discount their fees, many practitioners felt that they were providing sufficient unpaid assistance without volunteering for charity work.[14]

Yet expanded government funding has by no means eliminated the need for charitable assistance. As subsequent discussion makes clear, tens of millions of individuals do not qualify for Medicare or Medicaid benefits, lack health insurance, and are unable to afford private care.[15] In the face of such unmet needs, leaders of the medical profession are placing renewed emphasis on physicians' public service responsibilities.

Current Ethical Rules

Like other professions, the medical profession has traditionally exercised considerable control over its own regulation, including its ethical standards. The most authoritative compilation of these standards is the Code of Medical Ethics of the American Medical Association. As initially adopted in 1847, the Code offered little more than general aspirations for professional education and etiquette. For many years, it remained "the last place anyone with a serious interest in the ethics of health care would be tempted to look for weighty moral analysis."[16] Over the last century, however, the Code has evolved into an extensive, two-part treatise that articulates seven "Fundamental Principles of Medical Ethics," and six "Fundamental Elements of the Patient-Physician Relationship." These are "not laws, but standards of conduct which define the essentials of honorable behavior for the physician."[17] Supplementing these standards are advisory opinions by the AMA's Council on Judicial and Ethical Affairs, which interpret and apply the Code's mandates. Although neither the Code nor the opinions have binding legal force, they serve as the profession's "authoritative voice" in legal opinions and have shaped significant judicial rulings on health care issues.[18]

Like the American bar, the American medical profession has resisted efforts to mandate a specified amount of charitable service as part of its ethical code. Instead, it has relied on aspirational norms. In 1992, the AMA considered and rejected a proposal that would have required physicians to devote 10% of their income or 50 hours a year to care for the indigent.[19] As it currently stands, the AMA Code identifies a "basic right to have available adequate health care" as one of the six fundamental elements of the patient-physician relationship.[20] To that end, the Code encourages physicians to "continue their traditional assumption of a part of the responsibility for the medical care of those who cannot afford essential health care." However, the Code also makes it clear that the major responsibility for access to services lies with the public not the profession: "Fulfillment of [the right to care] is dependent on society providing resources so that no patient is deprived of necessary care because of an inability to pay."[21]

In June 1994, the AMA's Council on Judicial and Ethical Affairs issued an advisory opinion clarifying doctors' responsibilities. It emphasizes that "[e]ach physician has an obligation to share in providing care to the indigent" and lists possible ways for meeting that obligation.[22] Examples include treating an indigent patient at no cost or at reduced cost, and donating time in hospitals, shelters, community clinics, and government programs that provide health care to the poor. Although the opinion maintains that "[c]aring for the poor should be a regular part of the physician's practice schedule," it specifies no minimum amount of assistance. Rather, it states simply that "[t]he measure of what constitutes an appropriate contribution may vary with circumstances such as community characteristics, geographic location, the nature of the physician's practice and specialty, and other conditions."[23]

The Extent of Charitable Services and Unmet Needs

The medical profession has done a better job than the legal profession in tracking the extent of charitable services, and the data available reveal higher levels of participation among doctors than lawyers. According to the AMA's most recent studies, about two-thirds of doctors provide such services, and those who contribute donate an average of about nine hours a week, some 14% of the total time they spend on patient care.[24] The Center for Studying Health System Change's Tracking Report reports somewhat higher levels of participation and substantially lower amounts of service; some 72% of surveyed physicians provided charity care, but the average commitment was only about 11 hours a month, about 5% of total practice hours, which included patient care as well as other services.[25] Disparities between the AMA and the Center findings may be largely attributable to differences in the sample size and methodology.[26] At any rate, the dollar amount of charity care is impressive; by the mid-1990s, it was estimated at over $11 billion annually.[27]

Yet other surveys suggest that physician involvement in charity care is on the decline.[28] And existing levels leave substantial room for improvement in both the extent and quality of services. Nearly 44 million uninsured individuals, and an almost equal number of low-income underinsured individuals and Medicaid beneficiaries, are in need of greater access to adequate health care.[29] Lack of services can have life-threatening consequences or can significantly impair patients' capacity to work and to function independently in society. Moreover, even those who receive some charitable assistance consistently receive lower-quality care than insured patients.[30] Community health centers, which operate under severe budget constraints, are often unable to provide crucial specialized treatment.[31] Although more than four-fifths of community health centers are "frequently" or "very frequently" able to provide "all necessary services" for their insured patients, only a third can do so as often for their uninsured patients.[32] Even teaching hospitals, traditionally leaders in caring for the poor, have had difficulty providing indigent patients with comprehensive treatment. One recent national survey found that nearly a quarter of teaching hospital faculty felt that they were unable to admit uninsured patients or had to limit their care because of insurance status.[33] Even if indigent patients are admitted, they face an additional hurdle: clinical faculty are often unwilling or unable to obtain referrals to specialists for uninsured patients.[34]

The disparity in care is due to a combination of problems, including not only inadequate resources, but also peer pressure, insurance restrictions, and institutional priorities. For example, some clinical faculty feel uncomfortable referring nonpaying patients to colleagues who have other priorities related to teaching and research.[35] Insurance companies place complex limitations on referrals for specialty services, particularly outpatient mental health care and substance abuse treatment.[36] As noted below, formal policies and informal practices in many medical settings also discourage practitioners from seeing too many indigent patients.

A related problem involves the distribution of charitable services. Many doctors, like many lawyers, prefer to channel their charity to individuals who may be sources of future paying services, rather than to low-income individuals who most need assistance. In one national survey, of the two-thirds of internists who provided unpaid treatment, over half mainly targeted previous patients who had lost their insurance because of unemployment or other circumstances.[37]

Influences on Charity Care

Various factors affect physicians' willingness to provide charity care. The first involves the availability of other sources of free assistance, which affects perceptions of unmet needs. Charitable contributions are lower in areas with a large number of public hospitals and emergency departments that accept low-income uninsured patients.[38] Conversely, physicians are more likely to donate services in areas with large numbers of university teaching hospitals.[39] Recent research suggests several reasons why these hospitals are particularly likely to encourage charity care by affiliated physicians. One of the most important involves public relations.[40] Media and community criticism concerning access issues can often prompt a "renewed interest in public service."[41] Other significant influences on charitable contributions include a commitment by hospital leaders, an infrastructure to support such work, student demand for service opportunities, interest among the clinical faculty, and recognition by peers and administrators, including favorable consideration in promotion and tenure decisions.[42]

On the other hand, the most frequently cited obstacle to charitable service is the widespread adoption of managed care systems that impose aggressive cost-control methods.[43] Such methods are in turn responsive to increased competition and financial pressures in health services, as well as decreased ability to shift the costs of uncompensated care on to third-party payers. These structural forces have had a corrosive effect on charitable commitments. Some evidence suggests that managed care plans are more likely to avoid contracts with physicians who serve large numbers of uninsured persons.[44] Unsurprisingly, heavy involvement in managed care significantly reduces the likelihood that a physician will provide unpaid services and decreases the number of charitable hours provided.[45] Similar pressure by insurance companies, employers, and government payers also causes many doctors to reduce or eliminate uncompensated assistance.[46]

A further obstacle to charitable involvement is the trend in ownership arrangements. No longer is the American health care system dominated by independent health professionals making autonomous decisions about their practice priorities.[47] Over the past half-century, market pressures and elimination of anticompetitive constraints on nonphysician ownership have led doctors to consolidate their practices and merge into larger and larger institutions. Hospitals now employ an increasing percentage of the health profession, and fewer physicians own their practices.[48] This has had a negative effect on charity care, because doctors who are full or partial owners are almost twice as likely to provide such care as doctors who are not.[49] Practice owners are also far more likely than physicians employed by others to adopt discretionary policies on charges and collection that accommodate uninsured patients.[50]

In the face of these market pressures, leaders of the medical profession have looked for other ways to support charitable commitments. As in law, promotion of public service in professional schools has been an obvious choice.

Service Learning in Medical Education

Service learning in medical education, like its analogues in undergraduate and postgraduate programs, combines community placements with classroom learning and guided reflection.[51] Service learning differs from medical schools' traditional clinical courses in several significant ways. First, clinical education generally emphasizes teaching while service learning also focuses on public needs. Second, service learning emphasizes more reciprocal exchanges of knowledge than clinical education; the goal is for community members, staff, faculty, and students to participate as partners in the educational process. Third, clinical education focuses on interactions with individual patients, while service learning also addresses broader community concerns. Finally, even when clinical education involves community placements, the curriculum is typically designed by faculty. By contrast, community groups play an important role in the design of service learning.[52]

Service learning is a relatively new concept in medical education. Although universities have long supported charity care, the integration of service with academic courses is a recent development.[53] No comprehensive information is available on the extent to which medical schools have incorporated service learning opportunities into their standard curriculum. Only

5 of the nation's 20 top-ranked medical schools advertise these opportunities. However, foundations and medical societies, including the AMA and American Medical Student Association, are actively promoting such programs.[54] The AMA's program, Reaching Equitable Access to Care for Health (REACH), is working with 10 medical schools to develop service learning opportunities for students and faculty to serve in free clinics as part of a larger effort to promote increased volunteer work by physicians.[55]

The justifications for integrating public service into the medical school curriculum parallel those for similar efforts in other educational contexts. One rationale is that students who have a positive service experience at the formative state of their professional careers will be more likely to seek comparable charitable opportunities during practice. A second rationale is that service learning can serve important academic goals, such as building interpersonal skills and appreciation of community health issues.[56]

The extent to which existing approaches fulfill these objectives is unclear. No comprehensive studies are available on the long-term effects of service learning in medical education. However, a number of individual projects report significant achievements.[57] One involves a first-year elective service learning course at Dartmouth Medical School.[58] Participants teach a public elementary school class concerning health issues and participate in seminars on teaching techniques, peer collaboration, and guided reflection.[59] Initial evaluation suggests that medical students have improved their communication styles in ways that predict increased ability to interact with patients and staff. Students also have reported increased interest in community service, as well as increased recognition of the social factors influencing health and related public education efforts.[60]

As Chapter 3 noted, evidence from other educational contexts finds similar benefits. But more systematic research is clearly needed to encourage schools to make the financial and administrative commitment necessary for effective programs. At a minimum, such programs require dedicated faculty and community members, as well as modification of traditional teaching methods and scheduling priorities.[61] A growing number of schools are moving in the right direction, but considerable progress remains to be made.

ENGINEERING

Historical Background and Ethical Codes

Unlike medicine and law, engineering has no long-standing tradition of public service. Nor has the concept yet achieved widespread acceptance even in principle, let alone in practice. Part of the reason may lie in engineering's philosophical and historical roots. Early practitioners tended to view their profession as ethically neutral. When the Royal Society of London was founded in 1663 to promote excellence in science, its curator of experiments, Robert Hooke, advised members that their business was "to improve the knowledge of natural things, not meddling with Divinity, Metaphysics, Moralls, Politicks, Grammar, Rhetorick or Logic."[62]

Until recently, that remained the dominant view. During its formative years, the American Society of Civil Engineers, the nation's oldest engineering society, adamantly rejected even the concept of a code of ethics; moral concerns should remain a "matter of an engineer's personal responsibility and honor."[63] When the ASCE finally adopted its first ethical code in 1914, the document focused on relationships between engineers and their clients or colleagues, not on responsibilities to the public.[64] Similarly, the code adopted in 1912 by a predecessor of the Institute of Electrical and Electronics Engineers (IEEE) provided that an engineer's first obligation was the protection of client and employer interests.[65] The code's only acknowledgment of broader social responsibilities was a provision stating that "[t]he engineer should endeavor to assist the public to a fair and correct general understanding of engineering matters."[66] None of the early codes made reference to public service. Nor does it appear that their admonitions had much practical significance. Engineering societies generally made no attempt to enforce their codes and little effort to promote understanding and compliance among their members. Indeed, when IEEE members set out to write a new code of ethics in the 1970s, they were not aware that one already existed.[67]

During the twentieth century, a greater sense of social responsibility gradually emerged. The growing consensus was that engineering inevitably affected public health, safety, and the environment. In 1947, the Engineer's Council for Professional Development published the first code of ethics explicitly recognizing the engineer's "duty to interest himself in public welfare and be ready to apply his special knowledge for the benefit of mankind."[68] The Council, now the Accreditation Board for Engineering and Technology, has become responsible for the accreditation of graduate engineering programs and has exercised significant influence over national engineering societies. Many of those societies have adopted its code, which has been revised twice since 1947 to include stronger language concerning the profession's social responsibilities. The current version directs engineers to "hold paramount the safety, health, and welfare of the public in the performance of their professional duties."[69] Virtually all other codes of major engineering organizations include similar provisions.[70]

Some ethics experts maintain that this responsibility to promote the public welfare entails an obligation to engage in public service. Two of the leading codes of conduct make explicit reference to such service. The National Society of Professional Engineers' (NSPE) Code of Ethics for Engineers provides that "Engineers shall seek opportunities to participate in civic affairs; career guidance for youths; and work for the advancement of the safety, health, and well-being of their community."[71] Similarly, ASCE's Standards of Professional Conduct advises that "Engineers should seek opportunities to be of constructive service in civic affairs and work for the advancement of the safety, health, and well-being of their communities and the protection of the environment through the practice of sustainable development."[72]

These societies have also launched corresponding service initiatives. The NSPE's 2003–2005 Strategic Plan identifies as one of the organization's seven core values "service to the public" and encourages "engineers to participate in civic, educational, community and governmental activities and projects."[73] The ASCE has established a Committee on Volunteer Community Service and a public service award series. It has also prepared publications and a Web site showcasing members' volunteer projects, such as redevelopment of low-income housing and design of safety features for a local senior center.[74]

Yet these societies' initiatives typically lack the moral foundations associated with public service mandates in other professional contexts. Rather than appealing to practitioners' altruism and sense of social responsibility, the NSPE and ASCE frame community work as a means of promoting professional status. The ASCE's community service Web page opens with the following acknowledgment: "One of ASCE's strategic goals is to enhance recognition of civil engineering as a highly respected profession and a desirable and rewarding career. It is our professional duty and obligation to engage in public service as an essential means of practicing civic leadership outside of our employment toward the goal of improving our image."[75]

Similarly, the NSPE 2003–2005 Strategic Plan places community service under "Goal 2: Enhance the image and stature of engineering professionals."[76] Other strategies listed beneath this heading include implementing an "image campaign," publicizing the achievements of engineers, and developing how-to guides instructing members on ways to improve the profession's public image.[77] How much effect these initiatives have had on charitable involvement remains unclear.

The Extent of Public Service in Engineering

No systematic research is available on the extent of engineers' participation in public service. A review of current engineering ethics literature suggests that charitable work is not a primary focus within the profession. Eleven leading engineering ethics guides and textbooks, with a total of 2813 pages, included only 11 pages (0.4%) with references to public service. Of those 11 pages, 8 simply described case studies with charitable opportunities or themes.[78] Only one text offered even a brief discussion of public service obligations; its point was to highlight the debate in the profession over whether such obligations exist. The text concluded by listing examples of volunteer service such as "tutoring disadvantaged students in mathematics and physics," participating in "'urban technology' interest groups," and "advis[ing] local governments on their engineering problems."[79]

Such a list hardly exhausts the potential types of services needed, particularly for low-income communities. Other obvious possibilities include construction and renovation of facilities in areas lacking adequate housing, public transportation, and environmental protection. However, these projects generally require collective efforts and resources, which is one reason engineers often give for why they are less likely to donate services than other professionals.[80] But most communities have an ample supply of individual volunteer opportunities, such as consulting for nonprofit and governmental organizations, or participation in programs like Habitat for Humanity. As more engineering societies begin to promote public service, an even broader array of opportunities are likely to become available, especially if engineering firms can be enlisted to provide financial support.

Service Learning in Engineering

An increased interest in public service among engineering schools could also contribute to increased public service among practitioners. Such a trend would be consistent with other forces that are reshaping traditional engineering curricula. Historically, engineering education focused on developing scientific and technical capabilities and devoted little attention to ethical and charitable concerns.[81] However, over the last two decades, leaders in engineering education as well as engineering societies have begun placing increased emphasis on ethical responsibilities and "soft skills," including collaboration and understanding of community and environmental concerns.[82] Since the mid-1990s, a growing number of schools have been increasing curricular attention to these capabilities, and incorporating service learning that addresses them. The Engineering Projects in Community Service, developed at Purdue University, now serves as a model for over 15 schools.[83] Another influential program, designed by Cornell, Encourage Young Engineering Students, has grown into a national community service organization that involves engineering students in teaching math and science skills to elementary, middle, and high school students.[84]

Changes in engineering accreditation standards have reflected and reinforced this interest in service learning and the capacities that it seeks to develop. As of 2000, to satisfy these standards, engineering programs must demonstrate that their graduates possess not only technical skills but also an ability to function on multidisciplinary teams; an ability to communicate effectively; an appreciation of the impact of engineering solutions in a global and societal context; and a knowledge of contemporary issues.[85] Some of these capabilities are difficult to teach well in conventional courses, which typically involve either lectures or laboratory formats. As a consequence, a growing number of educators have turned to service learning as a way to meet the new accreditation requirements.[86]

No national data are available on the prevalence of service learning in engineering schools. Experts generally describe engineering as "lagg[ing] behind most other disciplines in the acceptance of this pedagogy."[87] Yet since the new accreditation criteria were announced, the number and scale of public service opportunities have dramatically increased. Nine of the nation's twenty top-ranked engineering schools now visibly advertise service learning projects and courses on their Web sites, and leading programs like MIT's have dramatically expanded their offerings.[88]

Such opportunities typically fall into one of two categories: teaching engineering, math, or science skills to younger students, often through collaborative projects; or working with community partners in responding to a specific public need. The range and depth of service learning courses are impressive. For example, students enrolled in MIT's Information and Communication Technologies in Community Development course collaborate with local nonprofit groups on urban planning issues.[89] Students learn about topics such as the digital divide, e-government, public participation, and race, class, and gender dynamics. At the University of Southern Alabama, students work with middle schools on designing projects and software systems to improve math and science instruction.[90]

The justifications for service learning in engineering parallel those advanced in other professional contexts but also reflect some distinctive concerns. The first rationale is that such approaches are effective ways of teaching skills now recognized as necessary by most educators as well as by engineering accreditation boards. Service learning requires students to collaborate with those of different backgrounds and to function as part of multidisciplinary teams. Well-designed projects also can build awareness of ethical issues and the "impacts of engineering solutions in . . . a societal context."[91]

A second rationale for service learning is that it may help increase retention rates.[92] The number of engineering degrees has declined in recent years, because of both lower initial enrollments and larger numbers of transfers to other degree programs.[93] Proponents of service learning argue that it can increase retention by demonstrating that engineering can be socially relevant and personally rewarding.[94] As one professor put it, "All too often, engineering is misrepresented as a boring field [in which] . . . the engineer has little contact with what is actually going on in the world."[95] Public service placements can help counteract this stereotype and make engineering more appealing to nontraditional candidates, including women and minorities, who have interests in community involvement.[96]

A related rationale for service learning is that it can address one of the root causes of declining enrollments by incorporating projects aimed at younger students. If interests in math and science drop off in middle and high school, fewer students will have the preparation necessary for college engineering programs. Community placements that build interest and skills among 12- to 18-year-olds can help recruit future degree candidates and compensate for curricular inadequacies in many resource-starved public schools.[97]

A final justification for service learning is that it can increase engineers' social understanding and social responsibility. Community placements often expand participants' awareness of the public consequences of professional decisions and enhance their appreciation of diversity-related concerns.[98] Many educators also hope to reinforce charitable commitments, creating a "new type of engineer—one for whom community service and volunteerism is a way of life."[99]

No comprehensive data are available on the effectiveness of service learning in advancing these objectives. However, as in other educational contexts, both faculty and students report significant gains, including enhanced collaborative skills and increased interest in community service.[100] With few exceptions, even students who were initially skeptical of public interest work generally believe that it was beneficial, and some indicate that they now feel they "should do more."[101]

Efforts are currently underway to obtain systematic data on the impact of service learning.[102] If the results are consistent with the information available to date both from engineering and from other disciplines, it may help to overcome the resistance of some faculty.[103] As skeptics note, well-designed service learning projects generally require a greater commitment of time, resources, and external support than conventional courses, and the projects develop skills that are harder to measure.[104] Evaluation of the concrete benefits of such projects could help persuade engineering schools that greater service investments are worth making.

BUSINESS

The Evolution of Corporate Philanthropy

Business involvement in charitable activities has less extended roots, but the last quarter century has witnessed a significant expansion of that role and an integration of public service in business education. To understand that evolution, a brief overview of the development of corporate philanthropy is necessary. The concept has been traced to medieval European guilds, which assumed some responsibility to care for members and their families during times of hardship.[105] However, when widespread charitable support of education and social welfare programs evolved during the nineteenth century, business played a very limited role. Several factors inhibited involvement. First, few large corporations existed with interests separate from their owners. If the wealthy individuals who controlled these businesses wanted to make a gift, they generally did so with their own funds. A second limitation involved legal doctrine prohibiting corporations from acting beyond their explicit chartered powers; any use of corporate funds that was not directly related to business purposes was considered "ultra vires," beyond the scope of legal authority.[106]

Judicial interpretations of this restriction were not entirely consistent. One leading New York 1896 decision allowed contributions to build homes, churches, and schools serving company employees, while a 1915 Georgia ruling disallowed a loan guarantee for public school and town development that would have yielded similar benefits.[107] Such conflicting judgments opened the way for legal challenges that discouraged corporate philanthropy. A further deterrent was the reaction among some potential recipients to "tainted money." A celebrated example was Jane Addams's rejection of a $20,000 donation for Hull House: the donor's "record as an employer made it unthinkable" to accept the subsidy.[108]

However, beginning in the early twentieth century, a number of forces converged to encourage greater corporate philanthropy. One was the rapid increase of reputable giving opportunities and pressures for contributions. The Progressive Era witnessed a dramatic growth in charitable organizations, as well as federations of widely acceptable charities that enabled businesses to contribute without fear of fraud or charges of undue favoritism.[109] World War I created further philanthropic opportunities and increased legitimacy for involvement. Widely respected authorities, such as retired Supreme Court Justice Charles Evans Hughes, argued that it was appropriate for corporations to support "worthy" causes that maintained "the very foundation of the corporate enterprise itself."[110] In 1924, the United States Chamber of Commerce conferred additional legitimacy on such charitable involvement by developing a code of ethics outlining businesses' obligations to their community, including philanthropy. This was the first widespread acknowledgment of corporate social responsibility, which was to develop more fully over the next decades.[111]

Other forces encouraging charitable involvement were the Great Depression and World War II, and law reforms that responded to the social needs of these eras. In 1935, Congress approved tax legislation allowing corporations to deduct up to 55% of their pretax earnings; in 1942 and again during the Korean conflict, it imposed an excess profits tax that created further incentives for charitable contributions. Decisions by courts and state legislatures both reflected and reinforced this trend. Between 1917 and 1960, almost all states amended their corporate laws to permit donations up to IRS-sanctioned levels without having to show a direct business purpose.[112] The significance of such legislation was confirmed in 1953, when the United States Supreme Court let stand a state court decision upholding a corporate gift to Princeton University's general fund. Under the court's reasoning, the "salvation" of business "rests upon [a] sound economic and social environment, which in turn rests in no insignificant part upon free and vigorous nongovernmental institutions of learning."[113] In effect, the ruling sustained statutes like the one at issue in the case, which made business philanthropy no longer ultra vires.

By the mid-twentieth century, the concept of corporate charitable involvement was well established, and it grew in importance as a corporate social responsibility movement developed in the latter part of the century. The social activism and consumer consciousness of the 1960s and 1970s, and the intermittent corporate scandals of more recent decades, gave rise to new emphasis on business ethics, including philanthropic obligations. Public opinion polls consistently indicated that most Americans believed that charitable involvement should be a standard part of corporate activities.[114] As the importance of corporate charity increased, so too did the profits available for distribution. Annual business giving increased from about $270 million in 1945 to about $6 billion in 1990, and $11 billion in the early 2000s.[115] Contributions have stabilized at about 1% of earnings.[116]

Paralleling the growth in contributions has been a growth in corporate-sponsored volunteer activity. Business leaders and their employees have, of course, long been involved in community affairs as individuals. What is distinctive about recent trends is that many companies now help staff community service projects. Although financial contributions and in-kind donations of equipment or merchandise are still the most common forms of support, a growing number of businesses also subsidize some employee volunteer activities. On company time, workers assist programs ranging from soup kitchens to community development and technology transfer.[117] More than a thousand businesses have joined Corporate Volunteer Councils, networks of employers that partner with community-based nonprofit agencies to help address local problems.[118] These service projects are increasingly becoming part of coordinated plans that integrate companies' philanthropic and business goals.

Indeed, the general trend in corporate workplaces is toward "strategic giving" that aligns profit and public service objectives. About four-fifths of surveyed companies report focusing volunteer programs on "core business functions."[119] In an increasingly competitive environment, businesses are attempting to ensure that their charitable activities provide "value added" to marketing, public relations, and human relations. Over the last two decades, many major corporations have targeted their philanthropy toward causes that are especially likely to appeal to their own investors, consumers, and employees. Such "cause-marketing" strategies are most likely to be effective when they relate in some obvious way to the company's product or services and can tap into its special expertise. Well-known examples include Avon's Women's Health Initiative, Chase Manhattan Bank's affordable housing project, and McGraw-Hill's literacy efforts.[120] Yet how much such philanthropic activities actually contribute to corporate performance remains a matter of debate.

Justifications and Critiques of Corporate Giving

The primary justifications for corporate charitable involvement parallel those for professionals, although the rationale for business contributions generally rests more on pragmatic than moral concerns. Although some advocates appeal to the ethical responsibility to "give back" to the society that sustains business, most arguments stress the instrumental value of good corporate citizenship.[121] One rationale is that philanthropy creates an image of social responsibility that attracts consumers, investors, and employees. The "halo effect" of association with attractive causes can build positive name recognition and help counteract the effect of any negative publicity arising from corporate activities. The concrete results of charitable contributions can also build good relations with local governments as well as influential nonprofit groups.[122] A second rationale stresses the value to employees of participation in charitable activities. Workers can acquire leadership, teamwork, strategic planning, and interpersonal skills. Many gain valuable business contacts and a better understanding of diversity-related issues. So too, employees' sense of shared purpose and identification with a respected employer can aid morale, recruitment, and retention.[123] Corporate decision makers may also receive less socially defensible but more personally valuable benefits, including public prestige, seats on nonprofit boards, and executive perks like preferential treatment at athletic or cultural events.[124]

A growing body of research has attempted to quantify these benefits, but without conclusive results. For example, public opinion surveys find that about two-thirds of consumers report considering social responsibility when making purchase decisions; three-quarters say that they would be likely to switch to a brand associated with a good cause; and about half say that they would be likely to pay more for a product or service associated with such a cause. However, only a fifth indicate that they actually bought a product or service in the last year because of such an association, and only a quarter could identify the "most socially responsible" companies.[125] So too, a number of studies have found that employee loyalty and morale is significantly higher in businesses that are involved in their communities, and that corporate giving levels correlate positively with public image and financial performance.[126] Although such correlations do not establish causation, many researchers believe that the consistency of the relationships, coupled with qualitative evidence of benefits, demonstrates that philanthropy is good for bottom lines.

Other experts are more skeptical; they emphasize the methodological limitations of data on financial performance and note that managers may have personal interests in making donations irrespective of concrete benefits to the corporation.[127] Some commentators view corporate philanthropy as a form of "social currency" among elite executives, or a way to shore up the legitimacy of activities that might otherwise prompt regulatory intervention. As these critics note, certain companies with poor reputations have spent more on advertising good deeds than on the donations themselves.[128] From this perspective, it is a mistake, both conceptually and legally, to treat business contributions as charity when they in fact function as a gussied-up form of advertising, public relations, or executive compensation.[129]

Many business ethics scholars as well as consumers are also critical of both the relatively low level of corporate donations in relation to capacity to give, and the way those funds are allocated. Although tax law permits up to 10% of pretax earnings, the average among companies that contribute is only around 1%, and many provide only token support for employee volunteer efforts.[130] The public also shares experts' doubts about the social value of some corporate philanthropy. In one representative poll, over half of those surveyed thought that business support might be "just for show to improve the company's image" and that it does not always help the causes it addresses.[131] Many empirical studies bear this out. For example, experts on hunger relief have noted that corporations are generally interested only in funding short-term emergency programs that promote a "shining corporate image" rather than long-term strategies that address underlying problems.[132] Other, more comprehensive overviews of corporate philanthropy point up recurrent problems, such as lack of information, expertise, and program evaluation.[133]

Corporate philanthropy also raises governance concerns that are typically less problematic in professional contexts. When law or engineering firms decide to support public interest work, they are doing so with their own money, and they can readily establish oversight structures to minimize the influence of supervising partners' self-interested preferences. By contrast, when corporations make charitable contributions, they are spending someone else's money, and it is extremely difficult for shareholders to exercise meaningful control. Recent surveys indicate that only 13% of Fortune 100 firms publicly report the amount of charitable contributions, and even fewer disclose recipients.[134] Moreover, although some professional service providers such as health maintenance organizations may also have external investors, the potential conflicts of interest in charitable priorities are less common in medicine than in business. The patients who need free medical care are not as likely to be in positions to reward executives with personal benefits as the nonprofit educational, cultural, and community organizations that many businesses support.

The accountability concerns that arise in corporate contexts are not, of course, entirely without remedies. Governance mechanisms are available to minimize the risks of self-interested decision making. For example, corporate boards could establish separate foundations or committees with shareholders, independent directors, and elected employee representatives who select charitable recipients. Such committees, along with boards, can establish procedures for evaluating the cost effectiveness of contributions. More support could target volunteer programs, which, because they depend on broad employee support, are less subject to inappropriate managerial bias. External regulatory authorities could require disclosure of corporate contributions and potential conflicts of interest. Public interest organizations could promulgate "best practices" guidelines as well as publicize outstanding or misconceived programs.[135] And business schools could do more to educate future managers about the value and structure of productive public service contributions.

Business Education and Public Service

As is true with professional education, serious attention to ethical issues is a relatively recent phenomenon in business schools, and only in the last decade have they begun to focus on charitable responsibilities. Not until Watergate and a series of corporate scandals in the 1970s and 1980s did ethical topics gain a curricular toehold. Part of the impetus came from accreditation standards of the predecessor of the Association to Advance Collegiate Schools of Business, International.[136] However, about a third of all schools still do not require a course on business ethics or business in society, and many of the courses that are offered do not include significant discussion of public service. Nor do the association's accreditation standards mandate coverage of service responsibilities. My own review of 13 recent corporate ethics texts revealed only 4 that even briefly addressed issues of public service, and none devoted even 1% of their pages to such discussion.[137]

Public service responsibilities are also missing or marginal in voluntary business ethics codes and in business schools' core curricula. For example, the Institute of Business Ethics, which was founded in 1986 "to encourage high standards" of corporate behavior, provides a general outline of content to include in a business' code of business practice and ethics, but it does not mention a commitment to community service or volunteer work.[138] So too, one survey of more than 100 leading MBA business programs found that none taught courses on corporate involvement in community economic development; only 13 even tangentially addressed the topic in classes about business ethics or business in society.[139]

Although the last two decades have witnessed a significant increase in extracurricular community service projects in business schools, service learning courses have been slower to develop.[140] Business ethics experts attribute resistance to a number of factors, which parallel those arising in professional schools. One is the general devaluation of teaching in comparison to research; faculty have inadequate incentives to invest the substantial time necessary for effective service learning courses.[141] A related obstacle is the priority that schools generally attach to measurable quantitative skills over the softer interpersonal capabilities, multicultural understandings, and ethical sensitivities that service learning fosters.[142] So too, many faculty doubt that they have the background or expertise to teach such courses, and worry about their ability to monitor, control, and evaluate community-based assignments.[143] A further barrier is resistance from some students who question the relevance of public interest placements, the fairness of grading procedures, or the appropriateness of required service.[144]

Yet despite these obstacles, interest is increasing, both in service learning and in nonprofit organizations generally. Although no comprehensive information is available concerning the extent of service opportunities for business students, the programs at surveyed schools reveal a growing range of options. For example, at Stanford's Graduate School of Business, about a quarter of students now concentrate on public management, a number that has doubled over the last decade; a majority are somehow involved with this program on nonprofit organizations through courses, volunteer activities, workshops, and international study trips.[145] Harvard Business School reports that about four-fifths of its students are "significantly involved" with nonprofit organizations, and a growing number participate in its Social Enterprise Initiative, which coordinates curricular and programmatic opportunities.[146] Scholarship on service learning in business is similarly increasing. Materials are now available describing topics and placement opportunities for virtually all areas of the core business school curriculum.[147] For example, students can develop marketing strategies and strategic plans, improve accounting, information and financial management systems, and address human relations needs in a wide range of nonprofit settings.

The benefits that students can gain from these experiences track those available in other service learning contexts, as well as certain capabilities that are especially important to future managers. First, participants gain knowledge and technical skills from the opportunity to connect abstract concepts with actual needs. As both education research and business school accreditation standards have noted, information acquired through experiential learning is more likely to be retained and extended to new situations than information conveyed through conventional classroom lectures.[148] In addition, community placements develop interpersonal capabilities such as teamwork, leadership, communication, and appreciation of cultural differences. Participants acquire useful managerial skills when they encounter diverse stakeholders with competing agendas, and complex trade-offs in circumstances of ambiguous or limited information. A related benefit is enhanced capacity for critical thinking. By requiring students to reflect on their experience and to share their assessments with others, service learning courses encourage a self-critical stance that is crucial in many business contexts.

Finally, service learning promotes social responsibility. It is particularly beneficial for students and faculty steeped in market values to confront market failures and their human consequences. Direct exposure to deep-seated social problems can expand participants' sense of understanding and empathy, which, as Chapter 3 notes, are foundations for altruistic activities. So too, a positive service experience during business school can encourage individuals' interest in future involvement.[149] Fostering a sense of social responsibility among future corporate leaders is especially critical in the face of increasing global interdependence and inequality. In the long run, neither businesses nor those who run them can thrive in societies that fail to address social welfare and environmental needs. Bringing that point home during a formative stage in managerial careers is an important step toward meeting those needs.

No research is available that assesses the long-term impact of public service experiences in business school. However, recent qualitative analyses give consistently positive evaluations, as well as strategies for structuring effective educational environments.[150] At the institutional level, business schools need to provide adequate resources and rewards for those who assume the special commitments of service learning courses. Faculty, for their part, should look for ways to leverage such teaching into research activities and to build networks of support. Outreach to other disciplines, alumni, community leaders, and potential corporate sponsors can expand funding, placement opportunities, and related programs. Well-designed screening and evaluation structures can help ensure a good fit between project needs and student capacities.

Finally, and most importantly, a service ethic must be reinforced throughout the educational experience. Faculty need to model the importance of public interest work through their own involvement, as well as through coverage in academic courses. Extracurricular volunteer programs, speaker series, awards, and publications are all necessary to convince students that corporate social responsibility is just that: a responsibility, not simply a public relations strategy.

A Comparative Assessment

Although more systematic research is necessary, the information available suggests a number of generalizations about public service in different occupational settings. Medicine clearly has the most extended history of charitable involvement, and the highest levels of current contributions. Although the AMA ethical code specifies no aspirational norms, participation rates are much higher than in law; some studies find that doctors' contributions average ten times the annual hourly contributions of lawyers.[151] Comparable data are lacking for engineers and managers, but their commitment to public service is more recent and less widely shared. Not all engineering and business ethics codes explicitly affirm such civic responsibilities, and the topic receives little attention in engineering and business ethics textbooks.

The Growing Focus on Public Service

Interest in public service has, however, increased substantially in recent years in both professional and managerial contexts. Membership organizations, accrediting bodies, and educational programs have all developed new initiatives. A number of common factors help account for this trend. One is the urgency of unmet needs and the inadequacy of governmental and nonprofit programs to address them. In medicine, the rise both in uninsured patients and in cost containment strategies has placed new pressures on the health care system. In law, recent cutbacks in legal aid and indigent criminal defense programs have exacerbated long-standing inadequacies in access to justice. One reason that these two professions have been more responsive than others to unmet needs is their monopoly over many forms of assistance. Charitable contributions have been one way to preserve that privileged status and to reduce demand for less expensive service providers. Many businesses have also seen social responsibility as a means to preempt greater regulation or taxation of their activities.

Moreover, for all occupations, public service advances other instrumental objectives, independent of its contributions to societal welfare. Charitable involvement enhances the reputation of individuals, their employers, and their occupations. For the professions, such pro bono work has been a primary feature distinguishing them from business, and entitling them to special societal status and regulatory autonomy. Service activities also enhance career development; they can build a variety of technical, leadership, and interpersonal skills, as well as expand personal contacts and networks.

Such benefits are also a primary rationale for public service opportunities in graduate and professional school. Over the last two decades, interest has increased across the disciplines, both in service learning and in extracurricular programs. A number of interrelated forces help account for this trend: public scandals and corresponding public image concerns; widespread discontent concerning access to professional services; and pressure by alumni, accrediting organizations, and professional associations for more ethics instruction, including service responsibilities. Law has gone the farthest in institutionalizing such obligations in its educational programs. Accreditation standards require the provision of pro bono opportunities, and a small but growing number of schools require some student service. However, many business and medical schools report greater success than law schools in attracting large numbers of volunteers; in some schools, participation rates are as high as 80%. Engineering programs have been the slowest to embrace service projects, perhaps because of the traditional focus on technical skills and the absence of strong societal pressure. However, unlike other disciplines, engineering confronts declining enrollments, and many of its leaders see expanded public service programs as a way to appeal to underrepresented constituencies like women and minorities.

By the same token, many other graduate and professional schools have found such programs to be an attractive strategy, not only for recruiting students, but also for building support from alumni, community leaders, and private foundations. The growing prominence of public service on university Web sites and its increasing presence in scholarly publications attest to widening interest among both students and faculty.

Common Challenges and Strategies for Change

That is not, however, to understate the difficulties of institutionalizing a service ethic. Outside of law, the topic is still largely noticeable for its absence in leading texts. Rarely does it figure in the core curriculum of graduate or professional schools. Accreditation standards have not been established or interpreted to ensure curricular coverage or broad participation among faculty and students. Academic reward structures discourage professors from assuming the burden of service learning, and many doubt that they have the expertise necessary to teach such courses.

Yet none of these obstacles is insurmountable. Chapter 7 sketches an extensive reform agenda for law that has relevance for other professional and business settings. At the educational level, professional associations, accrediting organizations, and media rankings could all put more pressure on schools to integrate service into the academic culture. More recognition should be available for individuals and institutions that demonstrate service commitments. At the organizational level, employers need to establish reward structures that encourage charitable work in practice as well as principle. Professional, business, and governmental agencies could develop reporting systems that make reliable information about service records publicly available. Clients and consumers could pay more attention to those records in purchasing decisions. And researchers could focus greater attention on cross-disciplinary experiences and on the strategies most likely to foster service commitments. This is not a modest agenda. But it is one in which the professions, business, and the public all have a substantial stake.

Chapter Five

PRO BONO SERVICE IN
AN INTERNATIONAL CONTEXT

Lawyers outside the United States have long provided some uncompensated legal representation. However, until quite recently, other nations generally lacked a strong tradition of pro bono service. Over the last decade, the concept has gone global. This chapter surveys the evolution of an international pro bono culture. Such a comparative perspective, largely missing from contemporary discussions of lawyers' public service, seeks to increase our understanding of the forces that can sustain it.

THE EVOLUTION OF PRO BONO SERVICE

As Chapter 2 noted, pro bono representation has deep historical roots, although its extent remains subject to dispute. In many European societies, the concept dates to the Middle Ages, when clergy and canon lawyers were expected to provide at least some assistance to the "worthy poor."[1] This expectation gradually spread to the bar generally and became one of the defining features of professionalism. By statute or assertion of "inherent power," European courts typically assumed authority to appoint uncompensated counsel in at least some cases.[2] Yet how often judges exercised that authority and how adequately lawyers served indigent clients remain unclear. Practices varied in different countries. As in some jurisdictions in the United States, courts occasionally upheld lawyers' objections to uncompensated appointments.[3] By contrast, beginning in the mid-nineteenth century, other nations such as France, Italy, and Germany established national legal aid schemes that relied heavily on appointment of uncompensated counsel, sometimes supplemented by government payment of certain litigation expenses.[4] However, these court appointment systems generally came nowhere close to meeting the needs of the poor, particularly in civil and nonlitigation matters.[5] Nor did the volunteer aid societies staffed by lawyers or trained lay specialists manage to fill the gaps.[6]

By the mid-twentieth century, the inadequacies of charitable assistance were prompting a variety of responses, which had the unintended effect of discouraging much needed pro bono work. The most important development was greater government support of legal aid in countries with justice systems most like our own. The rise of the welfare state in Western Europe and in former British Commonwealth nations led to comprehensive systems for access to law by low- and middle-income groups.[7] Unlike the United States, most of these nations have recognized a right to counsel in civil cases, a right that is also affirmed by the Council of Europe's interpretation of the European human rights law. According to Resolution 78 of the Ministers of the Council of Europe, a "right to necessary legal aid" and a "right of access to justice and to a fair hearing" both constitute "an essential feature of any democratic society." Such rights should "always include the assistance of a person professionally qualified to practice law" and that person "should be adequately remunerated."[8]

As noted below, almost no nation has come close to full realization of these rights. However, Western European and English-speaking countries such as Canada, Australia, and New Zealand have established civil legal aid systems that are more comprehensive than their American counterpart. These systems have involved government-subsidized fees for private lawyers who accept eligible clients, publicly supported legal advice centers, sometimes staffed by nonlawyers and citizen volunteers, and legal insurance schemes that cover large percentages of the population.[9] The use of sliding income scales to determine eligibility has meant that a far greater number of individuals are entitled to assistance than in the United States. Per capita expenditures on legal services also have generally been far greater in Europe, Canada, and Australia than in America. For example, at the turn of the twenty-first century, Great Britain was spending almost 17 times as much per person on legal aid as the United States.[10]

Yet as many commentators have noted, the evolution of these comprehensive legal aid systems diminished the pressure on the bar to contribute voluntary services.[11] Moreover, lawyers who represented indigent clients for statutorily fixed fees, generally well below market rates, often felt that they were making a sufficient pro bono contribution without volunteering for unpaid work.

The absence of well-developed pro bono traditions in many nations is also partly attributable to the less dominant role of law and lawyers. Compared with the United States, most other countries do not rely so heavily on the legal system to meet basic welfare needs and to address social problems.[12] For example, many nations use administrative structures and no-fault insurance coverage to handle claims that Americans pursue through litigation.[13] Almost all nations rely more extensively on trained nonlawyers to handle routine needs.[14] Outside of the United States, providing legal advice does not constitute the unauthorized practice of law. Cross-national studies also find that citizens of other nations are more willing than Americans to trust a centralized government, and less willing to trust courts to resolve contested social issues and to enforce individual rights and statutory guarantees.[15] The United States is unique in the extent to which lawyers, particularly public interest lawyers, are involved in shaping and implementing environmental, health, safety, consumer, and antidiscrimination protections.[16] Because most countries grant the legal profession a less pivotal governance role, their need for pro bono legal assistance has been less pressing.

However, the last 15 years have witnessed a dramatic increase in pro bono work throughout Europe, Canada, and Australia, and to a lesser extent South America and Asia. Principal reasons are a persistent, and in some countries growing, inadequacy in legal services and a growing influence of American law firms and legal culture.

Beginning in the mid-1980s, many countries began curtailing social welfare entitlements, including legal aid, and a further wave of funding cuts in the mid-1990s led to increasing restrictions.[17] For example, Great Britain reduced eligibility levels by almost a third, with the result that only those poor enough to qualify for state support remained entitled to services.[18] In Canada, budget reductions have led to a situation aptly characterized by the title of a 2000 Canadian Bar Association report, *The Legal Aid Crisis: Time for Action*.[19] Cutbacks in the cases eligible for assistance and the fees available for service have left millions of Canadians without legal remedies for basic needs; racial, ethnic, and linguistic minorities have had particular difficulty finding qualified providers.[20] Similar budget reductions have occurred in Australia and European nations.[21] The resulting gap in coverage has fueled interest in expanding bar pro bono contributions.

In some countries, such interest is primarily attributable not to budget cuts but to concerns about long-standing unmet needs. In France, for example, public pressure and the work of humanitarian nongovernmental organizations led to the 1995 formation of a pioneer pro bono association, Droits d'Urgence. The group coordinates volunteer barristers, solicitors, judges, and law professors, who provide free legal assistance to marginalized groups that had previously lacked access, such as immigrants, drug addicts, prostitutes, and the homeless.[22]

A further influence on the growth of pro bono programs abroad has been the influx of American lawyers steeped in public service traditions. Many attorneys in international branch offices of U.S. firms have looked for volunteer opportunities. Their example, and the pro bono structures that they have helped to create, has inspired involvement by the local bar.[23] For example, American firms' Paris offices were key initial participants in Droits d'Urgence. As its founder notes, in the mid-1990s, "when I met with managing partners in French firms [to talk about pro bono work] they didn't even understand what I was saying."[24] Now the organization has a broad base of local and international participants. In Eastern Europe, American lawyers have been equally crucial in launching a pro bono movement. The Public Interest Initiative, formed in 1997 by Columbia Law School, works with volunteer lawyers and law schools in Poland, the Czech Republic, Slovakia, and Hungary to staff legal clinics for the poor.[25] Similarly, the New

York–based Cyrus R. Vance Center for International Justice, along with other American bar organizations, is helping to establish a pro bono culture in Latin America.[26] Comparable efforts in other regions are attributable to local lawyers who became interested in public service while pursuing graduate degrees at U.S. law schools. In Germany and Israel, for example, American-trained lawyers have been influential in establishing pro bono programs or pressuring their employers to do so.[27]

Although the same forces supporting public service have been at work in many countries, each has followed a path shaped by its own particular history and needs. In order to draw useful generalizations, it is helpful to look more closely at the nations for which the most information is publicly available. To that end, the following discussion focuses first on two countries with legal systems similar to our own: the United Kingdom and Australia. The discussion then turns to China, which is unique in requiring lawyers to perform pro bono service. The different experiences of these nations may, in turn, shed light on how best to expand pro bono programs in this country.

The United Kingdom

Policies and Practices of Pro Bono Service

Little systematic research is available about the frequency of pro bono work in the United Kingdom. In 1989, a Law Society survey indicated that 41% of solicitors offered free legal services, although the majority gave one hour or less of their time per week.[28] Beginning in the early 1990s, in response to cutbacks in publicly funded legal aid and an increased governmental emphasis on volunteer activity, and inspired by the example of London-based United States firms, the English bar developed a range of initiatives designed to increase pro bono contributions.[29] In 1992, the Bar Council in the United Kingdom established a Pro Bono Unit and asked barristers to contribute two to three days a year.[30]

How many attorneys responded to the Pro Bono Unit's challenge remains unclear. Many large firms established or expanded pro bono programs, but little effort has been made to track participation rates.[31] The most systematic study, published in 2001, involved some 1000 junior solicitors and trainees, individuals who had been practicing for no more than five years. Of those who responded, only 38% reported doing at least some pro bono work. The amounts of service were modest, and most firms allocated pro bono work to the least experienced practitioners. About a quarter of the responding solicitors provided less than 2 hours a month; slightly under half provided 2 to 5 hours.[32]

The number of practitioners reporting charitable service is significantly lower than the 64% rate found in an earlier Law Society study. This discrepancy may be related to its extremely broad definition of pro bono contributions. Unlike the junior solicitors' survey, the Law Society study encompassed not only unpaid services, but also work performed "at a rate substantially below that normally charged." As commentators noted, that definition could have included many paying clients. Moreover, most of the practitioners providing services did so outside the context of an organized pro bono program for low-income groups; a substantial portion of assistance may have benefitted family, friends, or sources of paying work. Very few experienced solicitors spent more than about an hour per week on pro bono matters.[33]

The influences on charitable participation were similar to those reported by American lawyers in the survey described in Chapter 6. About half of British solicitors cited commitments to the community (53%), client contacts (57%), and personal development (48%). Almost half (44%) agreed that pro bono work was "part of a solicitor's professional and ethical obligations," and over four-fifths (88%) believed that such work would "improve the profession's public image."[34]

As has been true for American lawyers, the main reasons for nonparticipation were lack of time and employer support. Half of the survey participants felt that their schedules could not accommodate additional work. Only 10% thought that pro bono service was given full recognition by their firms, and only 30% felt actively encouraged by partners to engage in such activities; 13% reported being actively discouraged from involvement.[35] As the study concluded, "pro bono participation will only be increased if firms are willing to . . . allow [participants] the time, provide them with supervisory support, and offer sufficient recognition for their efforts."[36] Other smaller-scale surveys have found similar inadequacies in law firm policies and have made similar recommendations about strengthening the commitment to public service.[37]

Yet efforts by the organized bar to mandate such commitments have encountered opposition similar to that arising in the United States. In 1994, the Law Society in the United Kingdom considered and rejected a requirement of 40 hours a year of pro bono service. The view of the Society's Pro Bono Working Party was that such an obligation would "relieve the government of its own obligation to ensure access to justice."[38] The Law Society has more recently reiterated this position, despite negative publicity, and in 2000 it rejected a proposed aspirational standard of 40 hours per year. Opponents were concerned that it might pave the way for required service as well as further cutbacks in government support for legal aid.[39] Internal bar reports also recounted resentment among some rank and file solicitors who felt that large firms could "easily afford" to do pro bono work for "PR reasons," and didn't care about the impact on practitioners who "engage in lowly paid private client work."[40]

In the absence of wider bar support, leading London firms have formed a Solicitors' Pro Bono Group, which seeks to expand participation in public service.[41] Some skeptics attribute the group's formation primarily to a desire to improve the profession's image and to preempt government regulations mandating pro bono contributions.[42] Other observers have worried that firms see pro bono programs as a way to train junior practitioners, letting them "make their mistakes safely away from commercial clients." As one specialist in civil rights and human rights law put it, "rich city firms should be giving money to support legal aid and law centres . . . rather than letting their youngsters loose on an unsuspecting public."[43]

The basis for such concerns is hard to gauge, given the absence of any systematic efforts to assess the quality of services. It is, however, clear that cash contributions would not advance some firms' objectives, including a desire to improve morale and to infuse professional life with greater meaning.[44] And whatever the participants' motives, the Solicitors' Pro Bono Group has clearly increased involvement in socially valuable service; it channels aid from some 60 firms to over 300 charities, runs legal service clinics, and finds service opportunities for foreign lawyers who are not licensed to practice in the United Kingdom. It also enlists clients to consider firms' pro bono records in selecting outside counsel.[45] Outreach to students also has high priority, because their interest will encourage development of pro bono initiatives by firms concerned about recruitment and retention. Such considerations have prompted more general attention to legal education as a means of fostering greater commitments to public service.

Legal Education

To compare the evolution of pro bono service in English legal education with the experience of other nations, some understanding of its underlying structure is also necessary. In the United Kingdom, preparation for the bar begins with a first degree in law (roughly the equivalent of an American undergraduate degree), followed by a one-year vocational course and then an apprenticeship. Those planning a career in trial work as a barrister take a bar vocational course and then serve as an apprentice in a two-year "traineeship." Those planning a specialty other than litigation take a legal practice course followed by a one-year "pupilage" as an apprentice.[46] This structure separates the theoretical and practical aspects of legal education; skills development and ethical training receive little attention at the academic level.[47]

Roughly half of the curriculum for a qualifying undergraduate degree is mandated by the bar and the Law Society, and the focus is on substantive, black-letter law. This basic course of study does not emphasize the profession's role in public service or public interest causes.[48] Part of the reason, as earlier discussion suggested, is the bar's less active role in addressing social problems, compared with the United States. A related factor may be orientation of law students. As two English legal ethics experts note, the law degree program in the United Kingdom is dominated by individuals seeking access to a "lucrative career": "The most popular objectives of law students are acquiring the legal knowledge and intellectual skills which it is assumed are appropriate preparation for practice. Personal development, understanding of the social context of law, law reform, and preparation as policymakers appear at the bottom of their list of objectives."[49] This focus, coupled with the bifurcation of academic preparation and skills training, has traditionally impeded the development of clinical and professional responsibility courses that might nurture public service commitments. However, the last decade has witnessed growing interest in expanding such curricular opportunities. In 1996, the Lord Chancellor's Advisory Committee on Legal Education and Conduct recognized the need for more clinical courses, and after the turn of the twenty-first century, high-level officials such as the attorney general began calling for pro bono programs.[50] Employers have also started pressuring schools to offer more pro bono and clinical opportunities that can increase practical skills such as problem solving, communication, and maintaining effective client relationships.[51] The Solicitors' Pro Bono Group has pushed in similar directions. Its Pro Bono Student Initiative, launched in July 1999, includes an annual award to the student who has contributed the most to advancing the cause in his or her university. The Group also makes an annual award to the academic institution with the most effective pro bono program.[52]

Such pressure has had a significant impact. By 2003, about 40% of surveyed institutions had some sort of pro bono or clinical program addressed to underrepresented groups.[53] Partnerships were common with local volunteer organizations, legal literacy initiatives, law centers, and Citizens Advice Bureaux. Over a third of institutions without a pro bono program were considering the establishment of one.[54] Yet student participation has remained relatively low. The most recent surveys available find that only about 950 out of 46,000 law students are actively involved in pro bono work. Hourly contributions are also modest. Only a third of 20 institutions reported an average annual contribution of over 31 hours. The others had average rates between 1 and 20 hours.[55]

Participants describe mixed motives for their involvement, but most emphasize pragmatic concerns. About a third of the students hope to enhance their résumés and their employment prospects; another quarter want to gain practical experience and develop legal skills. Only a quarter report a desire to give back to the community or some other altruistic consideration.[56] Of those who run pro bono programs, a majority stress their usefulness in teaching legal skills or substantive law. Only a quarter cite a commitment to address unmet legal needs, and only a fifth hope to convey a professional responsibility to engage in public service.[57]

The main obstacles to effective student pro bono programs are similar to those arising in the United States in both law and other professional schools. The most common explanations for English universities' failure to adopt a public service program are "staff time and willingness to volunteer, supervision and the resources available to run such schemes."[58] Only about half of surveyed faculty at schools without pro bono projects believe that they are useful ways of enabling students to gain practical experience and legal skills.[59] Many professors have reservations about the appropriateness of public service programs in an academic setting, as well as their schools' ability to provide adequate supervision.[60]

Yet the growing experience with successful programs, both in Great Britain and other nations, may help dispel such concerns. British universities that have partnered with local community organizations have often avoided substantial supervisory burdens. And surveys of student participants in a wide range of American contexts generally find high levels of satisfaction with skills development.[61] Replicating such surveys in the United Kingdom, and stressing the educational value of experiential learning, may be the most promising strategy for attracting greater academic interest. It may also be possible to increase bar and governmental support for pro bono initiatives by demonstrating concrete benefits, such as meeting crucial public needs and improving the profession's status and practitioners career satisfaction. Giving students a positive service experience at a formative stage in their career is one of the best ways to build on recent progress toward a more socially responsible profession.

AUSTRALIA

Pro Bono Practice and Reform Strategies

Although lawyers in Australia have long been involved in charitable activities, their participation in organized pro bono legal work is a relatively recent development.[62] As in other nations, concern about access to justice increased greatly in Australia during the 1970s. A wave of progressive social reform included greater support for legal aid. One major initiative was the establishment of community legal centers, typically associated with law schools, and staffed by paid solicitors and social workers, as well as volunteer lawyers and students.[63] Such centers supplemented the limited government-funded legal aid schemes and the pro bono assistance intermittently provided by private practitioners as an "unstructured" "hit or miss affair."[64] By the end of the 1970s, a patchwork of service providers had developed, along with pressure for a more coherent and well-supported system. To that end, the federal government established independent legal aid commissions in each state, with funding from state and national revenues.[65] One unintended by-product of this comprehensive system was diminished pressure for volunteer assistance from private practitioners.[66] It was not until the government cut legal aid funding in the mid-1990s that state bar societies began developing formal pro bono programs to coordinate and expand volunteer efforts.[67]

One focus of these programs has been to extend the work of community legal centers. Although such centers are primarily funded by the government, they often rely heavily on volunteer lawyers and law students.[68] For example, New South Wales, a state with a population of approximately 6.5 million, has 26 such centers; the largest operates with about 10 paid staff, 40 volunteer lawyers, and 80 students.[69] Over the last decade, the scope of pro bono efforts has also expanded through centralized organizations such as the Public Interest Law Clearing House in Melbourne and the National Pro Bono Resource Centre.[70] Founded in 1994, the Clearing House screens and refers requests for aid from individuals and nonprofit groups. It also operates a Homeless Persons' Legal Clinic staffed by volunteers from participating firms. During the most recent year for which data are available, some 100 lawyers provided over 3000 hours of services.[71] The National Pro Bono Resource Centre, founded in 2002, promotes pro bono initiatives in law firms, law schools, and bar organizations throughout the country.[72]

The frequency of pro bono work is difficult to gauge. In 2002, almost two-thirds of law practices (63%) reported that they had contributed pro bono services, defined as free or reduced-fee services for a client who "has no access to the legal system" or whose case "raises a wider issue of public interest." On average, attorneys reported 42 hours of such work annually.[73] However, the Australian Bureau of Statistics, which collected the data, cautioned that it may not be accurate because most firms did not keep adequate records.[74] Nor were they asked who received assistance, and other research suggests that the majority of beneficiaries may have been former paying clients who were unable to afford full fees.[75] These clients are the main recipients of unpaid or partially paid work by solo practitioners. And according to both Bureau statistics and other studies, these practitioners average four times as much unpaid or reduced-fee work as lawyers in firms with over 10 members, which target more of their pro bono work to indigents and public interest causes.[76] How much of the bar's total aid is truly "charitable" by conventional definitions remains unclear.

What is clear, however, is that the demand for pro bono services far outstrips the supply. Surveys of pro bono clearinghouses find that they generally can make referrals for only about a third of the requests they receive, and those requests reflect only a small portion of unmet needs. The primary problem is the lack of volunteers who are willing or qualified to take cases in areas where demand is greatest, such as criminal and family law.[77] A second problem involves conflicts of interest, particularly in small, rural communities, or in matters involving the government, such as immigration.[78] Government agencies have sometimes instructed firms not to accept a pro bono case involving an adversary, even when there is no direct conflict of interest. Firms have also reported being penalized for taking such cases when the government awards contracts for legal work.[79]

Bar leaders are taking a variety of steps to address these limitations. One is to expand the network of providers and match them with opportunities in their areas of expertise. So, for example, Web sites now link volunteers with a broad range of matters including law reform, community education, and transactional work for nonprofit organizations. New groups such as the Institute of Chartered Accountants have joined these Web-based clearinghouses to provide assistance in financial, administrative, and fund-raising matters.[80] The National Pro Bono Resource Centre offers publications and assistance to firms, and a growing number are developing policies, procedures, and administrative positions to facilitate service.[81] One Victoria government program supports the six-month loan of law firm lawyers to community legal organizations. Participating firms can count such contributions in meeting new pro bono requirements in government legal contracts. These contracts obligate firms to commit at least 5% of fees from government work toward pro bono service.[82]

A second strategy is to alter the incentive structure for pro bono work. A National Pro Bono Task Force, formed by the Attorney General in 2000, has made a number of recommendations along these lines. For example, court procedures should be modified to reduce filing fees and awards of costs in pro bono matters. Governments should consider practitioners' records of public service when awarding legal work. Protocols should be developed to discourage the overbroad application of rules governing conflicts of interest. Additional resources should be available from the bar and the government to support pro bono efforts. And, as noted below, more efforts should be made to enlist law schools in inspiring public service commitments among their students.[83]

Of equal interest is what the Task Force did not recommend: mandatory service. In explaining that omission, the chair's introduction to the report noted that there is "strong opposition in Australia to any element of compulsion in the performance of pro bono legal work. . . . There is less opposition, but certainly no groundswell of support for any statement of 'aspirational targets' such as the American Bar Association's Model Rule urging lawyers to perform at least 50 hours of pro bono work per year."[84] Accordingly, the Task Force chose not to "press for such targets, noting that this approach may be inconsistent with the essential voluntariness of pro bono work."[85]

As in other nations, opponents of mandatory service also worry that pro bono contributions would be "treated as a replacement for government funding of legal aid" and would force private practitioners to assume what should be a public responsibility.[86] Support for an aspirational standard is growing, led by organizations including the Australian Law Reform Commission, the National Pro Bono Resource Centre, and the Law Institute of Victoria.[87] However the issue of standards is resolved, the limitations of the profession's current voluntary approach are apparent. Bar leaders are accordingly seeking new ways to inspire public service commitments. One obvious strategy is to encourage a pro bono ethic among law students at the formative stage of professional careers.

Legal Education

Preparation for the bar in Australia is similar to that in the United Kingdom. Traditionally, Australian law schools, like their British counterparts, placed little emphasis on clinical education or public service. Skills training and professional responsibility issues were largely relegated to postgraduate training. At the turn of the twenty-first century, almost half of 28 Australian law schools did not offer clinical programs, and those that were available often severely limited the number of placements.[88] According to research summarized by the National Pro Bono Task Force, "very few schools have a considered or coherent policy in relation to developing a pro bono ethos in law students."[89]

However, as in the United Kingdom, support for clinical and pro bono programs has been growing. One reason is that the bar's leadership views these programs as ways to build long-term commitments to social justice and public service.[90] An influential 2000 report by the Australian Law Reform Commission on the civil legal system explicitly endorsed clinical courses as an opportunity for students "to undertake pro bono work as part of their academic . . . requirements."[91] The National Pro Bono Task Force similarly recommended that law schools expand both clinical and pro bono opportunities, and proposed that the Council of Australian Law School Deans consider requiring every student to have a public service placement before graduation.[92]

Although the concept of pro bono requirements has not attracted much support, efforts to expand voluntary opportunities have had greater success. For example, by 2004, the National Pro Bono Resource Centre had announced a new law school initiative. A prominent law foundation had created a student pro bono award as well as a public service internship, which recruits and trains students for pro bono placements.[93] What limited information is available suggests that participants' experience with clinical and pro bono programs has been positive; such involvement increases students' understanding of the role of lawyers in assisting disadvantaged groups, their interest in future pro bono work, and their belief that such work is a professional obligation.[94] Further research documenting the benefits of public service programs may help convince legal academics that promoting pro bono service should be both an educational and ethical priority.

CHINA

The development of pro bono responsibilities in China has been shaped by distinctive attitudes toward law and the unique relationship between Chinese lawyers and the state. Traditional Chinese culture held neither the legal system nor the legal profession in high esteem. In 1820, the emperor issued an edict condemning the trend toward unbridled litigation and blaming "rascally" "litigation tricksters" who "entrap people for the sake of profit." The edict concluded that those who made a profession of preparing legal documents for others should be severely punished. As a result, some lawyers ended up with three years of imprisonment for their efforts.[95] Popular distrust of the profession was further reinforced during decades of communist rule.[96] For most of the last half century, the government either suppressed or extensively regulated legal practice. Those regulations generally included obligations of public service. Although China's sweeping reforms of the legal system in the mid-1990s liberalized restrictions on lawyers' practice, the government retained requirements of pro bono work.

The Emergence of Legal Aid and Pro Bono Service

Although the term *legal aid* was largely unknown in China until the 1990s, the concept dates to the 1920s, when a small but flourishing legal profession in major cities included a number of assistance programs run by private attorneys.[97] However, the small number of lawyers for the nation as a whole, and the frequently poor quality of their training and services, limited the effectiveness of such programs.[98] The government's role in legal aid took shape during the 1950s, as part of a system that socialized the profession. Lawyers became state employees, who practiced out of some 800 offices established by the Ministry of Justice and local justice bureaus.[99] The small size of the profession (under 3000 full-time attorneys) made widespread legal assistance unfeasible. However, the state made some effort to broaden access to justice through a pro bono requirement. The 1956 Temporary Provisions Regarding Lawyers' Fees required practitioners to provide free services to "persons seeking compensation for injuries due to a 'production accident,' to persons seeking alimony, child support, or elderly support payments, to parties whose legal questions could be answered orally, and to persons who were unable to afford lawyers' services."[100] How much effect the requirement had in practice remains unclear, particularly given its limited scope and the society's similarly limited reliance on law. Service obligations did not apply to criminal cases, the government generally avoided civil litigation, and few disputes ended up in the legal system. Of those that did, most did not have parties represented by lawyers.[101] Criminal justice was often dispensed by administrative agencies or ad hoc people's tribunals. To the extent that lawyers were involved, their function was limited to seeking leniency in punishment.[102]

Lawyers' role in providing legal aid, or services of any kind, was soon curtailed even further. An antirightist movement in the late 1950s began persecuting lawyers as "class enemies," and the Ministry of Justice was abolished in 1959. During the Cultural Revolution, from roughly 1966 to 1976, law schools and law offices were closed, and many lawyers were executed or sent to labor camps for "rehabilitation."[103] By the mid-1970s, only a few thousand attorneys remained in practice. In the late 1970s, however, the more liberal leaders who succeeded Mao Zedong recognized the need for lawyers in the transformation of the centrally planned economy to a market system that could participate in international trade. To that end, the government reinstated the Ministry of Justice, urged colleges and universities to reopen law schools, and instituted training programs for other legal specialists.[104]

The new framework also included a comprehensive set of Lawyers' Regulations and Provisions on Lawyers' Fees. Under their terms, lawyers were "state legal workers" with obligations to support the socialist system and to protect both the interests of the state and the lawful rights of citizens. The fee provisions expanded the range of matters eligible for unpaid assistance beyond those specified in 1956; certain economic benefits, such as claims for labor insurance and retirement payments, could qualify for aid. However, unlike the earlier pro bono requirement, the 1981 provisions no longer mandated that lawyers "shall" provide aid, but rather stated that lawyers "could reduce or waive fees."[105] The government reinstated mandatory language when it revised the provisions in 1990.[106] No statistics were collected on levels of pro bono work, so it was never clear how much unpaid assistance lawyers actually provided, or whether changes in statutory language had any significant effect.[107]

What became increasingly clear, however, was that more legal assistance and more lawyers are necessary to assist China's economic growth and to protect its most vulnerable citizens. Indeed, the Ministry of Justice recognized as much in 1990, in announcing a "rectification program" to address problems of corruption and incompetence in the profession. While acknowledging that a "small number" of lawyers had been infected by bourgeois liberal thinking and were overly concerned with money, the ministry recognized that the bar in general had become "an important force in social democracy."[108] To facilitate its role, the government began a process of liberalization in the late 1980s and 1990s. This wave of reform permitted lawyers to form private for-profit firms, enabled foreign firms to establish offices, upgraded qualifications for practice, and expanded state-supported legal aid and legal training.[109]

Such reforms have helped to increase the size and status of the profession, as well as the accessibility of legal services, but considerable challenges remain. The number of lawyers has grown dramatically from about 5500 in 1981 to 120,000 in 2003, and the government hopes to more than double that number by 2010.[110] But because lawyers account for such a small percentage of the population (0.009%) in China (as opposed to 0.32% in the United States), they represent clients in only about 10% to 25% of civil cases; only 4% of registered Chinese businesses have regular legal advisors.[111] Given the nation's large poverty population and the government's limited social welfare budget, providing adequate legal aid is a daunting task. As the Ministry of Justice has noted, "It is not practical for the government to afford all the legal aid expenses. We have to combine the government budget, the donations from society and certain lawyers' free services."[112]

That combination is now in place. The Ministry of Justice developed China's first comprehensive legal aid plan in the early 1990s, and by the close of the decade, over 900 centers were providing services.[113] In 1996, China also enacted comprehensive legislation regulating the legal profession. One provision of this new Lawyers' Law imposes a pro bono obligation. Article 41 provides that individuals who cannot afford to hire an attorney are entitled to legal aid in a range of civil and criminal cases. This entitlement is coupled with Article 42, which requires lawyers to undertake legal aid work "in accordance with state regulations."[114]

The extent and type of pro bono service are largely specified by state regulation, although standards on Lawyers' Services Fees and Lawyers' Professional Morality and Professional Discipline promulgated by the Ministry of Justice set forth some general mandates. Under these standards, lawyers may not refuse a criminal case assigned by a court. And under criminal codes, counsel must be assigned if the defendant is indigent and also blind, deaf, dumb, underage, or potentially subject to the death penalty.[115] Other pro bono procedures are spelled out in local regulations. In general, lawyers and law firms either staff legal aid programs for a specified period each month, or receive case assignments from those programs or from local courts. Some jurisdictions also require financial contributions or permit lawyers to make a contribution in lieu of service at a level roughly comparable to its economic value. To be eligible for assistance, clients must demonstrate economic hardship and reasonable grounds of prevailing in a matter falling within statutory entitlements.[116] Some localities require a lawyer to accept any eligible case; others allow a lawyer to exercise some discretion in the types and amount of pro bono work to be performed. Localities also differ as to whether attorneys should receive any compensation for the expenses incurred in legal aid work. However, this difference "may be more ideological than financial" because payments are minimal and do not cover the costs of lawyers' time.[117]

Each jurisdiction has a somewhat different process for implementing pro bono requirements. In Beijing, the first city to impose a specific pro bono obligation, attorneys must take one case per year. Law firms must also provide a minimum of two days of free legal advice per month, or else make a contribution to the city's legal aid fund. The buyout provision seeks to accommodate firms with a transactional practice, whose members lack expertise to handle routine individual needs. A centralized center coordinates pro bono work, and each of the city's law firms is responsible for helping to staff the center on a rotating basis. Although the city is willing to offer partial compensation for the expenses of handling legal aid cases, the amounts are small, and most lawyers do not bother seeking reimbursement.[118] Other localities have variations of this process: Pudong requires lawyers to take at least one legal aid case per year; Jiangsu requires them to take any case assigned by the local justice bureau; Wuhan assigns at least one case per year to firms; and Guangzhou keeps a list of lawyers willing to take cases and assigns matters on the basis of that list.[119] Some jurisdictions require law firms to contribute designated amounts to legal aid funds—for example, 1% of the firm's annual business incomes. Provincial and municipal bar associations subsidized by lawyers may also be asked to donate a specified percentage of their budgets.[120]

No systematic information is available concerning compliance with pro bono requirements. Accounts vary. According to one researcher, "there are clearly understood consequences" for lawyers who refuse a legal aid case, including suspension of the license to practice if the offense is repeated. However, he also acknowledges that officials often fail to impose any such discipline for noncompliance with pro bono requirements.[121] Another scholar notes that although local justice bureaus may fine or refuse to renew law firms' licenses for failing to take pro bono cases, no such sanctions have been reported.[122] In criminal matters, courts generally respond to a lawyer's refusal to take a case by assigning it to another lawyer.[123]

A related problem involves the frequently poor quality of required service. Many firms allocate pro bono assignments to their most junior members even though they lack sufficient expertise and supervision.[124] However, the problem of incompetent assistance is by no means limited to pro bono matters and reflects more general inadequacies in bar regulatory processes. As one expert notes, "To date, the Chinese bar has been largely undisciplined, with little enforcement of ethical or legal standards. Indeed, support for mandatory legal aid requirements appears to stem at least partially from the belief that lawyers have been neglecting their obligations to society. Given the failure of many in the legal profession to honor existing ethical and legal obligations, the effectiveness of mandatory legal aid obligations is questionable."[125] These problems can be somewhat mitigated by the provision of a buyout option in lieu of service. Although data on the frequency and level of financial contributions are unavailable, the consensus is that most law firms in cities like Beijing prefer financial payments to personal assistance.[126]

Experts offer a number of explanations for why the Chinese government insists on imposing pro bono requirements and why so many lawyers appear willing to comply despite the inadequacies of enforcement. The most obvious reason is the traditional view of attorneys as servants of the state, a view still reflected in the Lawyers' Law. It defines lawyers as professionals who "provide services to society"; its drafters deliberately rejected language appearing in other nation's ethical codes referring to a "free and independent profession."[127] The Ministry of Justice also justifies the pro bono requirement as a quid pro quo for lawyers' relative affluence and their right to form for-profit firms.[128] So too, the absence of a well-established tradition of professional ethics suggests why the government sees a need for specific public service requirements.[129]

Yet it is also the case that the bar in China, as in other nations, has its own reasons for providing pro bono work and a significant number of its members have done so outside the requirements of the legal aid system.[130] Public service is a way to build reputations in the community and to accommodate those who may be the source of referrals or paid work. Assistance at reduced fees may also be a practical necessity for lawyers in poor regions where most potential clients cannot afford the full cost of legal services. Moreover, many attorneys are genuinely committed to the rule of law, access to justice, and an independent profession, and see legal aid contributions as a way of furthering all of these principles.[131] Indeed, a widespread failure to comply with reasonable pro bono requirements could invite more intrusive government regulation and undermine progress toward greater professional autonomy.

From a societal standpoint, the current mandatory pro bono system is a mixed blessing. On the one hand, it clearly helps ensure essential services. In addition, by providing assistance within the context of a government program, lawyers can avoid some of the backlash that might occur if they represented unpopular clients or causes as a matter of choice.[132] On the other hand, many lawyers limit their public service to the routine individual matters that qualify for government aid and satisfy pro bono requirements. Because most localities do not allow lawyers to select the cases that fulfill these requirements, there is insufficient incentive for participation in the broad social justice causes that receive bar support in other nations. This limitation on pro bono work, coupled with the risks of retaliation against lawyers who challenge state authorities, has impeded the development of a strong public interest legal movement.[133] To the extent that the bar is involved in social justice causes, they are generally ones that further central governmental policy.

Some of the strongest support for those causes comes from a small but growing number of university-based public interest law clinics. In many experts' view, building support for such service opportunities in law schools is a key part of broadening and deepening China's pro bono tradition.

Legal Education

To understand the role of public service in Chinese legal education, some general background is necessary. Historically, standards for admission to the bar were lax, and the quality of preparation was relatively poor. The public's low esteem for the profession both reflected and perpetuated the problem. Because the profession was not held in high regard, it did not attract the most gifted candidates or encourage rigorous education. The low caliber of practice that resulted further reinforced public disfavor. Suspension of legal training during the Cultural Revolution exacerbated the problem.

When the government sought to rebuild the profession in the 1980s, it faced a tension between the need both to upgrade standards and to increase the number of practitioners as quickly as possible. The compromise was to institute a national bar exam, but to allow a broad range of applicants to take it and to provide an alternative means of qualification. Individuals can obtain admission to the bar by approval without passing the exam if they have had significant experience in law as academics or equivalent professionals. To sit for the exam, candidates need either a college degree or else two to three years of legal education in an institution of higher learning or a "study course" that includes options for self-study, correspondence classes, and adult education programs. Applicants must also complete a one-year apprenticeship and demonstrate good conduct.[134] At the turn of the twenty-first century, only about a quarter of practicing lawyers had college degrees, and even those that did often were insufficiently equipped for practice.[135] Law schools and study courses have emphasized memorization of black-letter law and focused little attention on practice skills or professional ethics; clinical courses generally have not been available.

Yet the country's need for legal aid and many faculty's interest in promoting social justice have also created public service opportunities in law schools that are better developed than in other nations. Since the early 1990s, many Chinese law students have engaged in substantial pro bono work. In 1992, Wuhan University, with support from the Ford Foundation, established China's first public interest legal organization, the Center for the Protection of the Rights of Disadvantaged Citizens.[136] Relying on faculty, students, and a small full-time staff, it accepts matters in six main areas: women's rights, administrative litigation, juvenile rights, environmental protection, elders' rights, and rights of the disabled. Unlike government legal aid programs, the Center does not limit its assistance to poor clients. It gives priority to non-routine cases where the effect is likely to be substantial. Students' work is purely pro bono; they receive no academic credit. Yet the Center attracts more volunteers than it can accommodate, partly because it offers unique opportunities in skills-based training.[137]

A growing number of other universities have established legal advice clinics or associations where law students provide information, research, document preparation, and referrals to local law firms.[138] Some have a substantive focus, like the Peking University's Center for Women's Law Studies and Legal Services, also funded by the Ford Foundation. A distinctive characteristic of this Center is its emphasis on impact litigation and law reform.[139] In general, these university centers have been careful to establish good working relationships with national and local government officials, and the Ministry of Justice has supported the development of additional law school programs. Yet a number of factors constrain their growth and effectiveness that have yet to be adequately addressed. One is the absence of opportunities for students to appear in court or to integrate their service experiences with academic course work. A second obstacle is the lack of widespread faculty participation. Many Chinese academics supplement their incomes through part-time consulting practices, which leaves insufficient time for pro bono service.[140] Other constraints involve cultural forces that are not limited to the law school context.

Challenges in Building a Pro Bono Tradition

Some of the challenges in encouraging public service among the Chinese bar are similar to those arising in other countries, particularly the increasing commercialization of legal practice and the focus on profits and income as measures of professional success. However, certain distinctive problems involve the lack of professional independence and the absence of a tradition in which law is an important strategy of protecting individual rights and promoting progressive social reforms. Lawyers must renew their practice licenses annually, and examples of physical abuse and license suspension for those who take unpopular positions have had a substantial chilling effect.[141] Other challenges involve the lack of strong professional associations and the government's resistance to influential nongovernmental reform-oriented organizations, particularly those supported by foreign funders that may have agendas inconsistent with official policies.[142]

Yet various social, economic, and political forces are also pushing in directions more supportive of pro bono and public interest work. One is the adoption of legal doctrines permitting class actions, contingent fees, and punitive damages, which makes cause-oriented litigation more feasible. The increasing presence of global law firms whose members support pro bono service and professional independence is encouraging those tendencies in the local bar. And the Chinese government's interest in broadening access to justice and mitigating international criticism of its human rights record is improving the climate for public interest work.

Connecting the Cultures

The increasing international influences on legal practice bring increasing opportunities to learn from other countries' pro bono experience. The United States has played a leadership role in exporting its own public service traditions, in part because those traditions are better established than in other nations, and in part because American law and lawyers play such a dominant role in the global community. Yet the American legal profession also has much to learn from viewing pro bono participation through an international lens. The preceding snapshots suggest a number of lessons that cut across geographical borders.

First, pro bono work holds substantial value for society, for the legal profession, and for individual and institutional providers. From a societal standpoint, involvement of the private bar is crucial in assisting underrepresented groups and promoting public interest causes. Although almost all nations are committed in principle to equal access to justice, almost none have been able to achieve it in practice. Government support of legal aid has never been adequate to meet the need, and cutbacks in many nations have widened the gap. The bar's willingness to help springs in part from its collective commitment to justice, but also from more pragmatic concerns about enhancing its status and preserving its independence. Legal employers, for their part, have similar reputational concerns and see pro bono work as a way to foster retention, recruitment, skills, and morale among their members. For law schools, such programs hold comparable value; they can be an effective form of recruitment and training and a way to build their reputations with local communities, governments, and bar associations. Individual lawyers and law students have similarly mixed motives; pro bono work promotes both professional development and ethical commitments.

The strategies that different countries have used to encourage public service have varied in accordance with their own traditions and needs. Chapter 8 summarizes the approaches that are most readily generalized across national boundaries. From a comparative perspective, a few common themes bear emphasis.

First, building a pro bono tradition requires support from multiple institutions. Whatever individuals' personal motives to serve, a widespread and sustained commitment will only occur if appropriate incentives are in place. One possibility is to mandate minimum pro bono contributions, a strategy employed at the most widespread level by the Chinese government, but also adopted at least intermittently by courts in Anglo-American and European countries, and by some law schools in the United States. The effectiveness of such requirements in securing broad compliance and competent assistance has been mixed. Much depends on the perceived legitimacy of pro bono obligations in the surrounding legal culture, and the personal and professional benefits from participation. For obvious reasons, such systems work best when participants have a range of ways to satisfy public service requirements, including buyout options for lawyers who lack the expertise and inclination to provide direct assistance.

In countries with a strong tradition of professional independence, the bar's widespread opposition to mandatory service makes other strategies more prudent. The government can play a role, but the most effective approach is likely to be enlisting involvement among its own employees, providing resources for voluntary programs, and linking awards of government work to the pro bono records of outside firms. Such initiatives in Canada, Australia, and the United States have had modest success.[143] Support from bar organizations is also crucial. They can adopt specific aspirational standards and best practices; enlist participants through challenge programs; and provide coordination, resources, and awards for pro bono initiatives. Corporate clients and prominent legal publications can exert pressure by monitoring public service contributions and awarding business or favorable publicity to those with distinguished records. Associations of law schools and academic accrediting bodies can place similar pressure on legal education to expand pro bono opportunities and to ensure that they are rewarding and rewarded experiences for both students and faculty. Finally, legal scholars and research organizations can focus greater attention on public service and the strategies that increase its frequency and effectiveness. A little knowledge is a dangerous thing, and in too many countries, that is all we have.

Chapter Six

An Empirical Analysis of
Pro Bono Service
Among American Lawyers

Despite the growing attention to pro bono work among the American legal profession, relatively little systematic research is available on how best to promote it. The objective of the empirical study was to provide the first broad-scale data about the personal characteristics, educational experiences, and workplace policies that influence pro bono participation.

Survey Methodology

To obtain such information, some 3000 detailed questionnaires went to three groups: (1) lawyers who were graduates of six schools that had different approaches to student pro bono work; (2) recent individual and law firm winners of the American Bar Association's annual Pro Bono Publico Award; and (3) firms for which annual pro bono data are available.

The first group of survey participants included law school graduates of Yale, the University of Pennsylvania, Fordham, Tulane, Northwestern, and the University of Chicago. All of these schools have had strong clinical programs but have varied in their approaches to pro bono work. Tulane and Pennsylvania were among the first to require student pro bono service and have consistently invested substantial resources in their programs.[1] Ford-

ham and Yale have strongly encouraged pro bono work, have designated administrators to coordinate such work, and have had high levels of student
involvement in public interest organizations.[2] Chicago and Northwestern
were identified by the Pro Bono Project of the Association of American Law
Schools (AALS) as schools with resources and student bodies comparable
to the others, but without a formal pro bono program or coordinator at the
time of the survey.[3] Two schools were selected in each category to minimize
idiosyncrasies that might be unique to either institution. However, the responses for each school were tabulated separately to reveal any statistically
significant differences between the graduates of the paired institutions. A
questionnaire, reprinted as Appendix 1, went to all the graduates from these
schools in the classes of 1993 and 1997. These classes were selected to include
lawyers who were at different seniority levels, who had been at their workplace long enough to have a good sense of its policies, priorities, and culture, and who included graduates of two law schools that required pro bono
service while they were students.

A second group of survey participants included individuals or law firms
that received the five annual American Bar Association (ABA) Pro Bono
Publico awards between 1993 and 2000 for outstanding pro bono service.
Names of recipients were obtained from profiles in the *ABA Journal*. The
time period was selected to correspond to the one used for the law school
graduates. Individual award winners received the same questionnaire that
was sent to these graduates. Firms received a similar questionnaire, which is
reprinted as Appendix 2. Individual recipients were also contacted by telephone to obtain the fullest possible information from lawyers who had dem-
onstrated exceptional commitment to pro bono work.

A third group of survey participants included firms consistently listed by
the *American Lawyer* as among the nation's 100 top law firms in terms of
gross revenue during the period 1993–2000. These were the only firms for
which data on pro bono service were publicly available. Firms that were in
the top 100 for at least four years, 94 firms in all, were included in the sample. The same questionnaire used for law firm ABA award winners went to
the pro bono coordinator or managing partner at those 94 firms. The initial

objective was to compare policies and practices at firms that had high, moderate, and low levels of average pro bono work per lawyer.[4]

The survey obviously was not designed to provide a random sample of lawyers or law firms. Rather, the point was to identify groups that could yield useful information about factors most likely to influence pro bono contributions. Although the respondents are not representative of the legal profession, they are either award winners or firm members who are particularly knowledgeable about practices affecting pro bono involvement, or they are part of a sample designed to determine whether different law school experiences influenced such involvement.

Characteristics of the Sample

Approximately 3000 individuals and firms received surveys, and 844 returned them, yielding an overall response rate of about 28%.[5] This rate is not unusual for large mailed surveys. For example, a recent widely reported study by the nonprofit research organization Catalyst, entitled *Women in Law: Making the Case*, also reported a 28% response rate.[6] As with any large survey with this level of response, the margin of error was greater than 3%, which means that the data may not be characteristic of the entire population surveyed. Some questions also had a high number of "not applicable" responses, which further increased the margin of error for those inquiries. Survey findings need to be interpreted in light of the nonrandom nature of the responses.

In general, however, biases in this survey's responses were likely to run in a direction that does not unduly limit the overall findings. The lawyers who took time to complete and return the questionnaire were, as noted below, individuals who were exceptionally likely to care about pro bono work. Because the primary objective of the study was to identify factors that contribute to such work, the most helpful perspectives were likely to come from those who were interested enough to respond.

In terms of demographic characteristics, the individuals who responded were roughly similar to lawyers in their general age cohort, except that the sample had a higher percentage of women, racial and ethnic minorities, law firm associates, and lawyers not engaged in legal practice.[7] About half (53%)

were in law firms, most of whom were associates (42% of the survey as a whole).[8] The participants in the study also earned more income and billed more hours than the average for the profession generally.[9]

These surveyed lawyers also made substantially greater pro bono contributions than the typical American attorney. The average number of pro bono hours per year for study participants was 70. However, contribution levels varied substantially within the sample subgroups: individual award winners, 255; firm award winners, 230; Tulane, 50; Pennsylvania, 114; Fordham, 59; Yale, 129; Chicago, 37; and Northwestern, 39. If graduates of schools with similar pro bono programs are combined, the average for lawyers who had either mandatory programs (Tulane and Pennsylvania), or well-supported voluntary programs (Yale and Fordham), is 81. For lawyers from schools without such programs, the average is 38 (Chicago and Northwestern). On the basis of the limited data available for the profession generally, summarized in Chapter 1, the sampled lawyers contributed well over three times as many hours as the national average; the award winners contributed over ten times as many hours.

It is less clear whether responding lawyers were also more generous than the bar as a whole in making financial contributions. Of the 180 lawyers who reported donations to organizations providing legal assistance for persons of limited means, a majority gave $100 or less. A quarter (23%) of the sample contributed $0 to $50; about a third (30%) contributed $51 to $100; a fifth contributed $101 to $200; and 4% contributed over $200 annually. As Chapter 1 noted, comparable data are not available for the nation as a whole. In the few states that compile statistics, the average annual lawyer contributions for roughly the same time period ranged from $32 to $82.

Data Analysis

To identify the most significant influences on pro bono service, the survey relied on two methods. One was to ask participants for their views; the other was to correlate various factors with the amount of charitable work that participants reported performing. Both measures have limitations, as is true of any empirical analysis relying on self-assessments. Nonetheless, these responses provide a more reliable profile of what affects public service contributions than the less systematic and comprehensive information currently available.

Questionnaire responses that were susceptible to statistical evaluation were analyzed to determine whether the dependent variable, hours of pro bono work, was correlated with independent variables such as law school programs, law firm policies, and respondents' demographic characteristics.[10] The open-ended questions were evaluated separately to identify insights about influences on lawyers' charitable activities and appropriate reform strategies. Regression analyses were used to determine the existence and strength of any relationship between pro bono work and the factors commonly thought to affect it.[11] On some questions, a low response rate prevented meaningful regression analysis. There were too few firms in each of the *American Lawyer* categories of low, middle, and high pro bono contributions, and too few individual ABA award winners, to permit such analysis. Accordingly, all the law firm responses were grouped together in order to provide general data about workplace practices. Because both groups of law firm participants—those who won awards and those responsible for pro bono programs—were likely to be strong supporters of such public service, their cumulative responses can be helpful in identifying strategies that contribute to that objective.

Once a regression analysis was performed on each individual group and on the combined responses, tests were run to see whether the independent variables had any effect, positive or negative, on the mean value for pro bono work.[12] Such an effect would not, of course, demonstrate that the independent variable caused an increase or decrease in pro bono work. However, the overall pattern of relationships, together with other questionnaire responses, can cast light on the factors likely to influence pro bono contributions.[13]

As subsequent discussion notes, almost none of the factors that surveyed lawyers or prior research identified as having the greatest influence on pro bono work were by themselves statistically significant in predicting such work. This lack of correlation may partly reflect noise in the data, but it may also highlight the interrelationships among forces that affect behavior. Individual characteristics, workplace practices, and educational experiences all play roles that are difficult to disentangle in professional settings.

PERSONAL CHARACTERISTICS AND MOTIVATIONS
OF SURVEYED LAWYERS

To gauge the relative importance of factors influencing pro bono participation, the questionnaire asked lawyers to rank commonly cited factors on a scale of 1 to 5, with 5 being "very significant" and 1 being "not significant." Table 6.1 summarizes the responses for the overall sample, the individual lawyer award winners, and the firm award winners.

In general, these rankings were consistent with the findings on altruistic behavior summarized in Chapter 3. The most commonly emphasized forces driving pro bono participation were the intrinsic satisfactions that came from the work (4.2) and a sense of obligation to pursue it (3.7). Of secondary importance were: employer policies (2.7) or encouragement (2.7); and professional benefits such as contacts, referrals, and training (2.7), trial experience (2.5), involvement with clients (2.4), and control over the work (2.4). Of slightly less significance were personal characteristics such as political commitment (2.3) or religious commitment (2.1). Awards by employers or bar associations had least importance (1.7). Regression analysis revealed that the only factors significantly correlated with the reported amount of pro bono service were political commitment and employer encouragement.[14] Regression analysis also examined whether any of the demographic characteristics of respondents were significantly correlated with pro bono work. No such correlations were present, a fact unsurprising in light of general patterns of altruistic behavior noted in Chapter 3. Race, ethnicity, gender, income, and the importance of religion did not predict involvement.[15]

Some lawyers also volunteered comments about the influences on their pro bono work, as did many of the ABA award winners. In general, these comments were consistent with the quantitative rankings noted above and with other research on altruistic behavior. The most significant motivations were a commitment to public service and the personal satisfaction that it provided. Some attorneys had gone to law school or had taken a particular job partly out of a desire to pursue public interest work.[16] For these lawyers, family influences, early volunteer involvement, or personal hardships often instilled a commitment to community service in general or to certain causes in particular.[17] Other attorneys developed interest while in law school or

TABLE 6.1

Positive Influences on Pro Bono Work

	Overall (n = 628)	Individual Award (n = 19)	Firm Award (n = 9)
Personal satisfaction	4.2	4.4	3.9
Sense of professional obligation	3.7	4.0	3.7
Employer policies (requiring/encouraging pro bono work, counting as billable hours)	2.7	2.3	3.8
Employer encouragement	2.7	2.5	2.9
Professional value of pro bono work (contacts, training, referrals)	2.7	2.1	3.5
Reputation/recognition	2.5	2.5	2.5
Opportunity for trial experience	2.5	2.2	2.9
Opportunity to work directly with client	2.4	1.8	3.4
Opportunity to exercise control over work	2.4	1.9	3.1
Political commitment	2.3	2.0	3.2
Religious commitment	2.1	1.4	2.5
Awards by employer or bar association	1.7	1.8	2.6

through exposure to pro bono programs at their firms.[18] A number of lawyers, mainly Tulane graduates and ABA award winners, expressed a conviction that such work was a "professional obligation" and part of the "price for lawyers' license to practice law."

A much larger group of lawyers, spread across the entire sample, mentioned the rewards of particular kinds of work. Examples included death row appeals, prison suits, sweatshop labor litigation, and political asylum claims. For many attorneys, pro bono matters provided their most rewarding professional experiences. As one ABA winner put it, after lawyers leave law school, the "altruistic sense of what the profession is about . . . disappears pretty quickly. Pro bono is a way to get this passion back. This makes you feel alive and like you are doing something worthwhile." Most award winners offered similar views, and some believed that they had benefited even more than their clients. One attorney noted, "If I couldn't do pro bono, I wouldn't practice law. It makes me feel like I am making a difference." Lawyers often contrasted their public service with their largely commercial practices and reported greater satisfaction from promoting social reform or helping a disadvantaged client than from wrangling over money. Some attorneys found it especially rewarding to work on matters within their field of expertise, such as helping a nonprofit organization protect its intellectual property. By contrast, others enjoyed the chance to focus on issues "not part of daily practice," particularly where the cases involved important constitutional questions or social justice causes.

Many lawyers also cited the professional benefits from pro bono work described in Chapter 2. For some attorneys, such work was a way to develop expertise in a particular area in which they wanted to practice. Others gained trial experience, which sometimes had direct payoffs in obtaining desirable paying cases. One lawyer credited his pro bono contributions with helping him achieve a leadership position in the local bar association. Others mentioned the benefits of networking and community involvement.

Lawyers were also asked about the relative importance of factors limiting pro bono work. Table 6.2 summarizes these responses. The most important factors were workload demands (4.5), family obligations (3.4), and billable hour expectations (3.0). Other factors included employer attitude (2.6), lack of opportunities in their practice area (2.6), lack of information about opportunities (2.4), lack of expertise (2.4), employer bonus policies excluding pro bono work (2.2), lack of interest (2.2), lack of resources and support staff (2.2), inconvenient or unpleasant aspects of such work (2.1), and lack of malpractice insurance (1.9).

Again, many attorneys' written comments and interview responses amplified these views. The disincentives for pro bono involvement resulting from employer policies and priorities are described below. Other, more personal reasons for declining public service clustered around five themes: a failure to see pro bono service as a professional responsibility; a lack of interest or confidence in the value of such service; negative pro bono experi-

TABLE 6.2

Negative Influences on Pro Bono Work

	Overall	Individual Award	Firm Award
Workload demands	4.5	3.8	4.1
Family obligations	3.4	3.3	3.7
Employer billable hour expectation	3.0	2.1	3.9
Employer attitude	2.6	1.9	3.3
Lack of opportunities in practice area	2.6	1.3	3.9
Lack of expertise	2.4	1.3	3.2
Lack of information about opportunities	2.4	1.5	3.2
Employer bonus policy excluding pro bono work	2.2	n/a	3.2
Lack of interest	2.2	1.5	3.2
Lack of resources (e.g., support staff)	2.2	3.0	1.7
Inconvenient or unpleasant aspects of work	2.1	1.8	3.3
Lack of malpractice insurance	1.9	1.2	3.5

ences; inadequate opportunities in the attorney's area of expertise; and financial or family constraints.

Some lawyers, especially those who did not find their legal careers intrinsically satisfying, explicitly denied that pro bono work was a professional responsibility. As one attorney put it, "I feel no moral obligation to perform such work as the quid pro quo of my license to practice law. It is merely my job." Another lawyer echoed that sentiment: "I hate practicing law and only do it to pay the bills. I refuse to undertake additional legal work."

Other attorneys simply registered their lack of interest in pro bono work or their sense that it was often "pointless," "unnecessary," or unlikely to do much good in the world. One lawyer noted: "I now realize how elusive the notion of 'social justice' is and have become more selfish—meaning less willing to sacrifice my own well-being in the interest of social justice. . . . I have grown discouraged about anything substantially changing." Even lawyers who did substantial pro bono work cited frustrations inherent in the work as a constraint on involvement. From their perspective, charitable legal assistance was an "inadequate band-aid" for social problems, and it was hard to take real satisfaction from outcomes where the "cards are stacked against the poor." For some attorneys, these frustrations, or a general lack of enthusiasm for legal practice, led them to prefer investing their volunteer efforts in projects unrelated to law. "Frankly," said one lawyer, these other activities feel "less like work."[19] Echoing these views, another attorney came to "really resent" his law firm's requirement of 40 hours of pro bono legal work because he was already very involved in other charitable activities.

Some attorneys cited negative pro bono experiences as the major factor limiting their participation. The work was uninteresting, unimportant, or emotionally draining, or the clients were unethical, unreasonable, or unappreciative. Some lawyers identified their field of practice as the main problem in finding appropriate cases. Attorneys who specialized in areas such as securities law, mergers and acquisitions, or trusts and estates could not find cases matching their expertise, or felt limited to routine "unrewarding" matters like incorporation of nonprofit organizations. So too, lawyers who ventured outside their field sometimes ended up with work that they found unchallenging, such as simple name changes or family law cases "too depressing to bear." The resources available in certain practice settings also imposed constraints. In the experience of one Chicago graduate, "Helping people avoid paying credit card bills is what you get in a small firm that doesn't spend millions on [pro bono programs]."

Other attorneys' negative feelings about volunteer work stemmed from client relationships. Some lawyers had represented individuals who seemed to be dishonest or to be "abusing the system." One attorney who handled landlord-tenant cases reported that his clients were "usually liable and often have lied in an effort to fashion a defense." Other lawyers believed that because individuals were not paying for the representation, they did not really value or appreciate the effort involved. This attitude often led to seemingly unreasonable rejections of settlement offers. Clients reportedly found "no downside to rolling the dice and going to trial."

Finally, some attorneys felt that they simply could not afford to do pro bono work. One partner in a two-person civil rights / criminal defense firm already represented many low-income clients on a contingent fee basis. The firm ended up with "a lot of 'de facto' pro bono work," and the partner found it impossible at this point in her career to build the practice, support its staff, and take on additional matters that she knew would be pro bono. Another lawyer, currently "a stay-at-home mother," would "love to do pro bono work," but the malpractice insurance and child-care costs were too great. Many lawyers cited family obligations, coupled with heavy workload pressures, as a primary constraint. The experience of one Chicago graduate with four young children was typical: "Between work and family obligations . . . I have absolutely no spare time." Attorneys who were willing to "stay at the office round the clock" when they were single had to establish different priorities when they had families. One lawyer, who found it impossible to find time for public service while combining 2400 billable hours a year with a family, added: "*I* need pro bono!" Or at least, as noted below, attorneys in this situation need a policy that counts pro bono work as part of their billable hour quota.

Not only did lawyers with families have competing demands on their time, they also had greater financial obligations, which pushed them to focus on paying work and client development activities that would generate it. However, the extent to which money mattered in constraining pro bono involvement was a matter of dispute. Some ABA award winners emphasized the need to make financial sacrifices—"to live a pro bono lifestyle"—and acknowledged the cultural pressures pushing in the opposite direction. As one attorney noted, "We live in a society in which what you make is what you are. When you encounter someone who by all other measures ought to be doing something to rack up the bucks and that person isn't doing it, there is this attitude 'what is wrong with him.'" Other award winners were less forgiving, and attributed the apathy of colleagues to simple greed. One put the point bluntly: "They are selfish narcissistic jerks who worship money." Another award winner felt that the primary reason for noninvolvement in pro bono work was political, not economic: "I think [these lawyers] enjoy their position of power in society and they don't have an interest in altering it."

In describing their own behavior, attorneys provided a more nuanced portrait. As Chapter 7 notes, many cited substantial educational debts and the high cost of living in cities like New York as major deterrents to public service. Summarizing a widespread view, one attorney noted, "Pro bono doesn't put bread on the table. When you get married and have kids, that pulls you quickly away." Some lawyers described themselves as "not driven by money," but rather as "realists" about the costs of supporting a family, especially if they had several educational tuitions to pay or children with special needs. A few interviewees were candid about their own lifestyle desires. As one attorney acknowledged, there are "certain comforts . . . [I don't] want to live without." By contrast, other lawyers, particularly ABA award winners, saw pro bono work as a way to reconcile their economic needs with their service commitments. Although they would have preferred a full-time public interest career, a well-paying private-sector job offering pro bono opportunities was the next best alternative.

Taken together, the data collected and reviewed for this study make clear that financial considerations are important but not decisive in explaining pro bono contributions. As is true with altruistic behavior generally, economic ability does not determine charitable involvement. Rather, the most powerful influences are a sense of satisfaction and obligation, together with the professional benefits or costs associated with pro bono work. Many of these benefits and costs are influenced by external factors, particularly workplace policies. Even seemingly personal motivations, such as the satisfaction that lawyers experience from pro bono involvement, may be in part a function of the opportunities, training, and support available. The negative pro bono experiences that some lawyers reported may reflect a mismatch between their interests or expertise and the volunteer options most readily accessible. So too, certain adverse reactions to clients may indicate a lack of understanding or "cultural competence" in dealing with low-income individuals, which could be addressed through better training and supervision. As discussion in Chapter 2 indicated, it is often counterproductive to assign poverty-related work to lawyers who have little appreciation of the life experiences that lead some impoverished clients to distrust their attorneys or "abuse" the system.

Not only could well-designed workplace programs affect satisfaction with pro bono work, they also could reduce the costs of pursuing it. And as the following discussion makes clear, most programs leave much to be desired.

PRO BONO POLICIES AND PRACTICES

The survey included a range of questions about employment practices that might influence pro bono activity. Lawyers were first asked whether their workplace had a policy concerning pro bono work, and if so, whether such work counted in full or in part toward billable hours. Tables 6.3 and 6.4 summarize the responses.

This overview of workplace cultures is striking in several respects. First, it is both surprising and disheartening that almost half of lawyers (47%)

TABLE 6.3
Policies on Pro Bono Work

	Overall ($n = 675$)	Individual Award ($n = 19$)	Firm Award ($n = 6$)
Formal policy	35.0	52.7	52.7
Informal policy	18.1	21.1	21.1
No policy	46.9	26.3	26.3

TABLE 6.4
Policies on Billable Hours

	Overall ($n = 379$)	Individual Award ($n = 11$)	Firm Award ($n = 4$)
Yes, all hours counted	25.3	50.0	27.2
Yes, certain number of hours	19.8	25.0	27.2
Yes, certain kinds of work	10.0	0	0
Other	44.9	25.0	45.6

were in workplaces with no pro bono policy, and only a third (35%) reported a formal policy. It may not be coincidental that formal policies were much more common among ABA award winners; three quarters of both individuals and firms reported a policy, and about half, a formal policy. Particularly in large or midsize organizations, lawyers often interpreted the absence of a formal policy as an absence of support for pro bono work. One put the point directly: "the lack of . . . policies (together with partners never speaking of pro bono work) silently discourages the practice. I think my firm's attitude is embarrassing."

Even more disheartening is the content of formal policies. Only a quarter of surveyed lawyers' workplaces (25%) fully counted pro bono work toward billable hours. Fewer than a third counted a certain number of hours (20%) or a certain kind of work (10%). Such findings are consistent with other recent survey data and send a signal that undermines public service commitments.[20] Many lawyers volunteered comments critical of their employers' failure to credit pro bono matters toward billable hour quotas. A common attitude was "do it if you want," but "don't expect to have less 'real' work" and "make sure you've got [your billables] at the end of the year." In effect, pro bono participation was permissible only if it occurred "outside the normal work hours."

Given what passes for "normal" in many firms, the price of public service is often prohibitive. For many lawyers, "between the billable [hour] quota and the emphasis on practice development . . . not much time [is left] for pro bono." In commenting on this dilemma, one attorney added, "I can hardly keep my head above water as it is." As noted earlier, lawyers with substantial family obligations were particularly likely to see nonbillable work as a "luxury" they could not afford.

Other limitations on pro bono participation arise from informal workplace norms and practices. To identify these factors, one question asked whether pro bono work was valued the same as billable work in promotion and bonus decisions or whether it counted positively in such decisions. Another question asked how much support the organization provided for public service in terms of staff, litigation costs, and other expenses. Tables 6.5 and 6.6 summarize the responses.

TABLE 6.5

Role of Pro Bono Work in Promotion and Bonus Decisions

	Overall (n = 477)	Individual Award (n = 11)	Firm Award (n = 6)
Valued equally to billable hours	10.0	36.4	16.7
Somewhat valued	17.2	36.4	33.3
Not viewed as important	18.1	9.0	50.0
Negatively viewed	43.5	9.0	0
Other	11.2	9.2	0

TABLE 6.6

Support for Pro Bono Work

	Overall (n = 529)	Individual Award (n = 15)	Firm Award (n = 6)
Provides full support	57.4	82.3	50.0
Provides partial support	11.2	5.8	0
Provides inadequate support	12.8	5.8	0
Other	18.7	6.1	50.0

Workplace policies concerning staff and financial resources for pro bono work were, on the whole, more generous than policies concerning billable hours, but were by no means fully supportive. Only about half of lawyers' workplaces (57%) subsidized all the costs of pro bono matters. Again, award winners had greater access to resources than the sample as a whole. Over four-fifths (82%) of the individual winners reported full subsidies. Many lawyers (n = 147) volunteered comments clarifying their organization's policy. About half (52%) indicated that their employer provided no support for pro bono work. A third indicated that some assistance was available, typically staff time, but that costs such as fees for experts were not covered.

Some employers provided resources for approved cases, but limited their approval to "small inexpensive matters."

A more pervasive limitation of workplace policies is the effect of pro bono work on promotion and bonus decisions. Only 10% of surveyed lawyers indicated that their organizations valued such work as much as billable hours. About a fifth (18%) believed that pro bono contributions were not viewed as important, and almost half felt they were negatively viewed (44%). Unsurprisingly, award winners were more likely to be in workplaces that valued, or at least did not penalize, public service. Almost three-quarters of the individual winners (73%) and half of the firm award winners (50%) reported that pro bono work was valued equally.

Again, a substantial number of lawyers ($n = 152$) wrote comments concerning their employer's treatment of pro bono service. Of these, two-thirds indicated that this work was a negative factor in promotion and bonus decisions. Positive comments tended to be brief and nonspecific: the firm was "fabulous" or "strongly encouraged" pro bono contributions. Most lawyers who provided details were in organizations with attitudes ranging from active discouragement to not-so-benign neglect. Sometimes the message was explicit. One associate was told by a partner that "I was putting myself at risk if I did too much public service work." Another similarly reported having to "squeeze out the time to do the pro bono work, and hide it, and fight people over priorities." In some firms, most attorneys viewed pro bono work "as a nuisance" or not a "proper use of billable time." In other firms, the negative attitude was conveyed through bonuses, which were linked to billable hours and which excluded charitable activities. As several lawyers emphasized, such policies created a "real financial disincentive to doing pro bono work." In these workplaces, "money has been the absolute bottom line, so pro bono has not been encouraged and is not rewarded."

Such financial disincentives were compounded by promotion practices that overlooked or undervalued pro bono service. As one attorney noted, the "overwhelming emphasis" in performance evaluations is "client work [which] makes it difficult to volunteer for unpaid matters." Another lawyer similarly observed that "you would never rise to the top on the basis of pro bono work, and a lack of pro bono work wouldn't be counted against you."

TABLE 6.7
Consistency of Policies and Practices

	Overall ($n = 324$)	Individual Award ($n = 11$)	Firm Award ($n = 4$)
Consistent	64.8	91.0	75.0
Not consistent	35.2	9.0	25.0

TABLE 6.8
Effect of Practices on Pro Bono Work

	Overall ($n = 235$)	Individual Award ($n = 7$)	Firm Award ($n = 2$)
Reduces pro bono work	59.7	71.4	50.0
Does not reduce pro bono work	40.3	28.6	50.0

In some practice contexts, volunteer activities could have more negative effects. As one lawyer observed, "If your time is taken up with pro bono, you will not have time to take on the . . . career-making deals which tend to be all consuming." Nor would it be possible to spend the hours necessary to develop the client base or practice expertise that many lawyers cited as a prerequisite for advancement.

In some organizations, these disincentives were at odds with formal policies. To identify the extent of the gap, the survey asked lawyers whether, if their organization's formal policy supported pro bono work, the policy was consistent with informal norms and reward structures, and if not, whether the informal practices significantly reduced individuals' willingness to accept pro bono work. Tables 6.7 and 6.8 summarize the responses.

Although most employers with supportive policies had consistent workplace practices (65%), about a third of respondents (35%) reported a gap. Of those who identified a disparity, over half (60%) felt that informal norms reduced lawyers' willingness to engage in pro bono work. Written comments often identified discontinuities between formal rhetoric and daily realities. Some attorneys believed that their firm simply paid "lip service" to pro bono work for purposes of recruiting or self-image. In these firms, public service was "actively encouraged on paper . . . [but not in] practice." Most notably, it was not credited toward billable hour requirements. Firm leaders "encouraged pro bono on the surface but [provided] . . . no incentive to do it."

Other partners simply failed to live up to their organization's stated policy. They "claimed to count pro bono work toward billable hours but in fact did not and associates who engaged in substantial pro bono work were sometimes criticized." The feudal management structure of some firms permitted a "disconnect" between the organization's stated policy and the "practical realities" enforced by supervising partners and department heads. In effect, pro bono participation was "encouraged formally but rarely actually accommodated." Other firms were selective in their accommodation. They permitted junior associates to take advantage of public service opportunities in order to gain useful practical experience, but gave upper-level associates no such leeway.

Part of the gap between principle and practice seemed a function less of design than neglect. The organization meant well but simply did not "have the infrastructure to support pro bono work" or had "not dedicated resources and leadership" to encouraging it. Some attorneys from small firms or corporate legal departments believed that financial constraints prevented adequate programs. But as one lawyer acknowledged, the problem was not simply a matter of size. It was rather that "small firms lack resources to do more without an impact on profits." The key impediment in these firms, as in many of their larger counterparts, was the choice to make profits preeminent. To help understand what drove such choices, the survey asked whether recent salary and billable hour increases had affected pro bono work. Table 6.9 summarizes those responses.

In general, the recent escalation in salaries and hourly work expectations caused more modifications in practices than in policies. Fewer than 10% of lawyers reported a change in formal policy (8%), and only 15% noted a

TABLE 6.9

Effect of Recent Increases in Salaries and Billable Hours

	Overall ($n = 479$)	Individual Award ($n = 17$)	Firm Award ($n = 5$)
Has caused change in formal policy	7.6	0	20.0
Has caused change in way pro bono involvement affects promotion and compensation decisions	14.8	24.9	0
Has caused lawyers to decline time-consuming pro bono work	45.5	25.2	40.0
Has not had significant impact	18.9	49.9	40.0
Impact is not yet clear	0	0	0

change in the way pro bono involvement affected promotion and compensation decisions. However, almost half of all lawyers (46%) felt that these pressures had caused practitioners to decline time-consuming pro bono work. Predictably, among award winners, the changes were not as important as for the sample as a whole. Still, 40% of firm winners reported a decline in willingness to take cases as a result of recent spikes in hours and salaries.

To gauge lawyers' reactions to current workplace norms, the survey also asked a series of questions about their satisfaction with the amount of pro bono work they did and their methods for obtaining it. Tables 6.10 and 6.11 summarize those responses.

Overall, these responses suggest that substantial progress remains to be made in most legal workplaces. Only about a fifth (22%) of surveyed attorneys were very satisfied with the amount of time that they spent on pro bono work. Another fifth (19%) were somewhat satisfied, and a quarter (25%) were neutral. A third of the sample was dissatisfied, slightly over a quarter somewhat dissatisfied, and about 10% very dissatisfied (11%).[21]

TABLE 6.10

Satisfaction with Amount of Pro Bono Work

	Overall ($n = 708$)	Individual Award ($n = 20$)	Firm Award ($n = 9$)
Very satisfied	22.1	44.9	33.3
Somewhat satisfied	19.0	30.7	33.3
Neutral	25.0	10.0	0
Somewhat dissatisfied	23.5	10.0	22.2
Very dissatisfied	10.8	4.9	11.1

TABLE 6.11

Satisfaction with Method of Obtaining Pro Bono Work

	Overall ($n = 533$)	Individual Award ($n = 20$)	Firm Award ($n = 6$)
Very satisfied	35.3	50.0	66.7
Somewhat satisfied	24.1	10.0	0
Neutral	29.3	34.9	0
Somewhat dissatisfied	9.3	4.9	33.3
Very dissatisfied	2.1	0	0

Assessments were more positive for the method of obtaining pro bono work, but only about a third of the sample (35%) was very satisfied. Another quarter was somewhat satisfied, and the remainder were neutral (29%) or dissatisfied (11%). Again, the award winners reported better experiences than other lawyers. Three-quarters of the individual winners (76%) and two-thirds of the firm winners (67%) were satisfied with the amount of time they spent on public service. Two-thirds of the firm winners (67%), and three-fifths (60%) of the individual winners were satisfied with how they obtained such opportunities.

The survey also asked more specific questions about lawyers' methods of obtaining pro bono work, their organization's structure for providing such work, and the effectiveness and desirability of such structures. Tables 6.12 through 6.15 summarize those responses.

The most common method for obtaining pro bono work was through an employer's pro bono committee or coordinator. About a third of the overall sample (35%), a third of the firm winners (34%), and a fifth (21%) of the individual award winners relied on this method. For the overall sample, the other most common sources of opportunities were bar association programs (17%), friends (12%), and supervising attorneys (8%). A smaller percentage obtained work from clients (6%), public interest organizations (4%), legal services providers (3%), or family members (1%). The patterns were slightly different for award winners; they relied less on employer programs and more on bar association programs, friends, clients, and legal service providers.[22] Many lawyers ($n = 101$) also wrote in responses that identified additional sources of referrals. The most common were court appointments, religious or charitable organizations, law schools, and networking activities.

A surprisingly high percentage of lawyers, about half of the overall sample (54%), worked in organizations with no pro bono committee or coordinator to facilitate pro bono placements. Half of the firm award winners and a third of the individual winners also lacked facilitators. Yet where such a structure was in place, it received reasonably favorable assessments; over a third (38%) of attorneys thought facilitators were very effective, and about half (49%) thought they were somewhat effective. Only 10% found them not effective. The small number of award winners who had such experience and responded to the question were even more positive; almost half of the individual winners (45%) and two-thirds of the firm winners (67%) rated facilitators as very effective. However, no consensus emerged in response to a follow-up question asking whether, if the lawyer's organization lacked a facilitator, it should appoint one; slightly under half advocated such a position (43%) and slightly over half (56%) did not. Award winners were also divided, with about two-thirds of firm winners (67%) but only 11% of individual winners recommending a facilitator.

TABLE 6.12

Method of Obtaining Pro Bono Work

	Overall ($n = 463$)	Individual Award ($n = 19$)	Firm Award ($n = 6$)
Employer pro bono committee or coordinator	34.8	21.1	34.4
Bar association program	16.9	21.1	0
Friends	11.9	0	22.9
Supervising attorney	8.4	10.5	0
Client	5.5	15.7	0
Public interest organization	3.7	0	0
Legal services provider	3.1	0	11.5
Family	1.0	0	0
Other	12.1	31.6	31.3

Lawyers' responses concerning the types of work available did, however, make clear the problems that can arise when no well-designed structure exists to screen pro bono opportunities and to handle concerns about the matters that lawyers can accept. One question asked attorneys how their organizations dealt with matters that might prove objectionable to clients, other lawyers, or the community. Another question asked how satisfied attorneys were with the types of cases that were permitted. A relatively small number of respondents answered these questions. Of those who did, about two-fifths (42%) were in organizations that discouraged work likely to advance positions inconsistent with client interests or values. Slightly over a third (37%) were in organizations that required matters to receive approval from a committee or coordinator. A small minority (11%) encouraged associates to work on cases selected by partners; others (11%) allowed attorneys to take any cases that did not pose conflicts of interests under bar ethical rules. Policies among award winners were more permissive. About four-fifths (83%) of

TABLE 6.13

Structure for Facilitating Pro Bono Work

	Overall (n = 589)	Individual Award (n = 19)	Firm Award (n = 6)
Pro bono coordinator	34.3	52.7	50.0
Committee	8.9	5.2	0
No facilitator	53.5	36.8	50.0
Other	3.3	5.2	0

TABLE 6.14

Effectiveness of Structure for Facilitator of Pro Bono Work

	Overall (n = 489)	Individual Award (n = 9)	Firm Award (n = 3)
Very effective	38.2	44.5	66.7
Somewhat effective	49.2	44.5	33.3
Not effective	9.5	11.0	0

TABLE 6.15

Desirability of a Facilitator for Organizations That Lack One

	Overall (n = 310)	Individual Award (n = 9)	Firm Award (n = 3)
Yes, desirable	42.5	11.0	66.7
No, not desirable	57.5	89.0	33.3

the individual winners and half of the firm winners (50%) reported that attorneys could take any cases that did not involve conflicts of interest; the remainder limited support to matters that had approval from committees or coordinators.

Close to half (43%) of respondents were dissatisfied with the types of pro bono work permitted. None was very satisfied, only 13% were somewhat satisfied, and 11% were neutral. Almost a third responded "other" and wrote comments identifying major concerns. One cluster of problems involved matters that lawyers classified as "not truly" pro bono, such as favors for clients and their relatives, or the personal legal matters of partners and their families. A related concern involved the use of pro bono resources to subsidize the "pet organizations" of certain partners, particularly when these matters were objectionable to other members of the firm. Some attorneys also reported ideological bias. One associate had found no opportunities for "conservative/libertarian" matters. By contrast, another complained that his firm took many "conservative causes but refused to allow associates to take liberal causes." An in-house attorney felt that his organization supported only projects that would benefit the corporate "image."

The problem with these practices is not simply that they discourage participation and skew the allocation of scarce charitable resources. It is also that such preferential treatment can undermine the legitimacy of pro bono programs. That risk is particularly great when the lawyers' self-interests are implicated. As one attorney observed, "Right now this firm's idea of pro bono is to handle a partner's personal matters for free. It's a joke."

Another limitation on pro bono opportunities was common in public sector workplaces. Internal codes of conduct, agency regulations, and conflict of interest legislation severely limit the volunteer legal activities that many judicial and governmental employees could pursue. One reported example involved a city charter that required special permission for representation of nonmunicipal clients. Another case in point was a public defender office policy banning representation in any outside legal matters. According to a United States Department of Justice employee, agency regulations prevented lawyers from litigating nongovernmental cases in their areas of expertise. An assistant U.S. attorney similarly believed that although his office formally encouraged community service, public interest legal matters were thought to pose too many conflicts of interest. A further problem for state employees was the risk of malpractice liability; sovereign immunity protected government lawyers only for their official work, and no insurance coverage was available for other matters.

However, not all public sector lawyers found such restrictions problematic. Some faced caseload pressures that already made additional work unfeasible. As it was, noted one public defender, there was "barely time to breathe at the end of the day, much less . . . do pro bono work." Other government lawyers believed that they were already contributing enough to society through their paid employment. As one put it, "I do feel that being a federal prosecutor is public service and involves some 'pro bono like' work —i.e., I accept a much lower salary." Another public defender similarly maintained that "all my work is pro bono."

Whatever the merits of that view, it bears emphasis that the number of attorneys holding public interest, public defender, prosecutorial, and legal aid positions represents a small proportion of the legal profession as a whole: well under 5%. For lawyers in most practice settings, the treatment of pro bono activities leaves much to be desired. Yet although many lawyers identify inadequacies in workplace policies, their criticisms have not been sufficiently pervasive or intense to force the necessary changes. When asked whether their organization's policies and practices on pro bono were factors in shaping their choice of employment, most lawyers indicated that those factors were not. Table 6.16 summarizes these responses.

Concerns about pro bono policies and practices rarely cause lawyers to vote with their feet. Only a third of attorneys considered such factors very important (13%) or somewhat important (20%) in making their choices of employment. Almost half (44%) indicated that pro bono policies and practices were not important, and almost a quarter (23%) had no information about them at the time of decision. Unsurprisingly, award recipients were far more likely to have cared about pro bono opportunities. Almost half of the individual winners (47%) and four-fifths (80%) of the firm winners considered such policies and practices to have been very or somewhat important in choosing an employer. Only about a third of the

TABLE 6.16

Effect of Pro Bono Policies and Practices on Choice of Employment

	Overall ($n = 628$)	Individual Award ($n = 19$)	Firm Award ($n = 5$)
Very important factor	12.8	31.6	40.0
Somewhat important factor	20.4	15.8	40.0
Not important factor	44.0	36.7	20.0
Had no information	22.8	15.7	0

individuals (37%) and a fifth of the firm winners (20%) indicated that these factors were not important.

STRATEGIES FOR CHANGE

The survey also gave lawyers an opportunity to indicate whether there was anything their organization could do to encourage more pro bono work. Of 237 responses to this open-ended question, about 15% thought that nothing much could be done. The most common reform proposal, cited by over a quarter (29%) of lawyers, involved modifying policies toward billable hours, either by reducing the amount of billable time required or by counting public service equally toward hourly requirements. About a fifth of responding lawyers suggested other changes in organizational policies (12%) or reward structures (7%). These changes included adopting formal policies, giving credit for public service in promotion and compensation decisions, and making it more prestigious. Smaller numbers of attorneys recommended requirements or stronger encouragement of pro bono work (5%); a more active role for pro bono committees or coordinators (5%); additional opportunities for corporate lawyers (4%); increased enthusiasm among partners (2%); and better use of local resources such as bar organizations or court-appointment programs (2%).

Award winners elaborated on these views. Some stressed the need for the organization's leaders to "set an example." Other lawyers emphasized the importance of crediting public service toward billable hour quotas and making it count in performance evaluations. Award winners also highlighted the necessity of identifying service opportunities that were a good match for participants' interests and expertise. Attorneys who felt "comfortable" and "connected" with their pro bono activities would be more likely to volunteer again and to provide a high quality of service. Adequate screening and supervision were equally critical to ensure that young lawyers who accepted legal aid assignments in order to develop skills and trial experience would not treat the matters like "batting practice" in which they "don't care where the ball goes" for the client.

Other proposed strategies included recognition for public service through awards and organizational newsletters. Enlisting support from corporate clients could also be helpful. As one attorney noted, if clients shopping for representation "made it clear that they expected their lawyers to be involved in pro bono, firms would respond." A minority of ABA award winners supported a bar or law firm requirement of pro bono service, but most did not. The greatest concern was that "clients in crisis" would be poorly served by reluctant lawyers; as one attorney put it, "it's not to the clients' benefit to have an attorney who is not truly interested in [their] welfare." Other lawyers cited the constitutional concerns and enforcement difficulties with pro bono requirements noted in Chapter 2.

MAJOR FINDINGS

Taken together, this study's findings help identify the major influences on pro bono work and the strategies most likely to affect it. The factors that lawyers believe are most critical in encouraging public service are the personal satisfaction that it brings and a sense of professional obligation to pursue it. Additional influences are employer support and encouragement; career benefits such as contacts, training, and trial experience; and previous service experiences, including those in law school. The factors that are statistically correlated with the amount of charitable work reported are political commitment and employer encouragement. These influences are, of course, interrelated. Whether attorneys find pro bono service satisfying may depend in part on their political commitments and the kinds of opportunities employers provide; whether attorneys view such service as a professional obligation may also depend on how it is treated in their workplace.

That treatment often leaves much to be desired. The major reasons that lawyers cited for not doing pro bono work were workload pressures, family obligations, and billable hour requirements. Other important factors were employer attitudes, as reflected in resources, bonus, and promotion practices, and a lack of rewarding public service opportunities. For some lawyers, the problem was that readily available options were outside their areas of expertise; other attorneys were unsatisfied with the kinds of cases and clients that they encountered. Among the reasons were employers who steered pro bono participants toward supervisors' own preferred causes or personal needs and discouraged work that might be inconsistent with client interests or values.

All too often, official workplace policies and informal practices played a major role in discouraging public service commitments. Only about a third of surveyed lawyers' workplaces had a formal pro bono policy, and only a quarter treated pro bono work as equivalent to billable hours. Only 10% of attorneys believed that their organizations valued pro bono contributions equally to paid work; almost half felt that such contributions were negatively viewed.

Given these norms, it is not surprising that many lawyers expressed dissatisfaction with their employers' treatment of public service. A third was dissatisfied with the amount of pro bono work; only a fifth was very satisfied. Only a third was very satisfied with the types of work available. Part of the problem may have been the lack of formal structure for public service. Over half of lawyers worked in organizations without a committee or coordinator to facilitate pro bono placements. Yet despite these limitations, attorneys rarely made satisfaction with pro bono opportunities a major factor in their employment decisions. Only a third cited pro bono policies and practices as even a "somewhat important" consideration.

Surveyed lawyers did, however, offer useful suggestions about improvements in workplace pro bono practices. The most common proposal was to alter policies regarding billable hours, either by reducing the amount of time required or by counting public service the same as paid work in meeting hourly targets. Other proposed changes included adopting formal policies and structures for facilitating pro bono work; weighing it positively in promotion and compensation decisions; making it more prestigious; and identifying additional opportunities that were a good match for attorneys' interests and expertise. Although a small number of survey participants, particularly award winners, proposed mandatory service, the vast majority did not. The consensus was to focus on strategies that would make voluntary participation a rewarding and rewarded experience.

The central question is, of course, how to make that reform agenda a more central priority. The evidence summarized in Chapters 1 and 2 suggests that many attorneys are underestimating the personal and professional rewards that well-designed programs can provide. If so, the question then becomes how best to educate attorneys about those benefits, and what role law schools can play in that effort.

Chapter Seven

An Empirical Analysis of
Law School Pro Bono Programs

Over the last 15 years, American law schools have substantially increased their focus on pro bono service. As Chapter 1 noted, about a fifth of accredited law schools now have pro bono or public service requirements for students, half have formal, administratively supported voluntary programs, and most others have student groups that sponsor charitable opportunities.[1] Although many students who participate in such public service activities indicate that the experience has increased their interest in future involvement, no research has attempted to measure whether such an effect occurs. Nor are data available about the long-term effect of service learning in other professional contexts.

To help fill this gap, the study described here asked pro bono award winners and graduates of law schools with different pro bono policies a range of questions concerning their educational experiences and public service involvement.[2] The schools included two with pro bono requirements (Pennsylvania and Tulane), two with well-supported voluntary programs (Fordham and Yale), and two without formal programs at the time of the survey (Chicago and Northwestern). Participants' responses yield useful information about the strengths and weaknesses of law schools' pro bono efforts, as well as the effect of those efforts on graduates' future service. Taken together, the findings identify strategies for improving public service programs in legal education, as well as assessing their likely influence on lawyers' pro bono contributions after graduation.

ATTITUDES TOWARD PUBLIC SERVICE

An initial series of questions focused on the extent to which law school may have affected motivations concerning public service. Attorneys were asked why they went to law school, whether their goals changed while they were there, and whether any such changes had affected their interest in pro bono or public interest work. Table 7.1 summarizes responses to the first question.

In identifying their main career motivations, over half of surveyed lawyers cited a desire for a financially rewarding and secure career (59%). The next most common responses were finding intellectual challenges (52%) and keeping options open (41%). Close to a third of the sample (31%) hoped to promote social justice, and just over a quarter (29%) wanted to prepare for public service. The aspirations of individual award winners were somewhat similar, including the desire for a well-paid and secure career (55%). However, a higher proportion was interested in promoting social justice (41%) and a lower proportion was concerned with intellectual challenge (32%).

Fewer than a third of the overall sample reported that their objectives

TABLE 7.1
Reasons for Attending Law School

	Overall (n = 844)	Individual Award (n = 22)
To prepare for public service	29.2	27.2
To keep my options open	41.1	40.9
To promote social justice	31.0	40.9
To establish a financially rewarding secure career	58.9	54.5
To find intellectual challenges	52.4	31.8

had changed during law school. Of those who did, many ($n = 172$) wrote comments indicating a shift in attitudes concerning pro bono or public interest work. Most disturbingly, only a fifth (22%) indicated that positive law school experiences had encouraged involvement in pro bono service. About a third (32%) reported that student loans (24%) or an understanding of differential salary levels (8%) had steered them away from public interest work. About a fifth (19%) reported that negative law school experiences had dampened their interest in pro bono service, or in a few cases, in legal practice generally.

Law School Culture and Public Service

Some lawyers took the opportunity to elaborate on positive or negative law school influences concerning pro bono service. Of the 46 who noted positive effects, a third mentioned law school culture; a fifth (22%) mentioned work or life experiences; and 15% cited personal beliefs and values. A smaller number identified opportunities to engage in pro bono or public service work in law school (4%) or financial support for such opportunities (7%). A supportive culture was conveyed through a graduation requirement or the attitudes of faculty and students. The service ethic appeared particularly strong at Yale. A disproportionate number of its graduates cited evidence of Yale's support, both "financially and philosophically," through curricular opportunities, public interest placements, and relatively generous loan forgiveness policies. As one attorney noted, "I started thinking more about public interest work because the law school valued it so highly and I loved my public interest job during the first summer (which my law school paid me to do)." Another Yale graduate credited classmates who "internally valued public service . . . [and] initiated and organized a variety of pro bono projects."

For the sample as a whole, the most positive comments typically focused on clinical experiences, which some graduates singled out as their "best" experience in law school. Others felt similarly about pro bono activities or did not indicate whether their public interest work was part of a pro bono or clinical program. Participants emphasized both the educational value of skills training and the personal rewards of assisting clients "desperately in need of legal representation." Graduates liked getting a "taste of what being a real lawyer was . . . like" and the chance for direct client contact, trial experience, negotiation, and drafting briefs. Learning about the "imperfections of the legal system" and the limitations of the "social safety net" was equally valuable. Some lawyers also singled out clinical professors or supervising attorneys as being especially "inspiring," "caring," or committed. Other lawyers cited positive relationships with clients or their own sense of "meaningfully contributing to society" and "making a difference in societal terms." One Tulane graduate gained an appreciation of "how much power lawyers have to help disenfranchised individuals and effect change." Another noted, "I helped some children have a better life—what could be more rewarding?"

Many attorneys, however, reported a far less positive experience, both with the law school culture in general and with their clinical or pro bono opportunities in particular. One of the most common complaints was that the majority of faculty did not promote or "appreciate" pro bono work. Nor did they reportedly emphasize lawyers' ethical responsibility to pursue it. According to one Yale graduate, although the school had a "terrific clinical program" and actively supported students seeking full-time public interest positions, "I don't remember any focus on pro bono work as I now conceptualize it, as part of a lawyer's professional obligation." Other graduates, including a few from Yale, felt that the "real," presumably tenured, faculty showed no serious "interest in or commitment to . . . public service." Still more lawyers criticized their school's inadequate support for clinics: the course opportunities were too limited; the time or credit allotted was insufficient; or the offerings were not "valued or promoted" by the tenured faculty.

A second cluster of criticisms involved the perceived elitism or ideological bias of faculty and students. Criticism came from graduates of all schools and from all points on the political spectrum. From the perspective of one Chicago alumnus, the school was filled with "upper-middle class white academics who relate to other upper-middle class white students." Some graduates felt that their schools' predominantly conservative attitudes "undermine[d] ethical values of students." Conversely, other lawyers complained that their schools' pro bono and public interest opportunities all had a "liberal agenda" that they did not share, and a few resented the "self-righteous[ness]" or "excessive preachiness" of program proponents.

Some graduates also felt that their institution's career service efforts were unduly biased toward private practice and that this orientation negatively influenced attitudes toward public service. Pennsylvania was characterized as "primarily a Wall Street feeder." Chicago reportedly "conveyed an impression of support for lucrative firm jobs and very little support for government and pro bono careers." Fordham's placement program was said to "heavily favor firm employment." Northwestern's career services office assertedly did "very little to promote public interest" employment. And Yale needed more of a "commitment to . . . helping students find public interest jobs." Although an orientation toward law firm positions is not necessarily inconsistent with support for pro bono work, graduates who voiced this criticism generally viewed the marginalization of public interest careers as part of a broader message about professional prestige that worked against public service in all forms.

However, many lawyers also acknowledged that these placement priorities were only part of a larger set of economic forces that undermined altruistic commitments. About two-thirds (65%) of survey participants agreed that market and financial constraints reduced their interest in pro bono and public interest work. Many individuals wrote comments elaborating on the impossibility of taking a public interest job while paying off student loans, supporting a family, or working in a city with a high cost of living. Some lawyers mentioned the effect of these economic factors on pro bono involvement as well. As one Tulane graduate noted, "I have paid back $78,000 in 8 years and still owe $33,000. Why should I do anything for free?"

A final set of negative influences on pro bono and public interest involvement arose from unrewarding clinical or pro bono experiences. The reasons were mixed. Some graduates cited inadequate supervision, support, or training. Others found their clients "unsavory" or undeserving for reasons similar to those arising in practice, described in Chapter 6. As one Tulane graduate put it, "some people create these problems for themselves." A

Yale graduate similarly noted that "I did not enjoy helping people who were basically trying to milk the system." Other lawyers, although more sympathetic toward their clients, cited the experience of working on seemingly unmeritorious claims as a deterrent to future pro bono work. A representative case involved a Chicago graduate who found it "frustrating and frightening" to obtain a community placement for a mental health patient who did not appear able to function safely outside an institution. Other lawyers found it depressing or "emotionally draining" to have such limited impact on systemic injustices or the overwhelming problems facing indigent clients. One Yale graduate who found domestic violence work "unrewarding" explained, "in most situations, a TRO [temporary restraining order] (or maybe any other legal remedy) is a drop in the bucket compared to the woman's needs."

PRO BONO POLICIES

The lawyers who cited these negative experiences did not, however, indicate whether they occurred in mandatory pro bono programs, voluntary activities, or clinical courses. In order to focus attention on public service, the survey asked attorneys to describe their school's policy and level of support for pro bono work. Tables 7.2 and 7.3 summarize these responses, combining data from schools with similar pro bono policies.

On the whole, graduates' descriptions were consistent with the three main approaches that the survey sought to assess: a pro bono requirement, a strong voluntary program, and the absence of a well-supported program. About four-fifths (83%) of the Tulane and Pennsylvania graduates recalled a requirement, and four-fifths (83%) of the Yale and Fordham graduates recalled strong encouragement for pro bono activities. Only half (55%) of the Northwestern and Chicago graduates remembered strong encouragement, and 40% remembered merely lip service or limited encouragement. It is, however, sobering that a substantial number of graduates either did not recall their school's pro bono requirement (17% of the Tulane and Pennsylvania graduates) or believed erroneously that they had been subject to one (8% of Yale and Fordham graduates; 2% of Northwestern and Chicago graduates).

It also bears note that regression analysis revealed no statistically signifi-

TABLE 7.2
Law School Policy Toward Pro Bono

	Overall ($n = 699$)	Individual Award ($n = 13$)	Yale/ Fordham ($n = 266$)	Tulane/ Pennsylvania ($n = 243$)	Northwestern/ Chicago ($n = 126$)
Required pro bono	36.5	0	8.3	82.7	2.4
Strongly encouraged pro bono	50.7	69.2	83.4	14.9	55.5
Paid lip service to pro bono service; gave limited encouragement	12.8	30.8	8.3	2.4	40.5
Did not encourage pro bono work	0	0	0	0	0
Discouraged pro bono work	0	0	0	0	1.6

cant correlation between law school policies and subsequent pro bono work. Although, as Chapter 2 indicated, between two-thirds and three-fourths of students in other surveys believe that participation in mandatory pro bono programs has increased the likelihood of their future service, this study fails to confirm that belief.[3] Such a result is not entirely surprising, given the research on volunteer activity summarized in Chapter 3, as well as the factors that lawyers themselves report as most important in influencing pro bono work. Personal values and the costs and rewards of pro bono involvement in particular workplaces are likely to dwarf the impact of law school policies. Although a positive student experience with public interest work can build interest in future involvement, such an experience need not come from pro bono activities; it could also occur in a clinic. Nor does a pro bono requirement ensure a positive experience.

Although the vast majority of graduates reported that their schools required (37%) or strongly encouraged (51%) pro bono work, the responses to specific questions suggest substantial room for improvement. For example,

TABLE 7.3

Law School Support for Pro Bono Programs

	Overall ($n = 707$)	Individual Award ($n = 10$)	Yale/ Fordham ($n = 238$)	Tulane/ Pennsylvania ($n = 241$)	Northwestern/ Chicago ($n = 154$)
Had a pro bono coordinator	60.3	42.9	60.4	83.0	19.1
Provided financial support for students' pro bono activities	17.3	28.6	18.4	7.1	32.2
Encouraged pro bono work through special programs	13.4	0	14.75	7.5	24.8
Included information on pro bono opportunities in orientation	1.0	0	0.5	0.43	3.3
Included coverage of pro bono in professional responsibility courses	1.3	0	1.7	0	2.0
Faculty members visibly committed to pro bono work	3.3	7.1	2.1	0.75	10.7
Adequate clinical opportunities for public interest work	3.3	21.4	2.2	1.28	6.8
Awards for outstanding pro bono work	0	0	0	0	0
Externship program with adequate public interest placements	0	0	0	0	0
Visible dean and administrative support for public interest work	0	0	0	0	0
Other	0	0	0	0	0

only about a third of the graduates from schools with voluntary programs and 7% of those with graduation requirements believed that their institution provided financial support for student pro bono activities. Only 1% of the sample as a whole reported that pro bono issues received coverage in orientation programs or professional responsibility courses. None of the graduates of schools with pro bono requirements recalled the subject arising in such courses. Nor did the vast majority of faculty convey substantial support for pro bono work. Only 3% of graduates observed a visible commitment or felt that their schools provided adequate clinical opportunities for public interest work. And none of the graduates responding to this question reported awards for outstanding pro bono contributions, externship programs with adequate public interest placements, or visible support by deans and administrators for public interest work. Given these responses, it is not clear what caused so many graduates to believe that their school strongly encouraged public service activities.

Nor is it clear whether a pro bono requirement is the most effective way for a school to promote public service. Much may depend on the nature of the program and the institutional culture. Tulane graduates voiced almost no objection to mandatory service, and many cited valuable experiences. By contrast, most Pennsylvania graduates who volunteered comments were highly critical, perhaps in part because the requirement was substantially greater (70 versus 20 hours). Typical observations included:

- A horrible experience, really embittered me about law firms and pro bono.
- It's a politically correct form of indentured servitude.
- The forced pro bono placement was an awful experience. Everyone seemed to hate feeling forced into it.
- Compulsory involuntary servitude . . . cheapened the experience and bred resentment.
- [T]he majority [of my classmates] found the requirement burdensome and a nuisance.

A smaller number of graduates voiced objections not to the requirement but to the way that it was implemented. According to some critics, a "broader spectrum of assignments" rather than the administration's "pet political causes" would help. Another graduate felt that grades were necessary: "Otherwise students will just blow it off."

How widely these perspectives were shared is impossible to assess. Such attitudes did not translate into lower rates of pro bono involvement after graduation. The average for Pennsylvania graduates was substantially higher (114 hours) than that of the sample as a whole (70 hours). Nor did the vast majority of Pennsylvania students seem to dislike their placements. As Chapter 2 noted, most exceed their minimum required hours, and the coordinator of the program, like her counterparts at other schools that mandate service, has not found student resistance to be a major problem. But neither is it clear how much systematic information they have for that perception, how much unvoiced resentment is present, or how reluctant students ultimately respond to their experience. Although this study cannot answer those questions, it does suggest strategies that could improve law school pro bono programs.

STRATEGIES FOR CHANGE

Many survey participants, both award winners and graduates of the sampled schools, volunteered comments about the role of legal education in encouraging public service. Of the 247 lawyers who responded to an open-ended question, two-thirds were largely satisfied with their law school's program. The most commonly proposed change, suggested by a quarter of responding lawyers, was greater financial support for pro bono and public interest work, including additional resources for volunteer opportunities, subsidized summer jobs, and loan forgiveness programs. About 10% of survey participants advocated other forms of support, such as more recognition for pro bono work, particularly by faculty, and greater assistance for students who were not planning full-time public interest careers. Smaller numbers of lawyers proposed further reforms including adoption of a pro bono requirement; less ideological bias in placements; increased service opportunities; and more support from career services offices. A very small minority (2%) suggested less emphasis on pro bono work, typically through elimination of required service or reduced pressure to volunteer. For example, one Fordham gradu-ate complained that "the guilt foisted upon students to do pro bono work is obnoxious—pro bono is a personal choice, not a professional obligation." By contrast, one Tulane graduate felt that the school's 20-hour requirement did not do enough to convey that sense of obligation; a local Jesuit high school mandate of 100 hours was "much more influential."

Some ABA award winners also volunteered reform strategies. About two-thirds advocated pro bono requirements for law students, a much higher per-centage than those supporting requirements for practicing attorneys. The general consensus was that students who are "still forming their view" of the lawyer's role would benefit from seeing how law affects those who cannot af-ford it and from having public service presented as a professional responsi-bility. Because students were "still being supervised," the risks of poor-quality service from reluctant participants would be lower than with practicing at-torneys. A minority of award winners believed that offering academic credit for public interest work would be preferable to requiring it. Additional pro-posals included showcasing volunteer activities by alumni; having deans and respected faculty talk about the value of public service; and educating stu-dents about the importance of considering prospective employers' records (not just rhetoric) in supporting pro bono participation.

Major Findings

The findings of this study underscore several key points about the influence of law school pro bono programs. First, the importance of such programs in promoting public service should neither be undervalued nor overstated. A positive experience with public interest work may increase participants' de-sire for future opportunities, their understanding of pro bono service as a professional obligation, and their attention to that issue when they are evaluating employment options. But any such positive influences may be trumped by a workplace reward structure that makes the cost of public ser-vice prohibitive. Still, as Chapter 2 noted, and this study confirmed, pro bono programs in law schools serve an educational value apart from their ef-fect on future charitable activities. For many surveyed lawyers, public interest work was a high point of their law school experience, both in terms of the skills that it imparted and the social justice commitments that it furthered.

However, this study also makes clear that pro bono service has not been fully integrated in American legal education. Many practitioners entered law school with interests in social justice and public interest work and encountered too little support for such concerns. Although a majority of surveyed graduates believed that their school supported pro bono service, responses to specific questions identified major institutional failures. Only about a third of responding lawyers believed that financial resources for pro bono activities were adequate; only 3% reported support from faculty, and only 1% recalled public service issues arising in orientation programs and professional responsibility courses.

Proposals for reforms follow clearly from these responses. Most of the survey participants' recommendations involved additional resources and recognition. Only a small minority of responding lawyers proposed adding or eliminating pro bono requirements. By contrast, about two-thirds of pro bono award winners supported mandatory public service for students, both because of its educational value and its symbolic message that public service is a professional responsibility. On the whole, the findings of this study do not support a preference for either mandatory or voluntary programs. Rather, this research makes clear that whatever approach is chosen, it should attempt to provide positive public interest experiences and ensure that they are available to the maximum number of students. Moreover, the value of pro bono service needs to be reflected and reinforced throughout the law school experience in both curricular coverage and resource priorities.

Chapter Eight

AN AGENDA FOR REFORM

Pro bono service expresses all that is best in the legal profession. Compared with other nations and other professions, the American bar has a distinguished record. Yet compared with the unmet need for legal assistance and attorneys' own ethical codes, considerable progress remains to be made. Most lawyers do not come close to meeting the American Bar Association's (ABA) modest standard of 50 hours a year of pro bono service. Most law students graduate without a pro bono legal experience. And much of the bar's charitable work goes not to the disadvantaged groups and causes most in need of assistance, but rather to friends, relatives, and potential or deadbeat clients.

This record reflects too many missed opportunities for both the profession and the public. A wide array of evidence documents the benefits of charitable work, not only for its direct recipients, but also for those who provide it, and for society generally. For individual practitioners and students, pro bono involvement serves both personal and professional interests. It assists career development by enhancing skills, reputation, and community contacts. And it enables practitioners to express deep-seated values and experience the psychological rewards associated with altruistic activity. For legal employers, pro bono programs can produce tangible benefits in

166

terms of retention, recruitment, and job performance. For the legal profession, public service is a way to enhance status and reputation and to reduce demand for mandatory alternatives. And for society generally, charitable assistance helps to protect individual rights; to meet basic health, education, and welfare needs; and to preserve the legitimacy of the justice system.

Given this range of benefits, there is much to be gained from an increased commitment to pro bono activities. And we do not lack for promising strategies. The preceding chapters offer a comprehensive account of what is likely to work, drawing on interdisciplinary research concerning altruistic behavior, the experience of other professions and other nations, and empirical data on pro bono programs in American law schools and legal workplaces. This account makes clear that institutionalizing ideals of public service requires strategies along two main lines. One set of initiatives involves increasing the pressures and incentives for lawyers, legal employers, and legal educators to translate pro bono principles into practice. In essence, that would entail reporting, requiring, and rewarding service. A second group of strategies involves making pro bono opportunities more accessible and effective. Both approaches will require greater collaboration among the judiciary, the organized bar, the law schools, and the public interest community. The challenge for all these groups is to foster a greater sense of urgency concerning access to justice, and a greater sense of professional obligation and capacity to respond.

REPORTING, REQUIRING, AND REWARDING SERVICE

A first step in expanding pro bono participation is to increase its visibility. Better information is needed about the extent (or lack) of public service by lawyers, legal employers, law faculty, and law students. One obvious option is to require lawyers and legal employers to report contributions of time or money to designated pro bono activities. Although the definition of qualifying activities is likely to provoke controversy, a reporting obligation would be less divisive than mandatory service. Given the urgent needs for assistance among low-income individuals, a strong case can be made for disclosure of assistance at least to those groups. Such a reporting obligation seems well worth the minimal costs of administration. As one legal ethics expert notes,

> If sufficiently reliable information about lawyers' pro bono work becomes publicly available, . . . commitment to pro bono work could increase as lawyers are pressured to meet pro bono needs. Municipal governments, foundations, nonprofit organizations and even corporations could withhold legal work from firms whose lawyers failed to perform a certain minimum number of hours of pro bono work. Failure to do adequate pro bono work might be a detriment to [employers' recruitment efforts or to individuals] seeking public office.[1]

Experience bears this out. Since the establishment of a reporting system in Florida, volunteer hours and financial contributions have grown substantially.[2] Disclosures and rankings of law firm pro bono activities in leading legal publications have had similarly positive effects, as have parallel initiatives by clients who require information on firms' recruitment and retention of minority lawyers. Many of the nation's largest corporations have begun to consider diversity records when channeling legal work.[3] But few American corporations, only 3% in one recent survey, have required information about the pro bono contributions of firms that are being evaluated as potential outside counsel.[4] Experience in other nations suggests that public service contributions would increase if more clients considered those contributions in channeling their work.[5]

Public or private sector organizations that purchase substantial amounts of legal services could also make pro bono assistance a condition of retainer agreements. For example, California has just passed legislation requiring such a condition in state contracts for legal services that exceed $50,000. Such contracts obligate the contracting law firm "to make a good faith effort to provide, during the duration of the contract, a minimum number of hours of pro bono legal services. . . . Failure to make a good effort may be cause for non-renewal of a state contract for legal services and may be taken into account when determining the award of future contracts."[6] Some California municipalities impose similar requirements.[7] Local governments in other nations not only consider pro bono participation, but also require a percentage of the profits on their legal work to be used for charitable legal activities.[8]

Further incentives for public service could come from law schools, bar associations, and other legal organizations. Law schools could, for example, require employers who use their placement facilities to disclose their pro bono policies and the average charitable hours and financial contributions of their members. Groups such as the Association of American Law Schools (AALS) Section on Pro Bono and Public Service Opportunities, the National Association for Law Placement, the ABA Standing Committee on Pro Bono and Public Service, and Equal Justice Works could do more to publicize employers' pro bono policies and performance. Legal periodicals could also provide more comprehensive information about public service records.[9] Readily accessible comparative information could assist law students in making pro bono opportunities part of their decision in selecting among employment options.

Such organizations could also develop best practices for pro bono service and publicize lists of employers who certify that they are in compliance. Appropriate practices, based on this study's research, could include:

- Adoption of a formal pro bono policy.
- Visible commitment by the organization's leadership.
- Credit for pro bono work toward billable hour requirements.
- Consideration of pro bono service as a favorable factor in promotion and compensation decisions.
- Recognition and showcasing of service.
- Establishment of a pro bono committee or coordinator that matches participants with appropriate placements and ensures adequate training, supervision, and performance.
- Compliance with the Law Firm Pro Bono Challenge of 3% or 5% of billable hours or the ABA Model Rules' standards of 50 hours per lawyer per year or the financial equivalent.

Analogous reporting requirements and best practice standards could also be developed for law schools. ABA accreditation standards already require schools to provide appropriate pro bono service opportunities for students and to encourage service by faculty. However, no information is available on what would constitute noncompliance, or on whether any schools have fallen short. Given that many schools neither keep nor disclose records on participation rates, enforcement does not appear to be particularly rigorous. Such records, as well as compliance with minimum standards, could be required as part of the accreditation process or as a condition for AALS membership. Schools that complied with best practice standards could also be acknowledged in publications of the AALS, ABA, and other lawyers' organizations, as well as in rankings like those by *U.S. News and World Report*. Although these ranking systems are deeply flawed, as long as they remain influential, they should acknowledge the importance of pro bono and public interest programs. The survey findings reported here, together with the AALS Pro Bono Project, suggest the following best practice standards:

- A formal policy concerning pro bono work by students and faculty.
- A program that makes available at least one significant well-supervised pro bono opportunity for every student and that involves the vast majority of students.
- Pro bono contributions by faculty at levels comparable to those expected of students.
- Visible support from faculty and administrators.
- Structures for ensuring appropriate supervision and quality control.
- Adequate funding for program expenses, summer opportunities, and courses with public service placements.
- Involvement of students in developing service options and in recruiting fellow classmates.
- Recognition of service through pro bono awards, notations on transcripts, and showcasing of student, faculty, and alumni projects in publications and special events.
- Curricular integration of materials concerning pro bono service in professional responsibility courses, orientation programs, and core courses.
- Consideration of pro bono contributions in faculty hiring and promotion decisions.

The message that public service is a professional responsibility needs to be reinforced not only in pro bono programs but also throughout the law school culture. Core courses can include discussion of unmet legal needs and prominent pro bono cases and projects; academic credit can be available for students who design service opportunities for their postgraduate workplace; placement offices can showcase firms that comply with best practice standards; and deans can highlight pro bono work in their communications with students, faculty, and alumni.[10]

So too, lawyers, judges, legal educators, and service providers need to work together to develop more effectively coordinated plans to expand pro bono participation. In some jurisdictions, impressive progress has occurred through law firm pledge drives led by prominent judges and parallel law school pledge drives organized by students.[11] In other jurisdictions, regional groups representing the bench, bar, and legal academy have collaborated in identifying unmet needs and developing a strategy to address them. One example is the Minnesota Justice Foundation, which oversees placements for law students from several Minneapolis schools.[12] A related approach is the Equal Justice Works Pro Bono Legal Corps, which uses AmeriCorps members to coordinate law student pro bono work with community groups in low-income areas.[13] Initiatives along these lines are needed in all jurisdictions.

More networks are also necessary to respond to emergencies and to sustain commitment after the crisis is over. One approach is the consortium of New York law firms that provided assistance related to the 9/11 terrorist attacks.[14] Another is Trial Lawyers Care, which recruited over a thousand lawyers to represent victims filing claims with the September 11 Victim Compensation Fund.[15] Although such initiatives have been extraordinarily effective in recruiting volunteers and providing temporary services, additional strategies are needed to inspire long-term public service commitments.[16]

Whether courts, bar associations, or law schools should take the further step of requiring pro bono contributions is a closer question. As the discussion in Chapter 2 suggested, mandating some modest contribution of services or financial support from practicing lawyers seems justifiable in principle. Without further experience and evaluation, it is impossible to know how effective such requirements would prove in practice. The small number of jurisdictions here and abroad with mandatory systems have not collected systematic information about costs, quality, and compliance. What evidence is available suggests that much depends on context: how much work is required, how competent lawyers are to provide it, how much backup assistance and supervision are available, how the requirement is enforced, and whether financial contributions are an alternative to service. On the whole, this study suggests that a modest obligation of time or money would be worth trying. At the very least, such a requirement could provide a catalyst for other workplace reforms and bar initiatives recommended here.

The major challenge in designing an effective mandatory system is political. As one veteran of the struggle notes, whenever bar discussions turn to pro bono requirements, "two things happen; the definition expands and the number of hours decline."[17] Unless and until we can build a broader base of support for obligations that substantially benefit the most underserved groups, the prudent alternative would be to focus on strengthening voluntary initiatives and on requiring lawyers to report their contributions.

Similar points could be made concerning law schools. Findings from this study provide a strong justification for exposing students to Americans' unmet legal needs, the profession's responsibility to address them, and the rewards of doing so. But survey results do not demonstrate that pro bono requirements are necessarily more effective in accomplishing those objectives than well-designed voluntary programs, coupled with strong institutional support and ample clinical opportunities. The chief value of a requirement is that it sends a message about the profession's service obligations, engages some students who would not otherwise participate, and forces schools to invest resources in developing effective programs. Yet the success of such programs can be compromised if the number of hours is too limited or too demanding, if the range and quality of placement options are inadequate, if preparation and supervision are insufficient, or if the importance of public service is not reinforced throughout the educational experience. The ultimate objective should be to institutionalize the best practices described above, however that can be achieved in a particular law school context.

STRENGTHENING PRO BONO PROGRAMS

Related strategies should focus on making public service opportunities more available, attractive, and effective. One approach is to target particular groups of attorneys whose services have been underutilized. Obvious examples include transactional lawyers, in-house counsel, government lawyers, legal academics, retired lawyers, and lawyers in American firms abroad.[18] Restrictions on pro bono work by public servants should be eased and more opportunities should be developed to avoid potential conflicts of interest.[19] New initiatives should target the rapidly growing sector of senior lawyers who are no longer in full-time practice.[20] More interfaith coalitions could enlist attorneys interested in partnering with religious organizations to assist low-income communities.[21] Further programs should be geared to law faculty willing to volunteer as experts, consultants, or co-counsel in their fields of expertise. More sabbatical and part-time pro bono programs could be offered by law firms seeking to recruit and retain talented, socially committed lawyers.[22] More employers could adopt the leave programs established by some law firms to cope with short-term economic downturns. Rather than permanently laying off associates and incurring the substantial recruitment and retraining expenses of hiring replacements when the demand for work increases, these firms lend underutilized attorneys to pro bono programs.[23]

Bar associations could also experiment with a "Public Service Alternative Bar Exam."[24] This pilot program, endorsed by the New York State Bar Association and the Association of the Bar of the City of New York, would give applicants to the bar the option of substituting pro bono service for the multistate exam. These applicants would work for 12 weeks under supervision in the state court system, and then provide an additional 150 hours of service in the three years after admission to the bar. Such a system would give applicants the opportunity to demonstrate more legal skills than the rote memorization tested by the multistate exam and would substantially expand the volunteer assistance available for unmet needs.[25]

Other strategies for strengthening pro bono programs involve improving support structures. More Web site matching services could alert potential volunteers to specific project needs and offer comprehensive educational materials.[26] More bar associations could offer backup assistance for inexperienced volunteers, free malpractice insurance for lawyers who otherwise would lack coverage, and continuing legal education credit for pro bono training. Greater attention could focus on increasing attorneys' sensitivity in dealing with clients from different class, racial, and ethnic backgrounds.[27] More courts could make special accommodations for pro bono cases, such as giving these cases priority on their dockets and permitting telephone conference calls in lieu of time-consuming personal appearances.[28]

Providers of voluntary services could also be more strategic in channeling their assistance. Further initiatives should target needs that often fall through the cracks of existing legal services networks. Groups such as impoverished rural residents, and cases like welfare claims and death penalty appeals, pose special challenges and require further initiatives.[29] Greater priority also should be given to needy individuals who agree to help themselves or their communities in exchange for legal assistance. For example, in Atlanta, indigent criminal defendants who want representation from the Georgia Justice Project must enroll in programs ranging from drug counseling to job training.[30] Since its inception, the Georgia project has assisted some 1500 defendants who have a recidivism rate of only 18%, compared with 45% in the surrounding area.[31] In a District of Columbia program, individuals seeking civil legal aid must agree to provide some community service themselves, such as helping with neighborhood cleanup or assisting disabled elderly citizens.[32]

More effort should focus on monitoring the quality of pro bono service and the effectiveness of various approaches to providing it. As Chapter 2 noted, rarely do programs seek systematic feedback from clients, and volunteers have little incentive to expose performance-related concerns. Given the vast demand for assistance, lawyers need not worry about ensuring favorable recommendations. Nor may they see much reason to divert scarce resources to program evaluations that could cast volunteers in a less than heroic light.[33] Yet in the long run, ensuring the most cost-effective use of limited charitable resources requires better information about their quality and impact. The ABA Standards for Programs Providing Civil Pro Bono Legal Services recognize as much and set forth guidelines for evaluation that should be the rule rather than the exception.[34]

So too, more comparative research is necessary to assess the merits of different pro bono delivery systems. We know far too little about what works best in our own profession and how it compares to initiatives in other nations and other professions. In the few jurisdictions here and abroad that compel service, how frequent is noncompliance, and what is the experience of clients? In professional settings that have exceptionally high rates of voluntary participation, what institutional structures sustain such commitment? Knowing more about the strategies that are most effective among other service providers could promote innovative bar approaches and better multidisciplinary collaboration.

All of these initiatives will, of course, require additional sources of funding. Lawyers' assistance is free, but the structures that make it successful are not. Pro bono programs require resources from nonprofit organizations to identify matters appropriate for volunteer services, to provide training and backup assistance, and to ensure some measure of quality control.[35] Research and evaluation require additional subsidies. If the bar remains unwilling to require pro bono financial contributions as an alternative to personal assistance, other funding possibilities merit consideration. For example, courts could increase filing fees for cases involving a substantial amount in controversy. Law firms could establish pro bono funds with expected financial contribution levels from lawyers who do not devote time to public interest legal work.[36] Legislatures could tax legal revenues above a certain minimum.[37] Whatever the strategy, the objective should be to ensure a closer match between the profession's resources and rhetoric concerning public service.

PRO BONO IN PERSPECTIVE:
BROADENING THE AGENDA

"Philanthropy is commendable," Martin Luther King Jr. once noted, "but it must not cause the philanthropist to overlook the circumstances of economic injustice which make philanthropy necessary."[38] Whatever the bar's success in strengthening pro bono programs, it must not lose sight of the broader inequalities to which those programs respond. Even if the vast majority of lawyers and law students made substantial charitable contributions, they would come nowhere close to meeting the legal needs of poor and middle-income Americans, let alone addressing the public interest concerns that are beyond the capacities of nonprofit organizations. Nor can a pro bono system relying on volunteers ensure the kind of deep knowledge and willingness to offend potential paying clients that would be necessary to guarantee truly equal representation. Lawyers' pro bono activities should serve as a catalyst, not a substitute, for adequate government funding and for broader changes in the delivery of legal services. Indeed, as noted earlier, one of the strongest justifications for such activities is that giving more attorneys exposure to the needs of the have-nots may lay foundations for reform.

Model projects and innovative project proposals are not in short supply. Examples include self-help resources such as online educational materials, pro se centers with interactive computer programs offering information and document preparation, and free assistance from court staff or volunteer lawyers.[39] Yet too few jurisdictions have adopted such reforms. The majority of surveyed courts have no formal pro se assistance services.[40] Many of the services that are available are not accessible by those who need help most: uneducated litigants with limited computer competence and poor English-language skills.[41] Nor has sufficient effort focused on establishing collaborative programs in which lawyers partner with health care and social service providers to meet the multiple needs of low-income communities.[42] Rather, bar leaders have rejected changes in ethical rules that would permit such multidisciplinary partnerships with nonlawyer professionals.[43]

Not only has the organized bar failed to press for necessary reforms, it often has actively blocked doctrinal change that would promote them. For example, the profession has supported sweeping prohibitions on unauthorized practice of law that have prevented nonlawyer specialists from offering services in areas where legal needs are greatest.[44] Yet research on the performance of such specialists here and abroad suggests that they are often at least as qualified as lawyers to provide routine assistance.[45] Concerns about incompetent and unethical providers could be met by regulation, not prohibition.[46] The organized bar, however, has resisted such regulatory proposals and has recently reaffirmed its support for strengthening unauthorized practice prohibitions.[47] The professional associations that celebrate lawyers' "selfless" pro bono contributions oppose reforms that would serve the same objectives on an even broader scale.

The organized bar has been equally unwilling to reconsider its norms of zealous advocacy in a world in which such representation is generally available only to those willing and able to pay. As law professor Scott Cummings has noted, "the time [lawyers] spend engaged in pro bono work provides a respite from this world but does not change it."[48] Ironically, the lucrative fees that come from exploiting inequalities in the legal system are part of what helps to finance pro bono correctives. The point was caricatured in a recent *New Yorker* cartoon. It pictured a well-appointed lawyer cheerily walking down courtroom steps, reminding a companion: "Remember, we can only afford to do all this pro bono because of how much antibono pays."[49]

A true commitment to the public good implies much more than the bar's traditional public service proposals. It demands not simply that lawyers increase the modest contributions of funds or time that are at issue in most pro bono debates. The profession must also direct more of its contributions to reforms in legal ethics and the delivery of legal services. This is not a modest agenda. But no issue could be more important for the profession. The extraordinary mobilization of talent and commitment that followed the 9/11 crisis reminds us of what the bar can accomplish when its highest ideals are engaged. One of the attorneys involved in that campaign, when asked why he volunteered, responded simply, "how could [I] not?"[50] More lawyers need to ask themselves that question, and more must be inspired to give the same answer.

REFERENCE MATTER

Appendices

Appendix One

PRO BONO SURVEY
Response Time: 12-15 Minutes

Individual Lawyer

For purposes of this survey, pro bono work includes services that meet the definition of the Law Firm Pro Bono Challenge: services undertaken normally without expectation of fees and consisting of the delivery of legal services to persons of limited means or to charitable, religious, civic, community, governmental, and educational organizations.

1. Current Employment

1.1 Describe your area of practice.

Solo Practice	1
Not practicing law	2
Government	3
Corporation	4
Law Firm	5
Other *(Explain)*_____	6

1.2 Approximately how many attorneys are there in your firm? _____

1.3 What is your current position?

Associate	1
Staff attorney	2
Partner (equity)	3
Partner (non-equity)	4
Self employed	5
Of Counsel	6
Other *(Explain)*_____	7

2. Pro Bono Work

2.1 Please estimate the number of hours that you spent in the past calendar year (January 2000 – December 2000) on pro bono work? _____

2.1a. If that number is not typical, please indicate the number that would be representative of the past three years. _____

2.2 Of the pro bono hours listed above, how many were spent helping individuals of limited means or non-profit organizations that focus on assisting such individuals? _____

2.2a. If that number is not typical, please indicate the number that would be representative of the past three years. _____

2.3 How satisfied are you with the amount of time you spend on pro bono work?

Very satisfied	1
Somewhat satisfied	2
Neutral	3
Somewhat dissatisfied	4
Very dissatisfied	5

2.4 Does your organization have a policy on pro bono work? Please enclose or describe it.

Formal policy	1
Informal policy	2
No policy	3
Description_____	
_____	
_____	4

2.5 If you work for an organization with a billable hour requirement, does time spent on pro bono count toward your requirement?

Yes, all hours	1
Yes, certain number of hours (please indicate how many)_____	2
Yes, certain kinds of work	3
Other *(Explain)*_____	
_____	4

2.6 Is pro bono work valued equally to billable hours in promotion and bonus decisions or does it count positively in those decisions?

Equally valued	1
Somewhat valued	2
Not viewed as important	3
Negatively viewed	4
Other *(Explain)*_____	5

2.7 If your organization's *formal* policy supports pro bono work, is this policy consistent with its informal norms and reward structures?

Yes *(If yes, skip to Q. 2.9)*	1
No	2
Explain_____	

2.8 If not, do the *informal* practices significantly reduce lawyers' willingness to accept pro bono work?

Yes	1
No	2

2.9 How much support does your organization provide for pro bono work in terms of staff, litigation costs, and other expenses?

Provides full support	1
Provides partial support *(Explain)*_____	2
Provides inadequate support *(Explain)*_____	3
Other *(Explain)*_____	4

1

2.10   Have recent increases in salaries and/or billable hours affected your organization's pro bono work?

Has caused change in formal policy
*(Explain)*_____
_____ 1
Has caused change in the way pro bono involvement
affects promotion and compensation decisions
*(Explain)*_____
_____ 2
Has caused lawyers to decline time-consuming
pro bono work 3
Has not had significant impact 4
Impact is not yet clear 5
Other *(Explain)*_____ 6

2.11   Please indicate whether the following factors have had a significant influence in encouraging you to do pro bono work. Rate each factor on a scale of 1 to 5 with 5 being very significant and 1 being not significant.

	Not Significant				Very Significant
Sense of professional obligation	1	2	3	4	5
Personal satisfaction	1	2	3	4	5
Employer encouragement .	1	2	3	4	5
Employer policies (requiring/encouraging pro bono, counting pro bono as billable hours, etc) . . .	1	2	3	4	5
Value of pro bono training/contacts/referrals .	1	2	3	4	5
Recognition/reputation . . .	1	2	3	4	5
Religious commitment . . .	1	2	3	4	5
Political commitment	1	2	3	4	5
Opportunity for trial experience	1	2	3	4	5
Opportunity to work directly with client	1	2	3	4	5
Opportunity to exercise control over the work	1	2	3	4	5
Awards by employer or bar association	1	2	3	4	5

Explain_____

2.12   Have other factors been significant influences in encouraging your pro bono work? *(Please explain)*

_____
_____
_____

2.13   Please indicate whether the following factors have limited your pro bono work. Rate each factor on a scale of 1 to 5 with 5 being very significant and 1 being not significant.

	Not Significant				Very Significant
Work load demands	1	2	3	4	5
Family obligations	1	2	3	4	5
Employer attitude	1	2	3	4	5
Employer billable(non pro bono) hour expectations	1	2	3	4	5
Employer bonus policy excluding pro bono work .	1	2	3	4	5
Lack of interest	1	2	3	4	5
Lack of expertise	1	2	3	4	5
Lack of information about opportunities	1	2	3	4	5
Lack of malpractice insurance	1	2	3	4	5
Lack of resources (e.g., support staff)	1	2	3	4	5
Inconvenient or unpleasant aspects of work	1	2	3	4	5
Lack of opportunities in your practice area	1	2	3	4	5

2.14   Have other factors been significant in discouraging your pro bono involvement? *(Please explain.)*

_____
_____

2.15   Were your organization's pro bono policies and practices factors in shaping your choice of employment?

Very important factors 1
Somewhat important factors 2
Not important factors 3
Had no information 4

2.16   How do you generally obtain pro bono work? *(Circle all that are applicable)*

Employer pro bono committee or coordinator   1
Supervising attorney 2
Bar association program 3
Family 4
Friends 5
Client 6
Community group 7
Legal services provider 8
Public interest organization 9
Other *(Explain)*_____ 10

2.17   How satisfied are you with this method of obtaining work?

Very satisfied 1
Somewhat satisfied 2
Neutral 3
Somewhat dissatisfied 4
Very dissatisfied 5
Explain_____

2

2.18 Does your organization have a committee or coordinator to facilitate pro bono work?

Pro bono coordinator 1
Committee 2
Other 3
No facilitator *(If no, skip to Q. 2.20)* 4

2.19 If your organization has a facilitator, how effective is that structure?

Very effective 1
Somewhat effective 2
Not effective 3
Explain_____

2.20 If your organization has no facilitator, should it have one?

Yes 1
No 2

2.21 How does your organization handle matters that might prove objectionable to other lawyers in the organization or to clients? *(Circle all that are applicable.)*

Organization allows attorneys to take cases,
   subject to conflicts of interest as defined
   by formal ethical rules 1
Organization allows attorneys to take cases,
   subject to potential conflicts of interest . . . 2
Organization limits support to cases approved
   by committee or coordinator 3
Organization encourages associates to
   work on cases selected by partners 4
Organization discourages work on cases likely
   to advance positions inconsistent with interests
   or values of current clients 5
Organization discourages work likely to prove
   objectionable to other lawyers or to hurt its
   reputation in the community 6
Other *(Explain)*_____ 7

2.22 How satisfied are you with your organization's policies concerning the types of pro bono work permitted?

Very satisfied 1
Somewhat satisfied 2
Neutral 3
Somewhat dissatisfied 4
Very dissatisfied 5
Other *(Explain)*_____ 6

2.23 Is there anything your organization could do to encourage more pro bono work?

_____

_____

_____

2.24 Please describe your recent pro bono work (What kinds of assistance have you provided in what kinds of matters? What have you found most and least satisfying?)

_____

_____

_____

2.25 In the past year, have you made any financial contributions to any nonprofit organizations providing legal assistance for persons of limited means?

Yes 1
No *(If no, skip to Q. 2.27)* 2

2.26 If you made a contribution, please indicate the amount and recipient

Contribution to a bar-affiliated program
   *(Please identify)*_____ 1
   Amount of contribution_____
Contribution to another organization
   *(Please identify)*_____ 2
   Amount of contribution_____

2.27 How important have the following factors been in influencing your interest in pro bono work? Please rate each factor on a scale of 1 to 5 with 5 being very significant and 1 being not important.

	Not Significant				Very Significant
Parental influences	1	2	3	4	5
Religious commitment	1	2	3	4	5
Childhood/early youth experiences in volunteer activities	1	2	3	4	5
Experiences in college	1	2	3	4	5
Experiences in law school . .	1	2	3	4	5
Employer policies and reward structure	1	2	3	4	5
Example of mentors or role model	1	2	3	4	5
Other *(Please explain)* _____	1	2	3	4	5

3. Law School

3.1 From what school did you receive your law degree?
_____

3.2 Year of Graduation_____

3.3 What was your main reason for going to law school? (Please rank all relevant factors. Indicate your primary reason with a "1", the next prominent reason with a "2", etc.)

To prepare for public service . . . . . _____
To establish a financially rewarding
   and secure career . . . . _____
To keep my options open . . . . . . _____
To find work with intellectually
   challenging people . . . . _____
To promote social justice . . . . . . _____
Other *(Explain)*_____ _____

3.4   To what extent have you achieved your objectives?

Substantially achieved 1
Somewhat achieved 2
Not achieved 3

3.5   What, if any, factors have prevented achievement of your objectives?

_____

_____

3.6a   Did your objectives change during law school?

Yes 1
No 2

3.6b   What factors caused them to change?

_____

_____

3.7   What was your law schools' policy toward pro bono?

Required pro bono
  If so, how many hours?_____ 1
Strongly encouraged pro bono.
  If so, how?_____ 2
Paid lip service to the value of pro bono service
  and made limited efforts to encourage it
  If so, how?_____ 3
Did not encourage pro bono work
  If so, how?_____ 4
Discouraged pro bono work
  If so, how?_____ 5

3.8   Did your law school support pro bono in any of the following ways? *(Circle those applicable.)*

Had a pro bono coordinator 1
Provided financial support for students'
  pro bono activities 2
Encouraged pro bono work through special
  programs 3
Included information on pro bono opportunities
  in orientation programs 4
Included coverage of pro bono in professional
  responsibility courses 5
Had faculty members who were visibly
  committed to pro bono work 6
Had adequate clinical opportunities for public
  interest/legal services work 7
Gave awards for outstanding pro bono work . 8
Had externship program with adequate public
  interest placements 9
Had adequate summer fellowship program for
  public interest work 10
Had visible dean and administrative support for
  public interest work 11
Other *(Please explain)*_____ 12

3.9   Describe what, if any, kinds of pro bono matters that you handled as a student.

_____

_____

_____

3.10   What was rewarding or not rewarding about the experience?

_____

_____

_____

3.11   Please estimate the total number of hours that you participated in the following activities during law school, and whether that participation significantly influenced your career choices or your pro bono work after graduation. *(Check those applicable)*

	No. of Hours	Encouraged Pro Bono	Discouraged Pro Bono	No Effect	Influenced Career
Clinics	_____	_____	_____	_____	_____
Pro bono or public interest legal work (uncompensated by credit or pay)	_____	_____	_____	_____	_____
Pro bono legal work (as part of paid firm employment)	_____	_____	_____	_____	_____
Pro bono or public interest legal work for graduation requirement	_____	_____	_____	_____	_____
Public interest legal work paid by fellowship or organization	_____	_____	_____	_____	_____
Public interest student organizations	_____	_____	_____	_____	_____
Non legal community service	_____	_____	_____	_____	_____

4

3.12a Did other law school influences *positively* affect your desire
to do pro bono work or to seek public interest employment?

	Yes	No
Pro bono work 1		2
Public interest employment 1		2

3.12b What were those *positive* influences?

Faculty 1
Friends 2
Law school atmosphere 3
Courses 4
Career services 5
Public interest office programs and counseling 6
Other *(Explain)* _____ 7

3.13a Did law school *negatively* affect your desire to do pro bono
work or to seek public interest employment?

	Yes	No
Pro bono work 1		2
Public interest employment 1		2

3.13b What were those *negative* influences

Faculty 1
Friends 2
Law school atmosphere 3
Courses 4
Emphasis placed on private practice by
career development 5
Inadequate public interest programs
and counseling 6
Other *(Explain)* _____ 7

3.14 Did market forces and financial constraints affect your interest
in doing pro bono or public interest work?

Yes 1
No 2
Explain _____

3.15 What was your amount of enforceable educational loans on
graduation?

Law School _____
Law School and undergraduate combined _____

3.16a Did your law school have a loan forgiveness program?

Yes 1
No *(If no, skip to Q. 3.17)* 2
Explain _____

3.16b If so, have you participated in it?

Yes 1
No 2
Explain _____

3.17 What if any changes would you recommend in your law
school's policy toward pro bono?

_____

_____

_____

4. Demographic

4.1 Sex:

Male 1
Female 2

4.2 Age: _____

4.3 Current Income

Under $39,999 1
$40,000 - $69,999 2
$70,000 - $99,999 3
$100,000 - $149,999 4
$150,000 - $199,999 5
$200,000 - $249,999 6
$250,000 - $499,999 7
Over $500,000 8

4.4a How many hours did you bill last year? _____

4.4b How much of that time was for *non* pro bono work?

_____

4.5 Racial/Ethnic Identity

Caucasian 1
African American 2
Asian American 3
Hispanic 4
Native American 5
Other *(Specify)* _____ 6

4.6 How would you describe your political affiliation?

Liberal 1
Moderate 2
Conservative 3
Other *(Specify)* _____ 4

4.7 How important is religion in your life?

Important 1
Somewhat important 2
Not important 3

5

Appendix Two

PRO BONO SURVEY

Legal Employers

For purposes of this survey, pro bono work includes services that meet the definition of the Law Firm Pro Bono Challenge: services undertaken normally without expectation of fees and consisting of the delivery of legal services to persons of limited means or to charitable, religious, civic, community, governmental, and educational organizations.

1.1   Please describe your organization.

Law Firm 1
    Number of lawyers _____
Corporate Law Department 2
    Number of lawyers _____

1.2   If your organization is a law firm, please indicate:

Gross Annual Revenues_____
Profits per partner_____
Partner/Associate Ratio (include non equity and equity partners)_____

1.3   If your organization is a private corporation, please indicate its size

Number of employees_____
Gross Annual Revenues_____

Pro Bono Work

2.1   Please estimate the average number of hours per lawyer that your organization spent in the past calendar year (January 2000–December 2000) on pro bono work._____

2.1a If that number is not typical, please estimate the average number that would be representative of the past three years._____

2.2   Of the pro bono work listed above, how many hours do lawyers at your organization spend on representing persons of limited means or other nonprofit organizations that focus on assisting such persons._____

2.2a If that number is not typical, please estimate the average number that would be representative of the past three years._____

2.3   How satisfied are you with the opportunities your organization provides lawyers to do pro bono work?

Very satisfied 1
Somewhat satisfied 2
Neutral 3
Somewhat dissatisfied 4
Very dissatisfied 5

2.4   Does your organization have a policy on pro bono work? Please enclose or describe it.

Formal policy 1
Informal policy 2
No policy 3
Description _____
_____
_____ 4

2.5   If your organization has a billable hour requirement, does time spent on probono work count towards your requirement?

Yes, all hours 1
Yes, certain number of hours
    (please indicate how many)_____ 2
Yes, certain kinds of work 3
Other *(Explain)*_____
_____ 4

2.6   Is pro bono work valued equally to billable hours in promotion and compensation decisions or does it count positively in those decisions?

Equally valued 1
Positively valued 2
Not viewed as important 3
Negatively viewed 4
Other *(Explain)*_____ 5

2.7   If your organization's *formal* policy supports pro bono work, is this policy consistent with its informal norms and reward structures?

Completely consistent 1
Somewhat consistent 2
Not consistent 3
Explain_____

2.8   If not consistent, do the *informal* practices significantly reduce lawyers' willingness to accept pro bono work?

Yes 1
No 2

2.9 How much support does your organization provide for pro bono work in terms of staff, litigation costs, and other expenses?

Provides full support 1
Provides partial support
   *(Explain)*_____
   _____ 2
Provides little or no support
   *(Explain)*_____
   _____ 3
Other *(Explain)*_____
   _____ 4

2.10 Have recent increases in salaries and/or billable hours affected your organization's pro bono work?

Has caused change in formal policy
   *(Explain)*_____
   _____ 1
Has caused change in the way pro bono involvement
   affects promotion and compensation decisions
   *(Explain)*_____
   _____ 2
Has caused lawyers to decline time-consuming
   pro bono work 3
Has not had significant impact 4
Impact is not yet clear 5
Other *(Explain)*_____
   _____ 6

2.11 Please indicate whether the following factors have had significant influence in encouraging lawyers at your organization to contribute to pro bono work. Rate each factor on a scale of 1 to 5 with 5 being very significant and 1 being not significant.

	Not Significant				Very Significant
Sense of professional obligation	1	2	3	4	5
Personal satisfaction	1	2	3	4	5
Employer encouragement	1	2	3	4	5
Employer policies (requiring/encouraging pro bono, counting pro bono as billable hours, etc)	1	2	3	4	5
Value of pro bono training/contacts/referrals	1	2	3	4	5
Recognition/reputation	1	2	3	4	5
Religious commitment	1	2	3	4	5
Political commitment	1	2	3	4	5
Opportunity for trial experience	1	2	3	4	5
Opportunity to work directly with client	1	2	3	4	5
Other *(Explain)*_____	1	2	3	4	5

2.12 Please indicate whether the following factors have limited pro bono hours by lawyers at your organization. Rate each factor on a scale of 1 to 5 with 5 being very significant and 1 being not significant.

	Not Significant				Very Significant
Work load demands	1	2	3	4	5
Family obligations	1	2	3	4	5
Employer attitude	1	2	3	4	5
Employer billable(non pro bono) hour expectations	1	2	3	4	5
Lack of interest	1	2	3	4	5
Lack of expertise	1	2	3	4	5
Lack of information about opportunities	1	2	3	4	5
Lack of malpractice insurance	1	2	3	4	5
Lack of resources (e.g., support staff)	1	2	3	4	5
Inconvenient or unpleasant aspects of work	1	2	3	4	5
Other *(Explain)*_____	1	2	3	4	5

2.13 Are your organization's policies and practices concerning pro bono significant factors in attracting and retaining lawyers?

Very important factors 1
Somewhat important factors 2
Not important factors 3
Have no information 4

2.14 How do lawyers in your organization generally obtain pro bono work?

Employer pro bono committee or coordinator   1
Supervising attorney 2
Bar association program 3
Family 4
Friends 5
Client 6
Community group 7
Other *(Explain)*_____
_____ 10

2.15 How satisfied are you with this method of obtaining work?

Very satisfied 1
Somewhat satisfied 2
Neutral 3
Somewhat dissatisfied 4
Very dissatisfied 5
Explain_____
_____

2.16 Does your organization have a committee or coordinator to facilitate pro bono work?

Committee 1
Coordinator 2
Other 3
No facilitator *(If no, skip to Q.2.18)* 4

2.17 If your organization has a facilitator, how effective is that structure?

Very effective 1
Somewhat effective 2
Not effective 3
Explain_____

2.18 If your organization has no facilitator, should it have such a service?

Yes 1
No 2

2.19 How does your organization handle matters that might prove objectionable to other lawyers or to clients? *(Circle all that are applicable.)*

Organization allows attorneys to take cases,
   subject to bar conflicts of interest rules . . . 1
Organization limits support to cases approved
   by committee or coordinator 2
Organization encourages associates to work on
   cases selected by partners or facilitator . . 3
Organization discourages work on cases likely to
   advance positions inconsistent with interests
   or values of current clients 4
Organization discourages work likely to prove
   objectionable to other lawyers or to hurt its
   reputation in the community 5
Other *(Explain)*_____
_____ 6

2.20 How satisfied are you with your organization's policies concerning the types of pro bono work?

Very satisfied 1
Somewhat satisfied 2
Neutral 3
Somewhat dissatisfied 4
Very dissatisfied 5
Other *(Explain)*_____ 6

2.21 Is there anything your organization could do to encourage more pro bono work?

_____
_____
_____

2.22 Please briefly describe the kinds of pro bono work that lawyers in your organization find most and least satisfying?

Most:

_____
_____

Least:

_____
_____

2.23 How has pro bono work affected your organization's other work? Please rate each factor on a scale of 1 to 5 with 5 being very significant and 1 being not significant.

	Not Significant				Very Significant
Has significantly helped through referrals	1	2	3	4	5
Has significantly helped through general reputation	1	2	3	4	5
Has significantly helped through improving workplace (e.g., improving morale, recruitment, training)	1	2	3	4	5
Has had no significant influence	1	2	3	4	5
Has had negative influence by reducing time available for fee-generating activities	1	2	3	4	5
Has had negative influence due to unpopularity of causes	1	2	3	4	5
Other	1	2	3	4	5

2.24 What accounts for your organization's attitudes toward pro bono work?

_____
_____
_____

2.25 Have there been major barriers to creating more support for pono work in your organization?

Yes 1
No 2

2.25a If yes, Please explain.

_____
_____
_____
_____

3

Notes

CHAPTER ONE

1. See text at notes 95–99.

2. See text at notes 91–94.

3. Deborah L. Rhode, Access to Justice 3, 7 (2004).

4. Omnibus Consolidated Rescissions and Appropriations Act of 1996: Legal Services Corporation, Public Law 104-134, Section 504(a). See Rhode, Access to Justice, 3–4, 13, 105–6, 110–11; Deborah L. Rhode and David Luban, Legal Ethics 855–60 (2004).

5. Roscoe Pound, The Lawyer from Antiquity to Modern Times 44–45 (1953); Roscoe Pound, Jurisprudence 697–704 (1959); J. M. Maguire, "Poverty and Civil Litigation," 36 Harvard Law Review 361, 385 (1923); Michael Millemann, "Mandatory Pro Bono in Civil Cases: A Partial Answer to the Right Question," 49 Maryland Law Review 18, 33–35 (1990).

6. Mauro Cappelletti, J. Gordley, and Earl Johnson, Toward Equal Justice: A Comparative Study of Legal Aid in Modern Societies 6-16 (1975); David L. Shapiro, "The Enigma of the Lawyer's Duty to Serve," New York University Law Review 735, 739–40 (1980).

7. Millemann, "Mandatory Pro Bono," 37–38.

8. William Holdsworth, A History of English Law, vol. 2, 491 (1936); Edwin James Thomas Matthews and Anthony Derek Maxwell Oulton, Legal Aid and Advice Under the Legal Aid Acts 1949 to 1964 (1971); Millemann, "Mandatory Pro Bono," 39–40; Donald Robertson, "Pro Bono as a Professional Legacy," in For the Public Good: Pro Bono and the Legal Profession in Australia 97, 111-12 (Christopher Arup and Katherine Ladler, eds., 2001).

9. 11 Hen. 7, chap. 12 (1495); Scottish Parliamentary Act of 1424, chap. 45.

10. Millemann, "Mandatory Pro Bono," 33–43 (1990). But see Shapiro, "Enigma."

11. Matthews and Oulton, Legal Aid, 11; Millemann, "Mandatory Pro Bono," 43, n. 134.

12. For the courts' civil power, see United States v. Dillon, 345 F.2d 633 (9th Cir.), cert. denied, 382 U.S. 978 (1968); Steven Rosenfeld, "Mandatory Pro Bono: Historical and Constitutional Perspectives," 2 Cardozo Law Review 255, 274 (1981). For the tradition of dock briefs, see Shapiro, "Enigma," 742.

13. For barristers' willingness to take unpaid cases, see Frederick Cecil Gurney-Champion, Justice and the Poor in England 8 (1926); Richard Abel, "Law Without Politics: Legal Aid Under Advanced Capitalism," 32 UCLA Law Review 474, 501 (1985).

14. For courts' power, see Scroggs, 1 Freeman 389, 89 Eng. Rep. 289 (Kings Bench 1674); Rosenfeld, "Mandatory Pro Bono," 274; William M. Beaney Jr., The Right to Counsel in American Courts 10 (unpublished dissertation, University of Michigan, 1951). For

the absence of discipline, see Shapiro, "Enigma," 468; Report of the Committee on Legal Aid and Legal Advice in England and Wales, Comt. No. 66412 (1945).

15. Geoffrey C. Hazard Jr., Susan P. Koniak, and Roger C. Cramton, The Law and Ethics of Lawyering 1100 (3d ed. 1999); Heather MacDonald, "What Good Is Pro Bono," 10 City Journal, Spring 2000, 2, 14.

16. American Bar Association (ABA) Canons of Professional Ethics, Canon 12 (1908).

17. Shapiro, "Enigma," 751–55; Rhode, Access to Justice 8–9, 50–58; Scott L. Cummings, "The Politics of Pro Bono," 52 U.C.L.A. Law Review 1, 10–11 (2004); and notes 18–42.

18. Beaney, "Right to Counsel," 124–48; Emery A. Brownell, Legal Aid in the United States 35 (1951); Patterson v. State, 25 So.2d 713 (Florida, 1947), cert. denied 329 U.S. 789 (1948).

19. For the standard, see Lassiter v. Department of Social Services, 452 U.S. 18 (1981). For the failure to appoint counsel, see Rhode, Access to Justice 51–53; Shapiro, "Enigma," 751.

20. For compensation, see Beaney, "Right to Counsel," 197; Charles S. Potts, "Right to Counsel in Criminal Cases: Legal Aid or Public Defender?," 28 Texas Law Review 491, 505 (1949); Brownell, Legal Aid, 124–25; Reginald Heber Smith, Justice and the Poor, 112 (1919). For the inexperience and poor quality of assigned lawyers, see Rhode, Access to Justice, 51–53; Beaney, "Right to Counsel," 327; Potts, "Right to Counsel," 503–4.

21. Edward Lumbard, New England Conference on the Defense of Indigent Persons Accused of Crime, Cambridge, October 31, 1963, quoted in Anthony Lewis, Gideon's Trumpet, 199–200 (1964). For jailhouse lawyers, see Smith, Justice and the Poor, 114; Clara Shortridge Foltz, "Public Defenders," 34 American Law Review 396, 397 (1897); David Mars, "Public Defenders," 46 Journal of Criminal Law, Criminology and Police Science 199, 207 (1955); Edward J. Dimock, "The Public Defender: A Step Towards a Police State?," 42 ABA Journal 219 (1956).

22. For discussion of the poor quality of representation, see Judith L. Maute, "Changing Conceptions of Lawyers' Pro Bono Responsibilities: From Chance Noblesse Oblige to Stated Expectations," 77 Tulane Law Review 91 (2002). For discussion of the inequitable burdens, see Charles Wolfram, Modern Legal Ethics 952 (1986).

23. Robert S. Hunter, "Slave Labor in the Courts," 74 Case and Comment 3, 9 (1969).

24. Shapiro, "Enigma," 755.

25. Millemann, "Mandatory Pro Bono," 65.

26. For early court decisions and commentary affirming courts' power, see Rowe v. Yuba County, 17 Cal. 61, 63 (1860) (Justice Field, J.); Thomas Cooley, A Treatise on the Constitutional Limitations Which Rest upon the Legislative Power of the States of the American Union 334 (1868). But see Webb v. Baird, 6 Indiana 13, 16 (1854). For other precedents, see Shapiro, "Enigma," 770–77; Millemann, "Mandatory Pro Bono," 67; - Rosenfeld, "Mandatory Pro Bono," 289.

27. Ex Parte Sparks, 368 So.2d 528 (Ala. 1979), appeal dismissed, 444 U.S. 803 (1979).

28. Hurtado v. United States, 410 U.S. 578, 588–89 (1973); Powell v. Alabama, 287 U.S. 45, 73 (1932).

29. United States v. Dillon, 346 F.2d 633, 635 (9th Cir. 1965), cert. denied, 382 U.S. 978 (1966); Accord, People v. Randolphe, 219 N.E.2d 337, 340 (Ill. Sup. Ct. 1966).

30. Mallard v. United States District Court, 490 U.S. 296 (1989); 490 U.S. 310 (Kennedy, J., concurring); 490 U.S. 311 (Stevens, J., dissenting).

31. Shapiro, "Enigma," 759–61; Millemann, "Mandatory Pro Bono," 68–69.

32. Family Division Trial Lawyers v. Moultrie, 725 F.2d 695 (D.C. Cir. 1984).

33. Pennsylvania Coal Company v. Mahon, 260 U.S. 393 (1922).

34. Pennsylvania Central Transportation Company v. New York City, 438 U.S. 104, 127 (1978).

35. Pennsylvania Central Transportation Company v. New York City, 438 U.S. 147 (1978); Pennsylvania Coal Company v. Mahon, 260 U.S. 393, 415 (1922) (opinion of Justice Holmes).

36. See cases discussed in Shapiro, "Enigma," 758–59.

37. For examples, see Rosenfeld, "Mandatory Pro Bono," 290–91.

38. Butler v. Perry, 240 U.S. 328, 332 (1915).

39. See United States v. Kozminiski, 487 U.S. 931, 943 (1988); Flood v. Kuhn, 407 U.S. 238, 265–66 (1972). See also United States v. Shackney, 33 F.2d 475, 485–87 (2d Cir. 1964); Steirer v. Bethlehem Area School District, 987 F.2d 989 (3d Cir. 1993).

40. Shapiro, "Enigma," 768; Millemann, "Mandatory Pro Bono," 485–87.

41. The Selective Draft Cases, 245 U.S. 366 (1918); Butler v. Perry, 240 U.S. 328 (1916); Bobilin v. Board of Education, 403 F.Supp. 1095 (D. Hawaii 1975). See also Steirer v. Bethlehem Area School District, 987 F.2d 989 (3d Cir. 1993).

42. See Rosenfeld, "Mandatory Pro Bono," 292–93; Shapiro, "Enigma," 768; Jennifer Murray, "Lawyers Do It for Free? An Examination of Mandatory Pro Bono," 29 Texas Tech Law Review 1141, 1161–62 (1998).

43. See John C. Scully, "Mandatory Pro Bono: An Attack on the Constitution," 19 Hofstra Law Review 1229, 12–58–59 (1990–91). See Cunningham v. Superior Court, 176 Cal. App.3d 349, vacated 177 Cal. App.3d 336 (1986).

44. Scully, "Mandatory Pro Bono," 1258–59, discussing the Committee to Improve the Availability of Legal Services, Final Report to the Chief Judge of the State of New York (1990), reprinted in 19 Hofstra Law Review 755 (1991).

45. See Family Division Trial Lawyers v. Moultrie, 725 F.2d 695 (D.C. Cir. 1984).

46. See, e.g., McGowan v. Maryland, 366 U.S. 420, 425 (1961); Semler v. Oregon State Board of Dental Examiners, 294 U.S. 608, 610 (1935); Williams v. Lee Optical, Inc., 348 U.S. 483, 488–89 (1955); Rosenfeld, "Mandatory Pro Bono," 295; Millemann, "Mandatory Pro Bono," 71.

47. Semler v. Oregon State Board of Dental Examiners, 294 U.S. 608, at 610 (1935).

48. Keller v. State Bar of California, 490 U.S. 1 (1995).

49. Scully, "Mandatory Pro Bono," 1250.

50. ABA, Model Rules of Professional Conduct, Rule 1.2 (2001).

51. Hazard, Koniak, and Cramton, The Law and Ethics of Lawyering, 1102; Rosenfeld, "Mandatory Pro Bono," 295; Millemann, "Mandatory Pro Bono," 66–71. See also Steirer v. Bethlehem Area School District, 987 F.2d 489, 996 (1993).

52. ABA Model Rules of Professional Conduct, Rule 6.1; ABA Code of Professional Responsibility, Ethical Consideration 2.25; Pound, The Lawyer from Antiquity to Modern Times, 5–7.

53. Jerold Auerbach, Unequal Justice: Lawyers and Social Change in Modern America 57 (1976); Bryant Garth, Neighborhood Law Firms for the Poor 18–19 (1980).

54. Auerbach, Unequal Justice, 57, 282.

55. For the ABA resolutions and lack of subsequent progress, see Brownell, Legal Aid,

8, 9, 230. For the Chicago campaign, see Auerbach, Unequal Justice, 57. For the New York effort, see Martha F. Davis, Brutal Need: Lawyers and the Welfare Rights Movement, 1960–1973 (1993). For the 1950 bar funding contributions, see Garth, Neighborhood Law Firms, 19.

56. For the NBA, see http://www.nationalbar.org/about/index.shtrml; J. Clay Smith Jr., Emancipation: The Making of the Black Lawyer 1844–1944, 541–85 (1993); Steven H. Hobbes, "Shout from Taller Rooftops: A Response to Deborah Rhode's Access to Justice," 73 Fordham Law Review 935 (2004). For other bar associations, see Rhode, Access to Justice, 52–55, and Cummings, "Politics of Pro Bono," 11, 25.

57. Smith, Justice and the Poor, 9.

58. F. Raymond Marks, Kirk Leswing, and Barbara A. Fortinsky, The Lawyer, The Public, and Professional Responsibility 15–16, 18 (1972). For the bar's early lack of support for legal aid services and hostility to government programs, see Auerbach, Unequal Justice, 53; Garth, Neighborhood Law Firms, 18–21, 26–34; Deborah L. Rhode and Geoffrey C. Hazard Jr., Professional Responsibility and Regulation 154–57, 162 (2002).

59. See Mark J. Green, The Other Government: The Unseen Power of Washington Lawyers 264–65 (1975).

60. Esther Lardent, "Pro Bono in the 1990s," in American Bar Association, Civil Justice: An Agenda for Reform in the 1990s, 424–25 (1989); Esther F. Lardent, "Mandatory Pro Bono in Civil Cases: The Wrong Answer to the Right Question," 49 Maryland Law Review 78, 88–89 (1990).

61. Auerbach, Unequal Justice, 282.

62. Joel F. Handler, Ellen Jane Hollingsworth, Howard E. Erlanger, and Jack Ladinsky, "The Public Interest Activities of Private Practice Lawyers," 61 ABA Journal 1388, 1389 (1975).

63. Handler et al., "Public Interest Activities," 1389; Marks, Leswing, and Fortinsky, The Lawyer, The Public, and Professional Responsibility, 8; Philip R. Lochner, "The No Fee and Low Fee Legal Practice of Private Attorneys," 9 Law and Society Review 431, 442–46 (1975); Joel F. Handler, Ellen Jane Hollingsworth, and Howard E. Erlanger, Lawyers and the Pursuit of Legal Rights 92–101 (1978); Richard Abel, American Lawyers, 130 (1989); Auerbach, Unequal Justice, 282; Barlow F. Christensen, "The Lawyers' Pro Bono Publico Responsibility," 1981 American Bar Foundation Research Journal 1, 14–18; Roger C. Cramton, "Mandatory Pro Bono," 19 Hofstra Law Review 1113, 1121–24 (1991).

64. ABA, Consortium on Legal Services and the Public, Legal Needs and Civil Justice: A Comprehensive Legal Needs Study (Chicago: American Bar Association, 1994). For earlier studies, see Barbara Curran, The Legal Needs of the Public (1977). For subsequent studies, see Rhode, Access to Justice, 3, 79–80, 105–6; and Deborah L. Rhode, "Access to Justice Connecting Principles to Practice," 17 Georgetown Journal of Legal Ethics 369, 373–77 (2004).

65. Lardent, "Mandatory Pro Bono," 89.

66. Lardent, "Mandatory Pro Bono," 92–93; Association of the Bar of the City of New York, Toward a Mandatory Contribution of Public Service Practice by Every Lawyer (1980), discussed in Rosenfeld, "Mandatory Pro Bono," 295.

67. "Text of Initial Draft of Ethics Code Rewrite Committee," Legal Times of Washington, August 27, 1979, 26, 45, col. 4.

68. Deborah L. Rhode, "Ethical Perspectives on Legal Practice," 37 Stanford Law Review 589, 610 (quoting opponent).

69. Ted Schneyer, "Professionalism as Bar Politics: The Making of the Model Rules of Professional Conduct," 14 Law and Social Inquiry 677, 701 n. 147 (1989). For accounts of the bar's opposition to any mandatory contribution or reporting system, see Scott Slonim, "Kutak Panel Report: No Mandatory Pro Bono," 67 ABA Journal 33 (1981); David F. Pike, "Don't Panic, Kutak Tells His Ethics Code Skeptics," National Law Journal, December 22, 1980, 2; John A. Humbach, "Serving the Public Interest: An Overstated Objective," 65 ABA Journal 564 (1979).

70. "Law Poll: Public Interest Legal Services," 68 ABA Journal 912 (1982).

71. ABA Model Rules of Professional Conduct Rule 6.1 (1983).

72. ABA Model Rules of Professional Conduct Rule 6.1 (1993).

73. ABA Model Rules of Professional Conduct Rule 6.1 (2002).

74. See Judith L. Maute, "Pro Bono Publico in Oklahoma: Time for Change," 53 Oklahoma Law Review 527, 572–73 (2000) (noting amendments in twenty-two states and the District of Columbia). For current state rules, see ABA Center for Pro Bono, State Pro Bono Service Rules.

75. Amendments to Rule 4-6.1 of the Rules Regulating the Florida Bar—Pro Bono Public Service, 696 So.2d 734, 735 (Fla. 1997); Maryland Rules of Procedure 16-903 (2002); Nevada Supreme Court Rule 191 (2003).

76. Madden v. Township of Delran, 601 A.2d 211 (N.J. 1992), available at http://www.judiciary.state.nj.lus/notices/madden.020301.pdf; "Revised Exemptions from Madden v. Delran Pro Bono Counsel Assignments for 2002," New Jersey Law Journal, March 11, 2002, 1.

77. California and Oregon Boards of Bar Governors have policy statements on pro bono. See ABA Center for Pro Bono, State Pro Bono Ethics Rules, available at http://www.abanet.org/legalservices/probono/stateethicsrules.html (October 17, 2003). See Maute, "Pro Bono," 572 nn. 267–68. Since Maute's article, Massachusetts revised its rules, so Illinois is now the only state that still has the pro bono language in the preamble only. See Massachusetts' Model Rule 6.1, available at http://www.mass.gov/obcbbo/rpc6.htm.

78. ABA Center, "Policies—State Pro Bono Ethics Rules"; Maute, "Pro Bono," 572, 581.

79. ABA Center, "Policies—State Pro Bono Ethics Rules"; Maute, "Pro Bono," 578; Voluntary Attorney Pro Bono Plan.

80. ABA Center, "Policies—State Pro Bono Ethics Rules"; Maute, "Pro Bono," 581.

81. ABA Center, "Policies—State Pro Bono Ethics Rules"; Maute, "Pro Bono," 582.

82. Rhode and Luban, Legal Ethics (2001).

83. Lardent, "Mandatory Pro Bono," 96–97; Barbara Glesner Fines, "Almost Pro Bono: Judicial Appointment of Attorneys in Juvenile and Child Dependency Actions," 72 University of Missouri at Kansas City Law Review 337 (2003).

84. Cummings, "Politics of Pro Bono," 145.

85. See SPAN (State Planning Assistance Network), Supporting Partnerships to Expand Access to Justice Report: Access to Justice Partnerships, State by State (March 2002). For examples, see Maryland Judicial Commission on Pro Bono Report and Recommendations (March 2000), available at http://www.courts.state.md.us/probono/history.html; Indiana Pro Bono Commission, available at http://www.in.gov/judiciary/probono/; and Indiana Rules of Professional Conduct Rule 6.5.

86. Exec. Order No. 12,988, 3 C.F.R. 159 (1996).

87. David Jackson DeVries, "Public Sector Obstacles Are Vanishing," ABA Journal, December 2000, 66.

88. "The Law Firm Pro Bono Challenge: Law Firm Performance in 1996 and 1997," What's New in Law Firm Pro Bono (The Pro Bono Institute, November/December 1999), 6; interview with Esther Lardent, Pro Bono Institute, July 2003.

89. See Corporate Pro Bono Org. available at http://corporateprobono.org/forms/news_full_record.cfm?newsID-1065 and ProBono.Net at http://probono.net/.

90. William J. Dean, "The 2000 Survey of Pro Bono Activity by New York Law Firms," New York Law Journal, May 7, 2001, A1; Elizabeth Amon, "Corporate Pro Bono Gets Boost," National Law Journal, September 11, 2000, A1; Orange County, Florida Bar Association, By-Laws, available at http://ocbanet.org; Robert A. Stein, "Leader of the Pro Bono Pack," ABA Journal, October 1997, 108.

91. National Law Journal, "Pro Bono NLJ Awards," January 5, 2004; Dee McAree, "Pro Bono Finds a New Edge," National Law Journal, January 3, 2005, A1; "Sizing Up the Am Law 200's Pro Bono Commitment," American Lawyer, September 2004, 113; "Cellar Dwellers," American Lawyer, September 2004, 103; "The AmLaw 200's Pro Bono Powerhouses and Laggards," American Lawyer, September 2003, 98.

92. Judith L. Maute and Cheryl Wofford Hill, "Delivery Systems Under Construction," 72 University of Missouri at Kansas City Law Review 377, 389 (2003).

93. See Carroll Seron, The Business of Practicing Law 129–33 (1996); Deborah L. Rhode, "Cultures of Commitment: Pro Bono for Lawyers and Law Students," 67 Fordham Law Review 2415, 2423 (1999). Less than one-half of New York lawyers provide pro bono services, and of these, three-quarters provided free legal services for a friend or relative, and about two-thirds provided services for a client who turned out not to be able to pay. Gary Spencer, "Pro Bono Data Show Little Improvement," New York Law Journal, March 5, 1999, 1; see also Denise R. Johnson, "The Legal Needs of the Poor as a Starting Point for Systemic Reform," 17 Yale Law and Policy Review 479, 480 n. 6 (1998); Maute, "Pro Bono Publico in Oklahoma," 527 (citing data indicating that little of Oklahoma lawyers' work goes to poor).

94. See sources cited in notes 62, 93, and 94.

95. Judith S. Kaye and Jonathan Lippman, Report on the Pro Bono Activities of the New York State Bar 12 (1999), available at http://www.courts.state.ny.us/probono/pbrpt.htm.

96. Maute, "Pro Bono Publico in Oklahoma," 562.

97. For Texas, see State Bar of Texas, Department of Research and Analysis, Volunteer Legal Services to the Poor, Voluntary Reporting, Final Report (October 2003), available at http://www.texasbar.com/attyinfo/probono/legpoor.htm. For New York, see Kaye and Lippman, Report. For Michigan, see Candace Crowley and Al Butzbaugh, "State Bar Coordinates Private Endowment and Operations Funding for Civil Legal Aid," 78 Michigan Bar Journal 1094, 1095 (1999). For Minnesota, see David E. Rovella, "Can the Bar Fill the LSC's Shoes?," National Law Journal, August 5, 1996, A1 (quoting Esther Lardent). For Florida figures over time, see Standing Committee on Pro Bono Services, Report to the Supreme Court of Florida, 2003, available at http://www.Flabar.org. Talbot D'Alemberte, "Tributaries of Justice: The Search for Full Access," 25 Florida State University Law Review 631, 633 (1998).

98. Correspondence from Mike Tartaglia, director, Programs Division, Florida Bar, June 2, 2004.

99. LSC Statistics: Private Attorney Involvement, All Programs, available at http://

www.lsc.gov/pressr/pr_pai.htm. See Spencer, "Pro Bono Data" (noting that only 14% of all New York lawyers took referrals from bar pro bono programs); Johnson, "Legal Needs of the Poor" (citing research indicating that only 10% of New York lawyers provide legal services to the poor); Elizabeth Amon, "The State of Pro Bono 2001," National Law Journal, January 7, 2002, A12.

100. Corporate Pro Bono Org., available at http://www.corporateprobono.org/.

101. Kaye and Lippman, Report; D'Alemberte, "Tributaries," 139; Standing Committee, Report to the Supreme Court of Florida (indicating that 74,323 Florida lawyers contributed $2,531,445 between July 1, 2001, and June 30, 2002). A "Generous Associates" campaign by the Washington, D.C., Legal Services Office has attempted to respond to recent cutbacks in pro bono. Such cutbacks have been encouraged by salary hikes advocated on the "Greedy Associates" Web site. The 2000 campaign generated only about $175,000. The 2001 campaign generated $250,826. Legal Aid Society of the District of Columbia, 2001 Annual Report 5 (2002); Joseph C. Zengerle, "Everybody Loses Without Pro Bono," National Law Journal, October 30, 2000, A20.

102. Katrina M. Dewey, "Of Porsches and Philanthropists," California Lawyer, October 2000, 96; Craig Anderson, "County Adopts Pro Bono Requirement," San Francisco Daily Journal, April 10, 2002, 1.

103. Cummings, "Politics of Pro Bono," 84; interview with Esther Lardent; Amon, "The State of Pro Bono 2001," A12 (reprinting pro bono average among surveyed large firms of 3.06% of billable hours).

104. David Jackson Devries, "Public Sector Obstacles Are Vanishing," 66; Dean, "2000 Survey of Pro Bono Activity," A1.

105. Aric Press, "Eight Minutes," American Lawyer, July 2000, 13.

106. Jack Wax, "No More Lawyer Jokes," National Law Journal, December 23–December 30, 2002, A17 (noting 42 hours as annual average for lawyers in top 100 firms); Press, "Eight Minutes," 13; Judicial Council of California, Chief Justice Urges More Lawyers to Donate Time to Pro Bono Efforts (press release, September 16, 2000), available at http://www.courtinfo.ca.gov/newsreleases/NR52-00.htm.

107. John C. Keeney Jr., "Where Have All the Partners Gone," Washington Lawyer, September, 2004, 5; Aric Press, "At the American Lawyer," American Lawyer, September, 2004, 9 (noting that at only about 15% of the 200 most profitable firms did half the lawyers perform at least 20 hours of service).

108. Press, "Eight Minutes," 13; Cameron Stracher, "Go Go Bono," American Lawyer, December 2000, 51. These figures represent the most recent data available.

109. Dee McAree, "Pro Bono Mini Boom," National Law Journal, January 5, 2004, 1, 23; Elizabeth Preis, "A Small Gain," American Lawyer, July 2002, 119; Susan Saulny, "Volunteerism Among Lawyers Surges, Encouraged by the Slumping Economy," New York Times, February 19, 2003, A27; Elizabeth Amon, "Experts See Lift in Pro Bono Work," National Law Journal, January 6, 2003, A1.

110. Marcus J. Lock, "Increasing Access to Justice: Expanding the Role of Nonlawyers in the Delivery of Legal Services to Low-Income Coloradans," 72 University of Colorado Law Review 459, 478 (2001).

111. See American Lawyer, "The AmLaw 200: Gauging Pro Bono Commitment," August 2002, 113; and sources cited in note 109.

112. Marc Galanter and Thomas Palay, "Public Service Implications of Evolving Law

Firm Size and Structure," in The Law Firm and the Public Good 19, 41–47 (Robert A. Katzman, ed., 1995); Esther Lardent, "Pro Bono Work Is Good for Business," National Law Journal, February 19, 2001, B20. Stanford law student Jacqueline Fink analyzed the correlation of pro bono work with profitability for the 100 most profitable firms according to 2000 American Lawyer data (unpublished paper, 2001). Of the twenty-five most profitable firms, three were at the top of the list and none were at the bottom (44). See also James L. Baillie, "It Helps the Bottom Line—Really," Business Law Today, January/February 1997, 50, 51.

113. Cynthia F. Adcock and Alison M. Keegan, A Handbook on Law School Pro Bono Programs: The AALS Pro Bono Project 7 (2001).

114. John Kramer, "Mandatory Pro Bono at Tulane Law School," in Pro Bono at Law Schools: New Solutions to Old Problems, The NAPIL Connection, 1990 Supplement.

115. Adcock and Keegan, Handbook, 8.

116. Recodification of ABA Accreditation Standards, Standard 302(e)(Curriculum).

117. ABA Accreditation Standard 404.

118. ABA Commission on Pro Bono and Public Service Opportunities in Law Schools, Learning to Serve: The Findings and Proposals of the AALS Commission on Pro Bono and Public Services Opportunities (1999), available at http://www.aals.org/probono/report.html; Cynthia F. Adcock, "Law School Pro Bono Partnership Formed," AALS Pro Bono and Public Service Section Newsletter 1 (Fall 2001). In the interests of full disclosure, I should note that the commission was the presidential initiative that I created during my term as president of the Association of American Law Schools, and that I helped secure funding for its work and for the subsequent follow-up project from the Open Society Institute.

119. Ellen Chapnick, chair, AALS Section on Pro Bono and Public Service Opportunities in Law Schools, Section Panel Presentation, Annual Meeting of the AALS, January 6, 2003 (Washington, D.C.).

120. Cynthia F. Adcock, Law School Pro Bono Programs, Fact Sheet, February 20, 2003 (available from the Association of American Law Schools).

121. Adcock and Keegan, Handbook, 9–10; Christina M. Rossas, "Mandatory Pro Bono for Law Students: The Right Place to Start," 30 Hofstra Law Review 1069, 1089 (2002). For the ABA Center for Pro Bono, Directory of Law School Public Interest and Pro Bono Programs, see http://www.abanet.org/legalservices/probono/lawschools/home.html.

122. Adcock and Keegan, Handbook, 23–30.

123. Adcock and Keegan, Handbook, 11.

124. Adcock and Keegan, Handbook, 11–12.

125. AALS Commission, Learning to Serve, 4; Notes of Focus Group Interviews conducted by the Association of American Law Schools' Commission on Pro Bono and Public Service Opportunities in Law Schools (1998) (on file with author).

126. AALS Focus Group Interviews.

127. AALS Commission, Learning to Serve, 4.

128. AALS Commission, Learning to Serve, 7.

129. AALS Commission, Learning to Serve, 10; Michael A. Mogill, "Professing Pro Bono: To Walk the Talk," 15 Notre Dame Journal of Law, Ethics and Public Policy 5, 33, n. 161 (noting that Stetson requires ten hours annually from faculty and students and

Southern Methodist specifies services "consistent" with the thirty-hour requirement for students).

130. Justin Herdman, "Students Face Pro Bono Obligation," Harvard Law Record, May 12, 2000, 1 (quoting Professor Andrew Kaufman concerning Harvard policy).

131. AALS Commission, Learning to Serve, 17.

132. AALS Focus Group Interviews.

133. AALS Commission, Learning to Serve, 17.

134. ABA Model Rules of Professional Conduct, Rule 6.1.

Chapter Two

1. See David Luban, Lawyers and Justice: An Ethical Study 263–64 (1988); Frank Michelman, "The Supreme Court and Litigation Access Fees: The Right to Protect One's Rights," part 1, Duke Law Journal 1153, 1172 (1973).

2. See Legal Services Corporation, Serving the Civil Legal Needs of Low-Income Americans: A Special Report to Congress 12 (2000); Alan W. Houseman, "Civil Legal Assistance for the Twenty-First Century: Achieving Equal Justice for All," 17 Yale Law and Policy Review 369, 402 (1998). See also California Commission on Access to Justice, The Path to Equal Justice (2002) (estimating that almost three-quarters of the needs of California poor are unmet); Jonathan Smith, "Community in Need: Securing Equal Access to Justice," Washington Lawyer, May 2003, 38 (estimating that 90% of the needs of poor District of Columbia residents are unmet); Roy W. Resse and Carolyn A. Eldred, Institute for Survey Research, Temple University for Consortium on Legal Services and the Public; American Bar Association (ABA), Legal Needs Among Low-Income and Moderate-Income Households: Summary of Findings from the Comprehensive Legal Needs Study 7–30 (1994).

3. See Deborah L. Rhode, Access to Justice 133, 139 (2004).

4. For representation of the poor, see David Luban, "Taking Out the Adversary," 209 California Law Journal (2003); Paul R. Tremblay, "Aiding a Very Moral Type of God: Triage Among Poor Clients," 67 Fordham Law Review 2475, 2481–82 (1995).

5. Code of Federal Regulation Sections 1610-42 (1999); Rhode, Access to Justice, 3–4, 13, 105.

6. Rhode and Luban, Legal Ethics, 849; Rhode, Access to Justice, 68; David Luban, "Taking Out the Adversary: The Assault on Progressive Public-Interest Lawyers," 91 University of California at Berkeley Law Review 209 (2003).

7. E. Allan Lind and Tom R. Tyler, The Social Psychology of Procedural Justice 102–3 (1998); Luban, Lawyers and Justice, 252–55.

8. Report of the Joint Conference on Professional Responsibility of the Association of American Law Schools and American Bar Association (1958).

9. Access to Justice Working Group, State Bar of California, And Justice for All: Fulfilling the Promise of Access to Civil Justice in California 33–34 (1996); Committee to Improve the Availability of Legal Services, "Final Report to the Chief Judge of the State of New York," reprinted in 19 Hofstra Law Review 755, 773 (1991); Karen Grisez, "Pro Bono, A Special Report: Summer on the Border," Legal Times [Washington, D.C.], August 2, 2004, 33.

10. "Final Report to the Chief Judge of New York," 776.

11. For example, nonlawyers in other countries can provide legal advice. See Rhode,

Access to Justice 89; Deborah L. Rhode, "Access to Justice: Connecting Principles to Practice," 17 Georgetown Journal of Legal Ethics 369, 408 (2004).

12. Deborah L. Rhode, The Interests of Justice 135–37 (2000).

13. Richard L. Abel, American Lawyers, 246 (1989); Charles Wolfram, Modern Legal Ethics, 953 (1986); Amendment to Rule 4-6.1 of the Rules Regulating the Florida Bar—Pro Bono Public Service, 696 So.2d 734, 738 (Florida, 1997); David Luban, "Faculty Pro Bono and the Question of Identity," 49 Journal of Legal Education 58, 65 (1999); Barlow F. Christensen, "The Lawyer's Pro Bono Publico Responsibility," 1 American Bar Foundation Research Journal 14–18 (1981); F. Raymond Marks, Kirk Leswing, and Barbara A. Fortinsky, The Lawyer, The Public, and Professional Responsibility, 288–93 (1972).

14. Walter Bennett, The Lawyer's Myth 143 (2001); Marks, Leswing, and Fortinsky, The Lawyer, The Public, and Professional Responsibility, 280–81; Michael Millemann, "Mandatory Pro Bono in Civil Cases: A Partial Answer to the Right Question," 49 Maryland Law Review 18, 65 (1990); Steven B. Rosenfeld, "Mandatory Pro Bono: Historical and Constitutional Perspectives," 2 Cardozo Law Review 225, 289 (1981).

15. Mallard v. District Court, 490 U.S. 311 (1989) (Stevens, J., dissenting); Roscoe Pound, The Lawyer from Antiquity to Modern Times 5–7 (1954); Luban, Lawyers and Justice, 286–87; Millemann, "Mandatory Pro Bono," 65.

16. "Final Report to the Chief Judge of New York," 782.

17. Richard C. Reuben, "The Case of a Lifetime," ABA Journal, April 1994, 73; Robert A Stein, "Champions of Pro Bono," ABA Journal, August 1997, 100.

18. Esther Lardent, "Pro Bono Work Is Good for Business," National Law Journal, February 19, 2001, B20; W. Terence Walsh, "Pro Bono 2000: A Bridge over Troubled Waters," Georgia Bar Journal, June 2000, 12; John Ryan, "Duty Calls," California Law Business, February 12, 2001, 17; Daniel Becker, "The Many Faces of Pro Bono," Washington Lawyer, May 2001, 22, 30; "The Role of the Private Bar and Pro Bono Service in Meeting the Legal Needs of the Twenty-First Century," 3 New York City Law Review 171, 186 (2000); "Lawyers of This Year," National Law Journal, December 25, 2000, January 7, 2001, A24; Cynthia Fuchs Epstein, "Stricture and Structure: The Social and Cultural Context of Pro Bono Work in Wall Street Firms," 70 Fordham Law Review 1689, 1693–94 (2002); Robert Granfield and Thomas Koenig, "'It's Hard to Be a Human Being and a Lawyer': Young Attorneys and the Confrontation with Ethical Ambiguity in Legal Practice," 105 West Virginia Law Review 495 (2003).

19. John B. Heinz and Paul S. Schnorr, with Edward O. Laumann and Robert L. Nelson, "Lawyers' Roles in Voluntary Associations: Declining Social Capital?," 26 Law and Social Inquiry 597, 599 (2001); Jill Schachner Chanen, "Pro Bono's Pros—and Cons: Rewards Are Great But It Takes a Deft Balance of Time and Effort," ABA Journal, May 1998, 80; Donald W. Hoagland, "Community Service Makes Better Lawyers," in The Law Firm and the Public Good 104, 109; Jack W. Londen, "The Impact of Pro Bono Work on Law Firm Economics," 9 Georgetown Journal of Legal Ethics 925 (1996); Thomas J. Brannan, "Pro Bono: By Choice or By Chance," Illinois Bar Journal, September 1996, 481; Ronald J. Tabak, "Integration of Pro Bono into Law Firm Practice," 9 Georgetown Journal of Legal Ethics 931, 932 (1996).

20. Ruth M. Bond, "Taking Time Out to Help Those in Need with Legal Burdens Brings Satisfaction, Pride," San Francisco Daily Journal, January 15, 2002, 4; Tanya Neiman, "Nothing Gives Like . . . ," San Francisco Attorney, February/March 2000, 44, 45;

Walsh, "Pro Bono"; Becker, "The Many Faces of Pro Bono," 22; Evelyn Apgar, "General Counsel, Pro Bono Gripes Galore," 6 New Jersey Lawyer, November 1997, 3.

21. ABA Young Lawyers Division, Career Satisfaction Survey, 28 (2000); ABA Young Lawyers Division, Career Satisfaction Survey (1995).

22. Vivia Chen, "Going Corporate," American Lawyer, September 2003, 94 (quoting William Fogg).

23. National Association for Law Placement (NALP) Foundation, Lateral Lawyers: Why They Leave and What May Make Them Stay 24, 43–52, 77 (2001); Austin G. Anderson and Arthur G. Greene, The Effective Associate Training Program: Improving Firm Performance, Profitability and Prospective Partners (1999).

24. NALP Foundation, Lateral Lawyers, 156, table A-22 (only 7.2% of lawyers cited lack of credit for pro bono work). For the effects on retention, see Talcott J. Franklin, "Practical Pro Bono: How Public Service Can Enhance Your Practice," South Carolina Laywer, January/February 1999, 17, 19; William J. Kelly Jr., "Reflections on Lawyer Morale and Public Service in an Age of Diminished Expectations," in Robert A. Katzmann, ed., The Law Firm and the Public Good, 90, 98–100 (1995); and sources cited in note 23.

25. Londen, "Impact of Pro Bono Work" 925; John Ryan, "Rescue Mission," California Law Business, February 12, 2001, 15 (quoting Jack Londen); Carrie Johnson, "When Pro Bono Is Not Just an Afterthought," Legal Times, June 30, 1997, S44; Memorandum to New York Partners of Clifford Chance, Re. Associates Concerns, October 15, 2002, available at http://news.com/servlet/ContentServer?pagesname=FT.comStoryFT/FullStory&c=Stor (noting that firm's unsupportive attitude toward pro bono was a "significant minus" in recruiting and adversely affected some associates' perceptions of firm culture).

26. Talcott J. Franklin, "Practical Pro Bono: How Public Source Can Enhance Your Practice," South Carolina Lawyer, February 1999, 15, 18.

27. Franklin, "Practical Pro Bono," 18.

28. Peter D. Hart Research Associates, Inc., A Survey of Attitudes Nationwide Toward Lawyers and the Legal System 18 (1993). See also Gary A. Hengstler, "Vox Populi," ABA Journal, September 1993, 61 (citing survey data finding that almost half of those surveyed believed that providing free legal services would improve the profession's image). A survey by the Oregon bar found when individuals were asked what information might cause them to have a higher opinion of the legal profession, they gave top ratings to knowledge that lawyers had given free legal advice to mass disaster victims and had made financial contributions to community legal services organizations. Karen Garst, "Reporting on Survey, Part II," Oregon State Bar Bulletin, December 1996, 39, 46.

29. ABA, Perceptions of the U.S. Justice System 59 (1999).

30. Tigran W. Eldred and Thomas Schoenherr, "The Lawyer's Duty of Public Service: More Than Charity?," 96 West Virginia Law Review 367, 390 and n. 94.

31. See Chapter 1; and the text accompanying notes 30–35.

32. See sources cited in Deborah L. Rhode, "Ethical Perspectives on Legal Practice," 37 Stanford Law Review 589, 609 (1985). Accord, "Is Pro Bono Work the Key to Equal Legal Access?," San Francisco Daily Journal, November 30, 2002, 4 (quoting Joseph Schwachter); Vito J. Titone, "A Profession Under Siege," New York Law Journal, May 20, 1992, 2; Ronald H. Silverman, "Conceiving a Lawyer's Legal Duty to the Poor," 19 Hofstra Law Review 885, 957 (1991) (summarizing testimony of New York lawyers).

33. For the gap, see Chapter 6.

34. "Few Attorneys Willing to Help with 'Access' Problem," California Bar Journal, November 1994, 16.

35. Charles Silver and Frank Cross, "What's Not to Like About Being a Lawyer," 109 Yale Law Journal 1443 (2000).

36. Silver and Cross, "What's Not to Like," 1481–82.

37. Silver and Cross, "What's Not to Like," 1483.

38. John C. Scully, "Mandatory Pro Bono: An Attack on the Constitution," 19 Hofstra Law Review 1229, 1235, 1244 (1990); Omar J. Arcia, "Objections, Administrative Difficulties and Alternatives to Mandatory Pro Bono Legal Services in Florida," 22 Florida State Law Review 771 (1995).

39. If we take Silver and Cross's figure of $150 as an average hourly rate, and if all of America's 900,000 lawyers complied with the ABA's suggested 50 hours per year, the total yield would be $6.75 billion per year, divided among 36 million poor people. That works out to roughly $3.60 per poor person per week.

40. John A. Humbach, "Serving the Public Interest: An Overstated Objective," ABA Journal, April 1979, 565. Accord, Arcia, "Objections, Administrative Difficulties," 781–82; Scully, "Mandatory Pro Bono," 1187.

41. George M. Kraw, "The Politics of Pro Bono," San Francisco Recorder, March 14, 2001, 4.

42. Scott L. Cummings, "The Politics of Pro Bono," 52 U.C.L.A. Law Review 1, 118–30 (2004); Robert W. Gordon, "Private Career-Building and Public Benefits: Reflections on 'Doing Well by Doing Good,'" 41 Houston Law Review 113, 133 (2004); David Wilkins, "Doing Well by Doing Good? The Role of Public Service in the Careers of Black Corporate Lawyers," 41 Houston Law Review 1, 76–77 (2004); Esther F. Lardent, "Positional Conflicts in the Pro Bono Context: Ethical Considerations and Market Forces," 67 Fordham Law Review 2279 (1999).

43. Kraw, "Politics of Pro Bono," 4; Accord, Humbach, "Serving the Public Interest," 564; Scully, "Mandatory Pro Bono," 1239. I have raised the same objection. Deborah L. Rhode, "Why the ABA Bothers: A Functional Perspective on Professional Codes," 59 Texas Law Review 689, 699–701 (1981).

44. See text accompanying note 27.

45. For a representative overview of this position, see Jonathan R. Macey, "Not All Pro Bono Work Helps the Poor," Wall Street Journal, December 30, 1992, A7.

46. Heather MacDonald, "What Good Is Pro Bono," 10 City Journal, Spring 2000, 14 (quoting New York lawyer Frances Menton Jr.).

47. MacDonald, "What Good Is Pro Bono," 22.

48. For assertedly counterproductive cases, see Jonathan R. Macey, "Mandatory Pro Bono: Comfort for the Poor or Welfare for the Rich?," 77 Cornell Law Review 1115, 1117 (1992) (quoting John A. Humbach); see also Douglas J. Besharov, ed., Legal Services for the Poor: Time for Reform, 3–29, 329–36 (1990); Kenneth F. Boehm, "The Legal Services Program: Unaccountable, Political, Anti-Poor, Beyond Reform and Unnecessary," 17 Saint Louis University Public Law Review 321 (1998); Richard Posner, Economic Analysis of Law 513–14 (5th ed. 1998); Silver and Cross, "What's Not to Like," 1481–84.

49. Silver and Cross, "What's Not to Like," 1484.

50. For representative criticisms, see Gerald N. Rosenberg, The Hollow Hope (1991); Donald L. Horowitz, The Courts and Social Policy (1977).

51. United States v. Carolene Products Co., 304 U.S. 144, 152 (1938); Luban, Lawyers and Justice, 358–70.

52. Deborah L. Rhode and David Luban, Legal Ethics 852 (2004); Joel Handler, Social Movements and the Legal System: A Theory of Law Reform and Social Change 210 (1978); Carrie Menkel-Meadow, "The Causes of Cause Lawyering: Toward an Understanding of the Motivation and Commitment of Social Justice Lawyers," in Cause Lawyering: Political Commitments and Professional Responsibility 31, 35–36 (Austin Sarat and Stuart Scheingeld, eds., 1998).

53. Steven Gunn, "Eviction Defense for Poor Tenants: Costly Comparison or Justice Served?," 13 Yale Law and Policy Review 385, 386 (1995); Carol Seron, Gregg van Ryzin, Martin Frankel, and Jean Kovath, "The Impact of Legal Counsel on Outcomes for Poor Tenants in New York City's Housing Courts: Results of a Randomized Experiment," 35 Law and Society Review 419 (2001); Steven Lubet and Cathryn Stewart, "A Public Assets Theory of Lawyers' Pro Bono Obligations," 145 University of Pennsylvania Law Review 1245, 1294 (1997); "Final Report to the Chief Judge of New York."

54. Lubet and Stewart, "Public Assets Theory," 1295.

55. Marvin E. Frankel, "Proposal: A National Legal Service," 45 South Carolina Law Review 887, 890 (1994); "Final Report to the Chief Judge of New York"; sources cited in Reed Elizabeth Loder, "Tending the Generous Heart: Mandatory Pro Bono and Moral Development," 14 Georgetown Journal of Legal Ethics 459 (2001); Rob Atkinson, "A Social-Democratic Critique of Pro Bono Publico Representation of the Poor: The Good as the Enemy of the Best," 9 American University Journal of Gender, Social Policy, and Law 129, 147–48 (2001); David Shapiro, "The Enigma of Lawyers' Duty to Serve," 55 New York University Law Review 784 (1980).

56. Yarbrough v. Superior Court, 702 P.2d 583, 590 (Cal. App. 1985).

57. Julie Murray, "Lawyers Do It for Free? Mandatory Pro Bono," 29 Texas Tech Law Review 1142, 1151 (1998); Silver and Cross, "What's Not to Like," 1490; Arcia, "Objections, Administrative Difficulties," 780; Shapiro, "Enigma," 735, 777; Debra Burke et al., "Pro Bono Publico: Issues and Implications," 26 Loyola Chicago Law Review 61, 67 (1994).

58. Arcia, "Objections, Administrative Difficulties," 780–81; Burke et al., "Pro Bono Publico," 67.

59. Shapiro, "Enigma," 777.

60. See Rhode, Access to Justice, 87; Rhode and Luban, Legal Ethics, 772–75.

61. See Rhode, Access to Justice, 88–89; Kendra Enri Nitta, "An Ethical Evaluation of Mandatory Pro Bono," 29 Loyola Los Angeles Law Review 909, 913 (1996); Richard Schmidt, "Nevada Bar Offers Pro Bono Plan to Stem Nonlawyer Competition," Wall Street Journal, January 9, 1995, B3.

62. See, e.g., Monroe Communications Corp. v. F.C.C. 900 F.2d 351, 353 (D.C. Cir., 1990) ("In deciding whether to award a renewal expectancy, the Commission focuses on non-entertainment programming broadcast by the station, including news, public affairs, and public service announcements").

63. Silverman, "Conceiving a Lawyer's Legal Duty," 1012–13; David C. Vladeck, "Hard Choices: Thoughts for New Lawyers," 10 Kansas Journal Law and Public Policy 351, 356 (2001).

64. American Medical Association, Council on Judicial and Ethical Affairs, Fundamental Elements of the Patient-Physician Relationship, 264 JAMA 3133 (1990), available

at their Web site, http://www.ama-assn.org/ama/pub/category/2510.html. In June 1994, the Council on Judicial and Ethical Affairs issued advisory opinion 9.065 "Caring for the Poor," which further clarified the physician's obligation and emphasized each individual physician's duty to provide charity care: "Each physician has an obligation to share in providing care to the indigent." Id. For a public discussion, see Chapter 4.

65. Lubet and Stewart, "Public Assets Theory," 246.

66. Luban, Lawyers and Justice, 286.

67. Frankel, "Proposal," 890; In re. Amendments to Rules Regulating the Florida Bar—1-3.1(a) and Rules of Judicial Administration, 598 So.2d 41 (Florida 1992).

68. Arcia, "Objections, Administrative Difficulties," 791; Loder, "Tending the Generous Heart," 459; Silverman, "Conceiving a Lawyer's Legal Duty," 1048–56.

69. Shapiro, "Enigma," 788.

70. See Scully "Mandatory Pro Bono," 1264; Nitta, "Ethical Evaluation," 928; State ex. rel. Scott v. Roper, 688 S.W.2d 757, 768 (Missouri, 1985) (en banc).

71. See sources cited in Rhode, "Ethical Perspectives," 610; Eldred and Schoenherr, "Lawyer's Duty," 391 n. 97 (discussing references to "Big Brother" and the Soviet Union); Frankel, "Proposal," 890.

72. Esther F. Lardent, "Structuring Law Firm Pro Bono Programs: A Community Service Typology," in The Law Firm and the Public Good, 59, 83–84 (noting absence of research). See Millemann, "Mandatory Pro Bono," 64 (noting experience with Maryland bar).

73. David Luban, "Mandatory Pro Bono: A Workable (and Moral) Plan," 64 Michigan Bar Journal 280, 283 (1985).

74. Millemann, "Mandatory Pro Bono," 70.

75. See the discussion in Chapter 1.

76. ABA, Model Rules of Professional Conduct, Rule 1.2 (2003).

77. Carolyn Elefant, "Can Law Firms Do Pro Bono? A Skeptical View of Law Firms' Pro Bono Programs," 16 Journal of the Legal Profession 95, 102–3 (1991); Philip R. Lochner, "The No Fee and Low Fee Legal Practice of Private Attorneys," 9 Law and Society Review 448–55 (1975); Esther F. Lardent, "Pro Bono in the 1990s," in ABA, Civil Justice: An Agenda for the 1990s, 423, 434 (Esther F. Lardent, ed., 1989).

78. An example is the suit by the Legal Foundation of Washington opposing the use of funds from interest on lawyers' trust fund accounts to subsidize legal services. Brown v. Legal Foundation of Washington, 538 U.S. 216 (2003).

79. Esther F. Lardent, "Mandatory Pro Bono in Civil Cases: The Wrong Answer to the Right Question," 49 Maryland Law Review 78, 82 (1990).

80. Concerns about fairness to lawyers with lowest incomes surface in virtually all the debates about pro bono requirements. See Silverman, "Conceiving a Lawyer's Legal Duty," 1007–8; Marcus J. Cook, "Increasing Access to Justice: Expanding the Role of Nonlawyers in the Delivery of Legal Services to Low-Income Coloradans," 72 University of Colorado Law Review 459 (2001); Arcia, "Objections, Administrative Difficulties," 783; Lardent, "Mandatory Pro Bono," 82.

81. Lardent, "Mandatory Pro Bono," 82; Arcia, "Objections, Administrative Difficulties," 785; Silverman, "Conceiving a Lawyer's Legal Duty," 1007–11; Cook, "Increasing Access," 479.

82. Standing Committee on Pro Bono and Public Service of the American Bar Asso-

ciation, Testimony Before the Ethics 2000 Commission, February 10, 2000, available at http://www.abanet.org/cpr; Roger C. Cramton, "Mandatory Pro Bono," 19 Hofstra Law Review 1137 (1991); Frankel, "Proposal," 890; Lardent, "Mandatory Pro Bono," 99; Marcus J. Lock, "Increasing Access to Justice: Expanding the Role of Nonlawyers in the Delivery of Legal Services to Low-Income Coloradans," 72 University of Colorado Law Review 479 (2001).

83. Doreen D. Dodson, chair of the ABA Standing Committee on Legal Aid and Indigent Defendants, testimony before the Ethics 2000 Commission, available at http://www.abanet.org/cpr/dodson10.htm; Report of the Committee to Review the Criminal Justice Act, January 29, 1993, reprinted in 52 Criminal Law Reporter 2265, March 10, 1993.

84. Norm Spaulding, "The Prophet and the Bureaucrat," 50 Stanford Law Review 1395, 1419 (1998); Sharon Tisher, Lynne Bernabei, and Mark J. Green, Bringing the Bar to Justice, 132–35 (1977).

85. Lori Tripoli, "The Hypocritical Oath? Why Some Associates Opt Out of Pro Bono," Of Counsel, May 17, 1999, 1, 10, 11. See also Stuart A. Scheingold and Austin Sarat, Something to Believe In: Politics, Professionalism, and Cause Lawyering 79 (2004).

86. Cummings, "Politics of Pro Bono," 50; Dodson, testimony.

87. Dodson, testimony.

88. Lardent, "Mandatory Pro Bono," 83–84; Arcia, "Objections, Administrative Difficulties," 789–80.

89. Ted R. Marcus, "Letter to the Editor," California Lawyer, August 1993, 12. See also Cramton, "Mandatory Pro Bono," 1128; Luban, "Mandatory Pro Bono," 280.

90. Rhode, Access to Justice, 19–23, 90–91, 95–102, 112–21, 185–94; "Access to Justice: Does It Exist in Civil Cases, Symposium Transcript," Comments of Esther Lardent, 17 Georgetown Journal of Legal Ethics 455, 481 (2004).

91. Millemann, "Mandatory Pro Bono," 62.

92. John Greenya, "Partners in Justice: Mentoring in the Pro Bono Program," Washington Lawyer, May–June 1997, 26–28 (describing the mentoring program of the Law Firm Pro Bono Clinic of the D.C. Bar's Public Service Activities Corporation); Eileen J. Williams, "PSAC in Action," Washington Lawyer, May–June 1996, 36–38 (describing training provided for attorney and paralegal volunteers).

93. Deborah L. Rhode, "Pro Bono in Times of Crisis: Looking Forward by Looking Back," 31 Fordham Urban Law Journal 1011 (2004); Judith L. Maute and Linda Wofford Hill, "Delivery Systems Under Construction," 72 University of Missouri at Kansas City Law Review 377, 391 (2003).

94. Barbara Glesner Fines, "Almost Pro Bono: Judicial Appointments of Attorneys in Juvenile and Child Dependency Actions," 72 University of Missouri at Kansas City Law Review 337 (2003); Lardent, "Mandatory Pro Bono," 97; Silverman, "Conceiving a Lawyer's Legal Duty," 893; Nitta, "Ethical Evaluation," 934.

95. Fines, "Almost Pro Bono," 383.

96. See Luban, "Mandatory Pro Bono," 280–82; Marc Galanter and Thomas Palay, "Let Firms Buy and Sell Credit for Pro Bono," National Law Journal, September 6, 1993, 17.

97. MacDonald, "What Good Is Pro Bono," 21.

98. Rhode, Access to Justice 24, 26; Greg Pierce, "Nation: Inside Politics," Washington Times, February 28, 2003, A5.

99. Silver and Cross, "What's Not to Like," 1488.

100. Silver and Cross, "What's Not to Like," 1488.

101. Silver and Cross, "What's Not to Like," 1493.

102. Harvey Berkman, "Past Struggles Echo as Clinton Makes a Pitch for Pro Bono Work," National Law Journal, August 2, 1999, A8.

103. See David E. Rovella, "Can the Bar Fill the LSC's Shoes?," National Law Journal, August 5, 1996, A1; Corporate Pro Bono.org (noting that almost half of survey respondents who reported that their department did no pro bono work believed that employees had an interest in doing it).

104. Standing Committee on Pro Bono, testimony.

105. Kellie Isbell and Sarah Sawle, "Pro Bono Publico: Voluntary Service and Mandatory Reporting," 15 Georgetown Journal of Legal Ethics 845, 860–61 (2002); Talbot D'Alemberte, "Tributaries of Justice: The Search for Full Access," 25 Florida State University Law Review 642 (1998).

106. ABA Center for Pro Bono, Overview of State Pro Bono Reporting Policies, available at http://www.abanet.org/legalservices/probono/reporting.html.

107. The Standing Committee on Pro Bono Services Report to the Supreme Court of Florida, The Florida Bar, and the Florida Bar Foundation, available at http://www.flabar.org.

108. ABA Standing Committee on Pro Bono.

109. Standing Committee on Pro Bono Services Florida Report.

110. ABA Center for Pro Bono, Overview of State Pro Bono Reporting Policies (quoting opponents from Massachusetts, and describing objections from lawyers in New York).

111. ABA Center for Pro Bono, Overview of State Pro Bono Reporting Policies. Illinois has the lowest rate; Arkansas has the highest.

112. ABA Commission on Pro Bono and Public Service Opportunities in Law Schools, Learning to Serve: The Findings and Proposals of the AALS Commission on Pro Bono and Public Services Opportunities (1999), available at http://www.aals.org/probono/report.html, 3.

113. David Hall, "Raising the Bar: A Campaign to Transform the Legal Profession," 22 Journal of the Legal Profession 7, 10 (1998); Thomas J. Schoenherr, Thomas M. Quinn, and Roslyn Myers, "The Fordham Model: Student Initiated Projects for the Public Interest" (unpublished manuscript, Fordham Law School, 2000); Stephen F. Befort and Eric S. Janus, "The Role of Legal Education in Instilling an Ethic of Public Service Among Law Students: Towards a Collaboration Between the Profession and the Academy on Professional Values," 13 Law and Inequality: A Journal of Theory and Practice 1, 7 (1994).

114. John Kramer, "Mandatory Pro Bono at Tulane Law School," National Association for Public Interest Law, Connection Closeup Newsletter, September 30, 1991, 1–2.

115. Committee on Legal Assistance, "Mandatory Law School Pro Bono Programs: Preparing Students to Meet Their Ethical Obligations," 50 The Record 170, 176 (1995); AALS Focus Group Interviews (1998).

116. Surveys of Louisville and University of Pennsylvania alumni who had taken part in mandatory public service programs yielded too small a number of completed questionnaires to provide generalizable findings. Neither attempted to compare the work done by graduates who were subject to requirements and those who were not.

AALS Focus Group Interviews; Kimberly M. Allen, "The University of Pennsylvania Public Service Program, Alumni Survey" (University of Pennsylvania, unpublished paper, 1994).

117. Deborah Moranville, "Infusing Passion and Context into the Traditional Law Curriculum Through Experiential Learning," 51 Journal of Legal Education 51–74 (2001); Paula Lustbader, "Teach in Context," 48 Journal of Legal Education 402 (1998). For the value of experiential "service learning" generally, see sources cited in Chapters 3 and 4.

118. Dina R. Merrell, "Pro Bono, Pro You," Student Lawyer, March 2001, 39, 40; Law School Affinity Group, From the Classroom to the Community: Enhancing Legal Education Through Public Service and Service Learning 5 (1999); Howard S. Erlanger and Gabrielle Lessard, "Mobilizing Law Schools in Response to Poverty: A Report on Experiments in Progress," 43 Journal of Legal Education 199, 224 (1993); Barbara L. Bezdek, "Legal Theory and Practice Development at the University of Maryland," 42 Washington University Journal of Urban and Contemporary Law 127, 131 (1992); AALS Focus Group Interviews.

119. Kramer, "Mandatory Pro Bono"; see also Kirsten Edwards, "Found! The Lost Lawyer," 70 Fordham Law Review 37, 60 n. 87 (2001); Christina M. Rosas, "Mandatory Pro Bono Publico for Law Students: The Right Place to Start," 30 Hofstra Law Review 1069 (2002).

120. For discussion of the erosion of social justice commitments in law school, see Richard D. Kahlenberg, Broken Contract: A Memoir of Harvard Law School (1992); Robert Granfield, Making Elite Lawyers: Visions of Law at Harvard and Beyond (1992); Robert V. Stover, Making It and Breaking It: The Fate of Public Interest Commitment During Law School (Howard S. Erlanger, ed., 1989).

121. Law School Affinity Group, From the Classroom to the Community, 5; Erlanger and Lessard, "Mobilizing Law Schools," 224. For an argument that professional responsibility is best taught in settings involving direct client contact, see David Luban and Michael Millemann, "Good Judgment: Ethics Teaching in Dark Times," 9 Georgetown Journal of Legal Ethics 31 (1995).

122. Merrell, "Pro Bono, Pro You," 40; University of Denver College of Law, Proposal for a Public Service Requirement, exhibit D, 15 (2002).

123. AALS Focus Group Interviews. At Stanford, although over a majority of third-year students reported interest in pro bono opportunities, only half knew anything about their future employer's pro bono policies, and much of their information was inadequate. Eric J. Lassen, "Public Good, Private Practice: A Study of Pro Bono in American Law Firms" (unpublished paper, Stanford, California, May 1998).

124. AALS Commission, Learning to Serve, 5–6; Law School Affinity Group, From the Classroom to the Community, 3–4.

125. Denver College of Law, Proposal, appendix D, 25–27, appendix E, 4.

126. Reshmi Basu, "Pay It Forward," American Lawyer, April 2001, 22; Katherine S. Mangan, "Not Guilty After All," Chronicle of Higher Education, June 11, 2004, 26.

127. Francesco R. Barbera, "Yard Work: Harvard Law Revives Mandatory Pro Bono Debate," ABA Journal, May 2000, 26 (quoting Fried); "Fried Explains Reservations About Committee Plan," 71 Harvard Law Record, February 18, 2000, 2 (quoting Fried).

128. Mark Twain, The Wit and Wisdom of Mark Twain 66 (Alex Ayers, ed., 1987).

129. Luban, "Faculty Pro Bono," 71.

130. Luban, "Faculty Pro Bono," 71.

131. Luban, "Faculty Pro Bono," 71.

132. Denver College of Law, Proposal, 10; Lucy E. White, "Pro Bono or Partnership?: Rethinking Lawyers' Public Service Obligations for a New Millenium," 50 Journal of Legal Education, 134, 142–45 (2000).

133. White, "Pro Bono or Partnership?," 142.

134. White, "Pro Bono or Partnership?," 144–45.

135. Susan Bryant, "The Five Habits: Building Cross-Cultural Competence in Lawyers," 8 Clinical Law Review 33 (2001); White, "Pro Bono or Partnership?," 144–45.

136. White, "Pro Bono or Partnership?," 144.

137. White, "Pro Bono or Partnership?," 144–45; Michelle S. Jacobs, "Full Legal Representation for the Poor: The Clash Between Lawyer Values and Client Worthiness," 44 Howard Law Journal 257, 258–59 (2001).

138. Melissa Faye Greene, Praying for Sheetrock: A Work of Nonfiction 178 (1991).

139. White, "Pro Bono or Partnership?," 145.

140. Allen, "University of Pennsylvania Public Service Program," 3–4.

141. Allen, "University of Pennsylvania Public Service Program," 4.

142. Pamela DeFanti Robinson, "Insurmountable Opportunities or Innovative Choices: The Pro Bono Experience at the University of South Carolina School of Law," 42 University of South Carolina School of Law Review, 959, 969–70 (1991). See New York Committee to Improve the Availability of Legal Services, "Final Report," 118; Commission on the Future of the California Bar, The Future of the California Bar 67 (1995).

143. Alan M. Slobodin, "Forced Pro Bono for Law Students Is a Bad Idea," 1 Boston University Public Interest Law Journal 199, 201 (1991).

144. Kenneth Lee, "Where Legal Activists Come From," American Enterprise, June 2001, 50; Washington Legal Foundation, In Whose Interest? Public Interest Law Activism in the Law Schools 48–49 (1990); Slobodin, "Forced Pro Bono," 199, 202–3.

145. For example, see Susan J. Curry, "Meeting the Need: Minnesota's Collaborative Model to Deliver Law Student Public Service," 28 William Mitchell Law Review 347 (2001).

146. AALS Commission, Learning to Serve, 10.

147. See text accompanying note 112.

148. Ellen Chapnick, director, Columbia Law School Pro Bono Program, Panel Presentation, AALS Section on Pro Bono and Public Service, January 4, 2004; Columbia Law School Web site, Columbia's Pro Bono Requirement, available at http://www.law.columbia.edu/center-program/public-interest/probono; Harvard Law School Web site, Pro Bono Services Program, available at http://www.law.harvard.edu; correspondence between Susan Feathers, University of Pennsylvania Law School Pro Bono Program, and Maureen Stimming, Director of Career Services, Chicago-Kent College of Law, October 18, 2004 (noting that three-quarters of law students at the University of Pennsylvania Law School exceed the required number of hours).

149. Denver College of Law, Proposal, appendix E, 2.

150. Denver College of Law, Proposal, appendix E, 9.

151. AALS Focus Group Interviews.

152. AALS Focus Group Interviews; Millemann, "Mandatory Pro Bono," 76–77.

153. Chapnick, Panel Presentation.

154. Schoenherr, Quinn, and Myers, "Fordham Model." At Yale, almost 45% of students participate in public service through a student group. See Yale Law School Web site, Public Interest Activities, available at http://www.law.Yale.edu/outside/html/PI/Pi-activities.htm.

CHAPTER THREE

1. For my earlier, more abbreviated summary of the literature, see Deborah L. Rhode, "Cultures of Commitment: Pro Bono for Lawyers and Law Students," 67 Fordham Law Review 2415, 2426–33 (1999). For the only other recent treatment, see Reed Elizabeth Loder, "Mandatory Pro Bono and Moral Development," 14 Georgetown Journal of Legal Ethics 459 (2001).

2. For example, much of the best clinical work involves children or single discrete acts of helping behavior, and much of the field research involves rescue work or full-time public service. See sources cited in notes 39–41, 46, 56.   ·

3. Robert Friedrichs, "Alter Versus Ego: An Exploratory Assessment of Altruism," 25 American Sociological Review 496 (1960); Mark Richard Templeman, A Life History Study of Social, Psychological, and Structural Determinants of Extraordinary Altruistic Behavior 2 (unpublished dissertation, Purdue University, 1988).

4. Templeman, Life History, 2; Lauren Wispe, "Toward an Integration," in Altruism, Sympathy, and Helping: Psychological and Sociological Principles 303, 304–5 (Lauren Wispe, ed., 1978).

5. C. Daniel Batson, The Altruism Question: Toward a Social-Psychological Answer 6 (1991); Jacqueline R. Macaulay and Leonard Berkowitz, "Overview," in Altruism and Helping Behavior: Social Psychological Studies of Some Antecedents and Consequences 1, 2–3 (Jacqueline R. Macaulay and Leonard Berkowitz, eds., 1970); Thomas Nagel, The Possibility of Altruism 79 (1970); Nancy Eisenberg, introduction to The Development of Prosocial Behavior 1, 3–6 (Nancy Eisenberg, ed., 1982); Lawrence Blum, "Altruism," in 1 Encyclopedia of Ethics 35–39 (Lawrence C. Becker and Charlotte B. Becker, eds., 1992).

6. Wispe, "Toward an Integration," 305.

7. See sources cited in Batson, Altruism Question, 5; Robert B. Cialdini, Mark Schaller, Donald Houlihan, and Kevin Arps, "Empathy-Based Helping: Is It Selflessly or Selfishly Motivated?," 52 Journal of Personality and Social Psychology 749, 756 (April 1987); Loder, "Mandatory Pro Bono," 467. See generally Melvin J. Lerner, "The Justice Motive in Human Relations and the Economic Model of Man: A Radical Analysis of Fact and Fictions," in Cooperation and Helping Behavior (Valerian J. Derlega and Janusz Grzelak, eds., 1982), 249.

8. See Batson, Altruism Question, 3–4; Dennis C. Mueller, Public Choice 1–4 (1979); David Gauthier, Morals by Agreement 1–20 (1986).

9. Jon Elster, "Selfishness and Altruism," in Beyond Self-Interest 44–52 (Jane J. Mansbridge, ed., 1990).

10. See, e.g., Richard J. Bentley and Luana G. Nissan, Roots of Giving and Serving 9 (1996); Alfie Kohn, The Brighter Side of Human Nature: Altruism and Empathy in Everyday Life 244 (1990); Ram A. Cnaan and Robin S. Goldberg-Glen, "Measuring Motivation to Volunteer in Human Services," 27 Journal of Applied Behavioral Science 269, 275–79 (1991); Elster, "Selfishness and Altruism," 44, 51; Jane J. Mansbridge, "On the Re-

lation of Altruism and Self-Interest," in Mansbridge, Beyond Self-Interest 133, 133–34; Neera Kapur Badhwar, "Altruism Versus Self-Interest: Sometimes a False Dichotomy," in Altruism 90, 93 (Ellen Frankel Paul, Fred Miller Jr., and Jeffrey Paul, eds., 1993).

11. See, e.g., Bentley and Nissan, Roots of Giving, 9; Margaret S. Clark, editor's introduction to Prosocial Behavior 7 (1991); Eisenberg, Development of Prosocial Behavior 6; Wispe, Altruism, Sympathy, and Helping, xiii.

12. Bernard Williams, Morality: An Introduction to Ethics 66 (1972).

13. Mansbridge, "On the Relation of Altruism and Self-Interest," 133, 136–37.

14. Loder, "Mandatory Pro Bono," 468; Batson, Altruism Question, 59; Mansbridge, "On the Relation of Altruism and Self-Interest," 136–37.

15. Robert D. Putnam, "Bowling Alone: America's Declining Social Capital," 6 Journal of Democracy 65 (1993); Sidney Verba, Kay Lehman Schlozman, and Henry E. Brady, Voice and Equality: Civil Volunteerism in American Politics 352 (1995); John Wilson and Marc Musick, "The Effects of Volunteering on the Volunteer," 62 Law and Contemporary Problems 141, 142–43 (1999).

16. Robert Putnam and Lewis Feldstein, Better Together: Restoring the American Community (2003).

17. Points of Light Foundation, The Corporate Volunteer Program as a Strategic Resource: The Link Grows Stronger, Executive Summary, 1–2 (1999); Debra E. Blum, Companies Link Business, Volunteering, Chronicle of Philanthropy, November 4, 1999, 14.

18. See research summarized in Alan Luks with Peggy Payne, The Healing Power of Doing Good, xi–xii, 17–18, 45–54, 60 (2d ed. 2001); Wilson and Musick, "Effects of Volunteering," 150–59; Marc A. Musick, A. Regula Herzog, and James S. House, "Volunteering and Mortality Among Older Adults: Findings from a National Sample," 548 Journal of Gerontology S173, S178 (1999).

19. Robert D. Putnam, Bowling Alone: The Collapse and Revival of American Community 333 (2000); Luks with Payne, Healing Power, xi–xiii, 17–18, 118–19; John M. Darley, "Altruism and Prosocial Behavior Research: Reflections and Prospects," in Clark, Prosocial Behavior, 312–27.

20. Cnaan and Goldberg-Glen, "Measuring Motivation," 276–78; Francis Ostrower, Why the Wealthy Give: The Culture of Elite Philanthropy 13–14 (1995).

21. Luks with Payne, Healing Power, 17–18, 118–19, 233.

22. See sources cited in notes 18 and 19.

23. Luks with Payne, Healing Power, 47–55.

24. Wilson and Musick, "Effects of Volunteering," 154–56.

25. Independent Sector, Giving and Volunteering in the United States: Key Findings 18, 36–37 (2001).

26. Ben Wildavsky, "Mandatory Volunteerism: Is There Harm in Having to Do Good?," American Enterprise, September/October 1991, 64, 70. See generally Independent Sector, Giving and Volunteering.

27. Wildavsky, "Mandatory Volunteerism," 70.

28. Michael Arnft and Harry Lipman, "How Americans Give," Chronicle of Philanthropy, May 1, 2003, 6.

29. Phyllis Moen with William Erickson, Madhurima Agarwal, Vivian Fields, and Laurie Todd, The Cornell Retirement and Well-Being Study Final Report 17 (2000).

30. Albert R. Hunt, "Charitable Giving: Good but We Can Do Better," Wall Street

Journal, December 21, 2000, A19 (summarizing Federal Reserve Board findings that the wealthiest quintile of Americans donates less than half of 1% while the second poorest quintile contributes about 1.5%). But see Eleanor Brown, "The Scope of Volunteer Activity and Public Service," 62 Law and Contemporary Problems 17, 31 (1999).

31. Brown, "Scope of Volunteer Activity," 17–42.

32. Carrie Menkel-Meadow, "The Causes of Cause Lawyering: Toward an Understanding of the Motivation and Commitment of Social Justice Lawyers," in Cause Lawyering: Political Commitments and Professional Responsibilities 31, 38 (Austin Sarat and Stuart Scheingold, eds., 1998); Center on Philanthropy, Giving USA 2004 15 (2004); Independent Sector, Giving and Volunteering, 127; Amy Caiazza, "Women's Community Involvement: The Effects of Money, Safety, Parenthood, and Friends," Institute for Women's Policy Research, Research in Brief, September 2001, 1; Hunt, "Charitable Giving," A19.

33. See Chapter 1, text accompanying notes 95–98.

34. Arnft and Lipman, How Americans Give, 6.

35. Arnft and Lipman, How Americans Give, 6.

36. Arnft and Lipman, How Americans Give, 6.

37. See Chapter 1, text accompanying note 99.

38. Virginia A. Hodgkinson and Murray S. Weitzman, with Eric A. Crutchfield, Aaron J. Heffron, and Arthur D. Kirsch, Giving and Volunteering in the United States (1996).

39. Anne Colby and William Damon, Some Do Care: Contemporary Lives of Moral Commitment (1992); Samuel P. Oliner and Pearl M. Oliner, The Altruistic Personality: Rescuers of Jews in Nazi Europe 165–67, 173–75 (1988); Robert Coles, The Call of Service: A Witness to Idealism 91–94 (1993); Eva Fogelman, Conscience and Courage: Rescuers of Jews During the Holocaust 155–60 (1994); Bentley and Nissan, Roots of Giving, 9; David Rosenhan, "The Natural Socialization of Altruistic Autonomy," in Macaulay and Berkowitz, Altruism and Helping Behavior 251.

40. Kohn, Brighter Side, 85–97 (1990); William Damon, The Moral Child 116–20 (1988).

41. Joan E. Grusec, "The Socialization of Altruism," in Clark, Prosocial Behavior 9, 13.

42. Colby and Damon, Some Do Care, 123; Michael L. Gross, Ethics and Activism: The Theory and Practice of Political Morality 96, 129 (1997); Mansbridge, "On the Relation of Altruism and Self-Interest," 133–37; text accompanying notes 53–55.

43. Nancy Eisenberg, Altruistic Emotion, Cognition, and Behavior 30–56; Oliner and Oliner, Altruistic Personality, 113, 165–67, 173–75, 228; Martin L. Hoffman, "Empathy and Prosocial Activism," in Social and Moral Values: Individual and Societal Perspectives 65–85 (Nancy Eisenberg, Janusz Reykowski, and Ervin Staub, eds., 1989); Menkel-Meadow, "Causes of Cause Lawyering," 39.

44. Nancy Folbre, Invisible Heart: Economics and Family Values 29 (2001); Gross, Ethics and Activism 97, 128; Kohn, Brighter Side, 96–98; David Horton Smith, "Determinants of Voluntary Association Participation and Volunteering: A Literature Review," 23 Nonprofit and Voluntary Section Quarterly 243, 251–52 (1994).

45. David B. Wilkins, "Two Paths to the Mountaintop? The Role of Legal Education in Shaping the Values of Black Corporate Lawyers," 45 Stanford Law Review 1981, 1996–2002 (1993).

46. Gross, Ethics and Activism, 132.

47. For the "avalanche" of giving among the public generally, see Catalogue for Philanthropy, Generosity in 2001, at http://www.catalogueforphilanthropy/org/cfp/generosity_index/2003.php. For an overview of lawyers' motives and efforts, see Association of the Bar of the City of New York Fund, Inc., et al., Public Service in a Time of Crisis: A Report and Retrospective on the Legal Community's Response to the Events of September 11, 2001 (2004), reprinted in 31 Fordham Urban Law Journal 1011 (2004); Deborah L. Rhode, "Pro Bono in Times of Crisis: Looking Forward by Looking Back," 31 Fordham Urban Law Journal 1011 (2004); and the five-part series in the New York Law Journal beginning with Thomas Adcock, "After Sep. 11, Record Number of Lawyers Answer the Call to Take on Pro Bono," August 8, 2002, 1.

48. Cnaan and Goldberg-Glen, "Measuring Motivation," 278–79; Coles, Call of Service, 91; Gross, Ethics and Activism, 128–32; E. Gil Clary and Mark Snyder, "A Functional Analysis of Altruism and Prosocial Behavior: The Case of Volunteerism," in Clark, Prosocial Behavior, 119, 125–26. In Colby and Damon's study, four-fifths of the moral heroes they interviewed attributed their core values to religion. Colby and Damon, Some Do Care, 78, 276–79.

49. Jerzy Karylowski, "Two Types of Altruistic Behavior: Doing Good to Feel Good or to Make the Other Feel Good," in Derlega and Grzelak, Cooperation and Helping Behavior, 397, 410; Janusz Reykowski, "Motivation of Prosocial Behavior," in Derlega and Grzelak, Cooperation and Helping Behavior, 355, 358–63.

50. Colby and Damon, Some Do Care, 200.

51. Kohn, Brighter Side, 80.

52. Kohn, Brighter Side, 80.

53. Robert M. Axelrod, The Evolution of Cooperation 88–105 (1984); James Q. Wilson, The Moral Sense 40–44 (1993); Robert Wuthnow, Acts of Compassion: Caring for Others, and Helping Ourselves (1991); Edward O. Wilson, "The Genetic Evolution of Altruism," in Wispe, Altruism, Sympathy, and Helping 11, 11–12.

54. Charles J. Morgan, Natural Selection for Altruism in Structured Populations, Ethology, and Sociobiology 211, 215–17 (1985); Matt Ridley and Richard Parkins, "The Natural Selection of Altruism," in Macaulay and Berkowitz, Altruism and Helping Behavior 19, 24–31.

55. Ann Colby, Thomas Ehrlich, Elizabeth Beaumont, and Jason Stephens, Educating Citizens: Preparing America's Undergraduates for Lives of Moral and Civic Responsibility 140 (2003); Damon, Moral Child, 13; Grusec, "Socialization of Altruism," 9, 13; Abraham Sagi and Martin L. Hoffman, "Empathetic Distress in the Newborn," 12 Developmental Psychology 175 (1976); Clark, Prosocial Behavior, 13; Jane J. Mansbridge, "The Rise and Fall of Self-Interest in the Explanation of Political Life," in Mansbridge, Beyond Self-Interest, 3.

56. Grusec, "Socialization of Altruism"; Hodgkinson et al., Giving and Volunteering, 12–13.

57. Bentley and Nissan, Roots of Giving, 9; Kohn, Brighter Side, 71; Doug McAdam, Freedom Summer 200 (1988); Templeman, Life History, 49; Sumru Erkut, Inside Women's Power: Learning from Leaders 45 (2001).

58. Fogelman, Conscience and Courage 253–70 (1994); Hodgkinson et al., Giving and Volunteering, 12–13, 87–88; Brown, "Scope of Volunteer Activity," 27, 35; Rosenhan, "Natural Socialization," 260–63; E. Gil Clary and Jude Miller, "Socialization and Situational Influences on Sustained Altruism," 57 Child Development 1358, 1359, 1365–66 (1986).

59. Hodgkinson et al., Giving and Volunteering, 87; Jacqueline R. Macaulay, "A Shill for Charity," in Macaulay and Berkowitz, Altruism and Helping Behavior 43, 43–44; Leonard Berkowitz, "Social Norms, Feelings and Other Factors Affecting Helping and Altruism," in 6 Advances in Experimental Social Psychology 63, 68 (Leonard Berkowitz, ed., 1972).

60. Kohn, Brighter Side, 91; James H. Bryan, Joel Redfield, and Sandra Mader, "Words and Deeds About Altruism and the Subsequent Reinforcement Power of the Model," 42 Child Development 1501 (1971); Joan E. Grusec, "Socialization of Altruism," in Eisenberg, Development of Prosocial Behavior 139, 154.

61. Batson, Altruism Question, 224–27; Loder, "Mandatory Pro Bono," 481.

62. Gross, Ethics and Activism, 133–135; Bentley and Nissan, Roots of Giving, 33–36; Francie Ostrower, Why the Wealthy Give, 14–16, 33–38, 59, 133; Lori Verstegen Ryan and Mark A. Ciavarella, "Tapping the Source of Moral Approbation: The Moral Referent Group," 38 Journal of Business Ethics 179 (2002); Mansbridge, "On the Relation of Altruism and Self-Interest," 136.

63. See sources cited in notes 65–69; Kohn, Brighter Side, 210; Templeman, Life History, 51–52; Bentley and Nissan, Roots of Giving, 10.

64. Fogelman, Conscience and Courage, 193, 273–98; Menkel-Meadow, "Causes of Cause Lawyering," 40.

65. Robert B. Cialdini, Influence: Science and Practice (2001).

66. Robert Kuttner, Everything for Sale (1997), quoted in Folbre, Invisible Heart, xi.

67. Over a hundred studies have analyzed this effect since the classic study by Bibb Latane and John M. Darley, The Unresponsive Bystander: Why Doesn't He Help? 38, 41, 90 (1970). See Kohn, Brighter Side, 68.

68. Henry Kaufman, "Legality and Harmfulness of a Bystander's Failure to Intervene as Determinants of Moral Judgment," in Macaulay and Berkowitz, Altruism and Helping Behavior, 77, 81.

69. Ostrower, Why the Wealthy Give, 25, 36–38, 133; Bentley and Nissan, Roots of Giving, 10. See the discussion of lawyers' motives for service in Chapters 2 and 6.

70. E. Gil Clary and Mark Snyder, "Functional Analysis," 119, 125; Smith, "Determinants of Voluntary Association," 251–52; Coles, Call of Service, 93–94; Menkel-Meadow, "Causes of Cause Lawyering," 59 n. 57.

71. See generally Mansbridge, "On the Relation of Altruism and Self-Interest," 137.

72. Bentley and Nissan, Roots of Giving and Serving, 8–9; Smith, "Determinants of Voluntary Association," 251; Nancy Eisenberg, Altruistic Emotion, Cognition, and Behavior, 207; Pearl M. Oliner, "Legitimating and Implementing Prosocial Education," 13 Humboldt Journal of Social Relations 391 (1985–86).

73. Independent Sector, Giving and Volunteering 44, 67; Bentley and Nissan, Roots of Giving, 8–9; Smith, "Determinants of Voluntary Association," 251; Hodgkinson et al., Giving and Volunteering, 109–10; Oliner and Oliner, Altruistic Personality, 135–36.

74. Kohn, Brighter Side, 71; Hoffman, "Empathy and Prosocial Activism," 82; Reykowski, "Motivation of Prosocial Behavior," 358–63.

75. Arthur Koestler, "On Disbelieving Atrocities," in The Yogi and the Commissar 88 (1945).

76. Kohn, Brighter Side, 202–3; Joan E. Grusec and Theodore Dix, "The Socialization of Prosocial Behavior: Theory and Reality," in Altruism and Aggression: Biological and

Social Origins 218, 219–21 (Carolyn Zahn-Waxler, E. Mark Cummings, and Ronald Iannotti, eds., 1986); Joan E. Grusec and Erica W. Redler, "Attribution, Reinforcement, and Altruism: A Developmental Analysis," 16 Developmental Psychology 525, 526–29 (1980); Clary and Miller, "Socialization," 1367; Richard A. Fabes, Jim Fultz, Nancy Eisenberg, Traci May Plumlee, and F. Scott Christopher, "Effects of Rewards on Children's Prosocial Motivation: A Socialization Study," 25 Developmental Psychology 509 (1989).

77. See sources cited in Kohn, Brighter Side, 92; Grusec and Redler, "Attribution," 526–29; Loder, "Mandatory Pro Bono," 472–73; Marc R. Lepper, David Greene, and Richard E. Nisbett, "Undermining Children's Interest with Extrinsic Reward: A Test of the 'Overjustification' Hypothesis," 28 Journal of Personality and Social Psychology 129 (1973); C. Daniel Batson, Jay S. Coke, M. L. Jasnoski, and Michael Hanson, "Buying Kindness: Effect of Extrinsic Incentive for Helping on Perceived Altruism," 4 Personality and Social Psychology Bulletin 86, 90 (1978). See also Richard M. Titmus, The Gift Relationship: From Human Blood to Social Policy (1971) (offering payment for giving blood reduces unpaid donations); Carol M. Werner and Natasha McVaugh, "Service-Learning 'Rules' That Encourage or Discourage Long-Term Service: Implications for Practice and Research," 7 Michigan Journal of Community Service Learning 117, 118–20 (Fall 2000).

78. See sources cited in Loder, "Mandatory Pro Bono," 474; and Mark Sobus, "Mandating Community Service: Psychological Implications of Requiring Prosocial Behavior," 19 Law and Psychology Review 153, 163–65 (1995).

79. Rosenhan, "Natural Socialization," 263–67.

80. Loder, "Mandatory Pro Bono," 473; William D. Crano, Daniel W. Gorenflo, and Susan L. Shackelford, "Overjustification, Assumed Consensus, and Attitude Change: Further Investigation of the Incentive-Aroused Ambivalence Hypothesis," 55 Journal of Personality and Social Psychology 12, 12–13, 20 (1988).

81. Crano et al., "Overjustification," 12–13, 20; Sobus, "Mandating Community Service," 177.

82. The first and most influential report was the National Commission on Youth, The Transition of Youth to Adulthood: A Bridge Too Long—A Report to Educators, Sociologists, Legislators, and Youth Policymaking Bodies (1980). For an overview, see Charles C. Moskos, A Call to Civic Service (1988); Gregory B. Markus, Jeffrey P. F. Howard, and David C. King, "Integrating Community Service and Classroom Instruction Enhances Learning: Results from an Experiment," 15 Education, Evaluation, and Policy Analysis 410–11 (1993); Marilyn W. Smith, "Community Service Learning: Striking the Chord of Citizenship," 1 Michigan Journal of Community Service Learning 37–43 (Fall 1994). For the intellectual foundations of community-based experiential learning, see John Dewey, Experience and Education (1938); Thomas Deans, "Service-Learning in Two Keys: Paulo Freire's Critical Pedagogy in Relation to John Dewey's Pragmatism," 6 Michigan Journal of Community Service Learning 15 (Fall 1999).

83. Colby et al., Educating Citizens, 7–19; Putnam, Bowling Alone.

84. 42 U.S.C. §12501 et seq (2004).

85. About 12% of work-study funding goes to "serve-study" programs. Joshua Green, "The Other College Rankings," Washington Monthly, January/February 2002, 11.

86. Markus, Howard, and King, "Integrating Community Service," 411. For the number of schools with required or voluntary programs see Brown, "Scope of Volunteer Activity," 29.

87. Sharon Jayson, "Building on Volunteerism," USA Today, December 9, 2004, 10D; Linda J. Sax, "Citizenship Development and the American College Student," in Civic Responsibility and Higher Education 3 (Thomas Ehrlich, ed., 2000). See generally Campus Compact, 2003 Service Statistics, Web site of the National Campus Compact, available at http://www.compact.org.

88. Colby et al., Educating Citizens, 134–35. Some commentators distinguish between *community service learning* and *community service volunteering.* The former term refers to service that is directly integrated into students' course work. The latter term refers to volunteer activity that is not part of the formal curriculum. See Daniel F. Perkins and Joyce Miller, "Why Community Service and Service-Learning? Providing Rationale and Research," Democracy and Education, Fall 1994, 11. For definitions, see generally 45 C.F.R. §2510.20 (2003) (defining community service); and Jeremy Cohen, "Matching University Mission with Service Motivation: Do the Accomplishments of Community Service Match the Claims?," 1 Michigan Journal of Community Service Learning 98, 100–2 (Fall 1994) (defining service learning).

89. Thomas Ehrlich, "Civic and Moral Learning," About Campus, September/October 1999, 6, 7. See also Diane P. Hedin, "The Power of Community Service," in "Caring for America's Children," 37 Academy of Political Science 201 (Frank J. Macchiarola and Alan Gartner, eds., 1989).

90. Colby et al., Educating Citizens, 14.

91. Loder, "Mandatory Pro Bono," 466, 481; Batson, Altruism Question, 18–19, 22–23, 25, 26–27, 35–36.

92. Stephen D. Papamarcos, "The 'Next Wave' in Service-Learning: Integrative, Team-Based Engagements with Structural Objectives," 23 Review of Business 31, 37 (2002).

93. Ehrlich, "Civic and Moral Learning," 7; see also Dennis D. Hirsh and Suzanne Goldsmith, "Community Service Builds Citizenship," National Law Journal, February 5, 1996, A19; Benjamin P. Barber, An Aristocracy of Everyone: The Politics of Education and the Future of America, 250–56 (1992).

94. Lori J. Vogelgesang and Alexander W. Astin, "Comparing the Effects of Community Service and Service-Learning," 7 Michigan Journal of Community Service and Service Learning 25–34 (Fall 2000); Susan Hayes Godar, "Live Cases: Service Learning Consulting Projects in Business Courses," 7 Michigan Journal of Community Service Learning 126–32 (Fall 2000).

95. Colby et al., Educating Citizens, 137–38; D. Neuman, P. Griffin, and M. Cole, The Construction Zone: Working for Cognitive Change in School (1989).

96. Colby et al., Educating Citizens, 138.

97. Lori J. Vogelgesang, "Diversity Work and Service Learning: Understanding Campus Dynamics," 11 Michigan Journal of Community Service Learning 34 (Spring 2004); Colby et al., Educating Citizens, 226.

98. See Jeremy Leeds, "Rationales for Service Learning: A Critical Examination," 6 Michigan Journal of Community Service Learning 112, 113 (Fall 1999); Ira Harkavy, "1994 as a Turning Point: The University-Assisted Community School Idea Becomes a Movement," 4 University and Community Schools 5 (1994); Cohen, "Matching University Mission," 102.

99. Markus, Howard, and King, "Integrating Community Service," 411; D. Conrad

and Diane P. Hedin, "School Based Community Service: What We Know from Research and Theory," Phi Delta Kappan 743, 747 (1991).

100. Wildavsky, "Mandatory Altruism," 70; Markus, Howard, and King, "Integrating Community Service," 411 (quoting Maryland School Board Vice President Jack Sprague); Vogelgesang and Astin, "Comparing the Effects," 25–34.

101. See Chester E. Finn Jr. and Gregg Vanourek, "Charity Begins at School," 100 Commentary 46, 48 (1995).

102. Leeds, "Rationales for Service Learning," 119.

103. Stanley Fish, "Why We Built the Ivory Tower," New York Times, May 21, 2004, A23.

104. Diane P. Hedin, "Power of Community Service," 37 Proceedings of the Academy of Political Science 201, 207 (1989); Werner and McVaugh, "Service-Learning,"120.

105. Wildavsky, "Mandatory Volunteerism," 69.

106. Leeds, "Rationales for Service Learning," 114 (quoting Ira Harkavey).

107. Harry C. Boyte, "Turning Youth on to Politics," Nation, May 13, 1991, 626–27; Robert C. Serow, "Students and Volunteering: Looking into the Motives of Community Service Participants," 28 American Education Research Journal 543, 555–56 (1991).

108. Anne Colby and Thomas Ehrlich, "Higher Education and the Development of Civic Responsibility," in Ehrlich, Civic Responsibility and Higher Education, xxi–xliii; Leeds, "Rationales for Service Learning," 119; Brown, "Scope of Volunteer Activity," 32; Markus, Howard, and King, "Integrating Community Service," 411; Janet Eyler and Dwight Gyles Jr., Where's the Learning in Service-Learning? (1999).

109. Vogelgesang and Astin, "Comparing the Effects," 30.

110. Vogelgesang and Astin, "Comparing the Effects," 30–31.

111. Hedin, "Power of Community Service," 207; Markus, Howard, and King, "Integrating Community Service," 413, 417; Cohen, "Matching University Mission," 100–101; Alexander W. W. Astin and Linda J. Sax, "How Undergraduates Are Affected by Service Participation," 39 Journal of College Student Development 251, 257–59 (1998); Colette Dumas, "Community-Based Service Learning: Does It Have a Role in Management Education?," 15 International Journal of Value-Based Management 249 (2002); Dasaratha V. Rama, Sue P. Ravenscroft, Susan K. Wolcott, and Edward Zlotkowski, "Service Learning Outcomes: Guidelines for Educators and Researchers," 15 Issues in Accounting Education 657, 669–72 (2000).

112. Astin and Sax, "How Undergraduates Are Affected," 257–61; Eyler and Giles, Where's the Learning.

113. Astin and Sax, "How Undergraduates Are Affected," 261 (noting small differences); Colby et al., Educating Citizens 114 (noting research where benefits disappear within five years); Leeds, "Rationales for Service Learning," 119 (noting absence of data on sustained benefits).

114. Arthur A. Stukas, Mark Snyder, and E. Gil Clary, "The Effects of 'Mandatory Volunteerism' on Intentions to Volunteer," 10 Psychological Science 59, 63 (1999).

115. Alexander W. Astin, Linda J. Sax, and Juan Avalos, "Long Term Effects of Volunteerism During the Undergraduate Years," 22 Review of Higher Education 187 (1999).

116. Frederick Rudolph, The American College and University 58 (1990); Ernest Boyer, Scholarship Reconsidered: Priorities of the Professoriate 3–5 (1990).

117. John B. Bennett, Collegial Professionalism: The Academy, Individualism, and the Common Good (1998); Donald Kennedy, Academic Duty (2000).

118. Werner and McVaugh, "Service-Learning," 117; Sobus, "Mandating Community Service," 181; Carol A. Marchel, "The Path to Altruism in Service-Learning Cases: Big Steps or a Different Kind of Awkwardness?," 10 Michigan Journal of Service Learning 15 (Fall 2003).

119. Werner and McVaugh, "Service-Learning," 117; Diana I. Cordova and Mark R. Lepper, "Intrinsic Motivation and the Process of Learning: Beneficial Effects of Contextualization, Personalization, and Choice," 88 Journal of Educational Psychology 713 (1996).

120. Sobus, "Mandating Community Service," 181.

121. Colby et al., Educating Citizens, 256.

Chapter Four

1. Rodney R. Porter, "Religion and Medicine," in Encyclopedia of the History of Medicine 1453 (W. F. Bynum and Rodney R. Porter, eds., 1993).

2. John Bell and Isaac Hays, "American Medical Association Code of Medical Ethics" (1847), in The American Medical Ethics Revolution: How the AMA's Code of Ethics Has Transformed Physicians' Relationships to Patients, Professionals and Society 334 (Robert B. Baker, Arthur L. Caplan, Linda L. Emanuel, and Stephen R. Lathan, eds., 1999).

3. Kenneth M. Ludmerer, Time to Heal: American Medical Education from the Turn of the Century to the Era of Managed Care 119 (1999).

4. American Medical Association (AMA), Council on Ethical and Judicial Affairs (CEJA), "Caring for the Poor," 269 Journal of the American Medical Association (JAMA) 2533 (May 19, 1993); Steven A. Schroeder, Jane S. Zones, and Jonathan A. Showstack, "Academic Medicine as a Public Trust," 262 JAMA 803 (August 11, 1989).

5. Ludmerer, Time to Heal, 23.

6. Ludmerer, Time to Heal, 118–19.

7. Ludmerer, Time to Heal, 119.

8. John E. Deitrick and Robert C. Berson, Medical Schools in the United States at Mid-Century 61–62 (1953).

9. Richard Kronick, "Valuing Charity," 26 Journal of Health Politics, Policy and Law 993, 995–96 (October 2001).

10. Schroeder et al., "Academic Medicine," 805.

11. Kronick, "Valuing Charity," 994–95.

12. AMA, CEJA, "Caring for the Poor," 2534; Kronick, "Valuing Charity," 996; Ludmerer, Time to Heal, 227.

13. Kronick, "Valuing Charity," 998.

14. Kronick, "Valuing Charity," 999.

15. Tanya Albert, Joel B. Finkelstein, and Markian Hawryluk, "Unfinished Business: Congressional Agenda 2004," American Medical News (February 2, 2004), available at http://www.ama-assn.org/amednews/2004/02/02/gvsa0202.htm. See also Ludmerer, Time to Heal, 227.

16. Arthur L. Caplan, "Medical Ethics: Code of Medical Ethics: Current Opinions with Annotations," 273 JAMA 1232 (April 15, 1995).

17. AMA, Code of Medical Ethics xiv (2000).

18. Robert Baker, Arthur Caplan, Linda Emanuel, and Stephen R. Latham, "Crisis,

Ethics, and the American Medical Association: 1847–1997," 278 JAMA 163–64 (July 9, 1997).

19. Lewis D. Solomon and Tricia Asaro, "Community-Based Health Care: A Legal and Policy Analysis," 24 Fordham Urban Law Journal 235, 277 (Winter 1997).

20. AMA, CEJA, "Fundamental Elements of the Patient-Physician Relationship," 264 JAMA 3133 (1990), available at AMA's Web site, http://www.ama-assn.org/ama/pub/category/2510.html.

21. AMA, CEJA, "Fundamental Elements."

22. AMA, CEJA, Advisory Opinion 9.0065 (1994).

23. AMA, CEJA, Advisory Opinion 9.0065.

24. Carol K. Kane, "Physician Provision of Charity Care, 1998–1999," AMA Physician Marketplace Report 1–2 (April 2002).

25. Peter J. Cunningham, "Mounting Pressures: Physicians Serving Medicaid Patients and the Uninsured, 1997–2001," Center for Studying Health System Change Tracking Report No. 6 (December 2002).

26. The CTS study excluded radiologists, anesthesiologists, and pathologists, whereas the AMA study did not. Peter J. Cunningham, Joy M. Grossman, Robert F. St. Peter, and Cara S. Lesser, "Managed Care and Physician's Provision of Charity Care," 281 JAMA 1088 (March 24, 1999).

27. Solomon and Asaro, "Community-Based Health Care," 277.

28. Marie C. Reed, Peter J. Cunningham, and Jeffrey J. Stoddard, "Physicians Pulling Back from Charity Care," Center for Studying Health System Change Issue Brief No. 42, 1 (August 2001).

29. Lynne D. Richardson and Ula Hwang, "America's Health Care Safety Net: Intact or Unraveling?" 8 Academic Emergency Medicine 1056, 1057 (November 2001).

30. See Gerry Fairbrother, Michael K. Gusmano, Heidi L. Park, and Roberta Scheinmann, "Care for the Uninsured in General Internists' Private Offices," 22 Health Affairs 217 (2003). See Michael K. Gusmano, Gerry Fairbrother, and Heidi Park, "Exploring the Limits of the Safety Net: Community Health Centers and Care for the Uninsured," 21 Health Affairs 188 (2002); Joel S. Weissman, Ernest Moy, Eric G. Campbell, Manjusha Gokhale, Recai Yucel, Nancyanne Causino, and David Blumenthal, "Limits to the Safety Net: Teaching Hospital Faculty Report on their Patients' Access to Care," 22 Health Affairs 156 (2003).

31. Weissman et al., "Limits to the Safety Net," 157.

32. Gusmano et al., "Exploring the Limits," 192.

33. Weissman et al., "Limits to the Safety Net," 159.

34. Weissman et al., "Limits to the Safety Net," 163.

35. Weissman et al., "Limits to the Safety Net," 163.

36. Weissman et al., "Limits to the Safety Net," 163.

37. Fairbrother et al., "Care for the Uninsured," 223.

38. Cunningham et al., "Managed Care," 1090.

39. Cunningham et al., "Managed Care," 1090.

40. Diane Coucoulus Calleson, Sarena D. Seifer, and Cheryl Maurana, "Forces Affecting Community Involvement of AHCs: Perspectives of Institutional and Faculty Leaders," 77 Academic Medicine 72, 75 (2002).

41. Calleson, Seifer, and Maurana, "Forces Affecting Community Involvement," 79.

42. Calleson, Seifer, and Maurana, "Forces Affecting Community Involvement," 78.

43. Cunningham et al., "Managed Care," 1087. For examples, see Jonathan Cohn, "Uncharitable," New York Times Magazine, December 19, 2004, 53–54.

44. Andrew B. Bindman, Kevin Grumbach, Karen Vranizan, Deborah Jaffee, and Dennis Osmond, "Selection and Exclusion of Primary Care Physicians by Managed Care Organizations," 279 JAMA 675, 675–79 (1998).

45. Cunningham et al., "Managed Care," 1089.

46. Fairbrother et al., "Care for the Uninsured," 223.

47. Edward H. O'Neil, "The Changing Health-Care System and Expectations of Physicians," in Creating Community-Responsive Physicians: Concepts and Models for Service Learning in Medical Education 9, 12 (Sarena D. Seifer, ed., 2000).

48. O'Neil, "Changing Health-Care System," 11.

49. Cunningham et al., "Managed Care," 1090.

50. Fairbrother et al., "Care for the Uninsured," 223.

51. Sarena D. Seifer, Kris Hermanns, and Judy Lewis, introduction to Seifer, Creating Community-Responsive Physicians, 1, 2.

52. Seifer, Hermanns, and Lewis, introduction, 3.

53. Sherril B. Gelmon, Barbara Holland, Beth Morris, and Amy Driscoll, "Evaluating the Impact of Service Learning: Applications for Medical Education," in Seifer, Creating Community-Responsive Physicians 139.

54. The Foundations are the Pew Charitable Trusts, the Robert Wood Johnson Foundation, and the W. K. Kellogg Foundation. Carrie L. Switzer, Service Learning in a Medical School: Psychosocial and Attitudinal Outcomes, 11 (unpublished dissertation, University of Pittsburgh, 1999).

55. Switzer, Service Learning, 2.

56. AMA Web site, available at http://www.ama-assn.org/ama/pub/category/11893. html.

57. See Seifer, Creating Community-Responsive Physicians, for articles on service learning projects at the following medical schools: Dartmouth University, Wright State University, University of Florida, Morehouse School of Medicine, Ohio State University, University of Connecticut, East Tennessee State University, University of Pittsburgh, and the University of Washington.

58. JoEllen Tarallo-Falk, "The Socialization of Medical Students in a Preventative Health Service-Learning Experience," in Seifer, Creating Community-Responsive Physicians 131.

59. Joseph F. Walsh, Jennifer Sage Smith, G. Christian Jernstedt, Virginia A. Reed, and Sara Goodman, "Partners in Health Education: Service-Learning by First-Year Medical Students," in Seifer, Creating Community-Responsive Physicians 35.

60. Gelmon et al., "Evaluating the Impact," 139, 150.

61. Gelmon et al., "Evaluating the Impact," 150.

62. Stephen F. Johnston, J. Paul Gostelow, and W. Joseph King, Engineering and Society: Challenges of Professional Practice 552 (2000).

63. American Society of Civil Engineers (ASCE), Ethics: Standards of Professional Conduct 10 (April 3, 2000).

64. ASCE, Ethics: Standards of Professional Conduct 10 (April 3, 2000).

65. Stephen H. Unger, "Codes of Engineering Ethics," in Ethical Issues in Engineering 105, 121 (Deborah G. Johnson, ed., 1991).

66. Unger, "Codes of Engineering Ethics," 105, 121.

67. Unger, "Codes of Engineering Ethics," 105, 121.

68. Unger, "Codes of Engineering Ethics," 121.

69. Unger, "Codes of Engineering Ethics," 122.

70. Engineering organizations with such provisions include: World Federation of Engineering Organizations (WFEO), National Society of Professional Engineers (NSPE), Institute of Electrical and Electronic Engineers (IEEE), American Society of Civil Engineers (ASCE), American Society of Mechanical Engineers (ASME), and American Institute of Chemical Engineers (AIChE).

71. National Society of Professional Engineers (NSPE) Code of Ethics for Engineers, section II (2)(a); Michael S. Pritchard, "Service Learning and Engineering Ethics," Online Ethics Center for Engineering and Science at Case Western Reserve University, available at http://onlineethics.org/essays/education/pritchard.html.

72. ASCE Standards of Professional Conduct, Canon 1(e).

73. NSPE 2003–2005 Strategic Plan, available at http://www.nspe.org/aboutnspe/ab1-plan.asp.

74. ASCE Public Service Award, available at http://www.asce.org/files/pdf/professional/cvcspubserviceaward.pdf.

75. ASCE Community Service, available at http://www.asce.org/professional/commservice.

76. NSPE 2003–2005 Strategic Plan.

77. NSPE 2003–2005 Strategic Plan.

78. The following engineering ethics textbooks were evaluated. Those that made reference to community service have the percentage of pages covering the topic noted in parentheses. Most texts include no reference. Alistair S. Gunn et al., Hold Paramount: The Engineer's Responsibility to Society (2003); Charles E. Harris et al., Engineering Ethics: Concepts and Cases (2000) (2%); Mike W. Martin and Roland Schinzinger, Introduction to Engineering Ethics (2000); Charles Fleddermann, Engineering Ethics (1999); Kenneth K. Humphreys, What Every Engineer Should Know About Ethics (1999); Caroline Whitbeck, Ethics in Engineering Practice and Research (1998); Michael Davis, Thinking Like an Engineer: Studies in the Ethics of a Profession (1998); Michael S. Pritchard et al., Practicing Engineering Ethics (1997); Mike W. Martin and Roland Schinzinger, Ethics in Engineering (1996) (1%); Eugene S. Schlossberger, The Ethical Engineer (1993); Deborah G. Johnson, Ethical Issues in Engineering (1991) (0.4%).

79. Martin and Schinzinger, Introduction to Engineering Ethics, 382.

80. Martin and Schinzinger, Introduction to Engineering Ethics, 381.

81. Johnston et al., Engineering and Society, 544.

82. Edmund Tsang, James Van Haneghan, Burke Johnson, E. Jean Newman, and Sandy Van Eck, "A Report on Service-Learning and Engineering Design: Service-Learning's Effect on Students Learning Engineering Design in 'Introduction to Mechanical Engineering,'" 17 International Journal of Engineering Education 30, 31 (2001).

83. See EPICS National Web site, available at http://epicsnational.ecn.purdue.edu/. See also Marydell Forbes, "Service-Learning Projects Expand at Purdue" (February 23, 2004), available at https://engineering.purdue.edu/EAA/article.php?story=20040223094426502&mode=print.

84. EYES (Encourage Young Engineering Students) Mission Statement, available at http://www.psc.cornell.edu/eyes-about.htm.

85. ABET Engineering Accreditation Commission, "Criteria for Accrediting Engineering Programs: Effective for Evaluations During the 2004–2005 Accreditation Cycle," available at http://www.abet.org/criteria.html.

86. William Oakes, John Duffy, Thomas Jacobius, Panos Linos, Susan Lord, William W. Schultz, and Amy Smith, "Service-Learning in Engineering," in Proceedings, ASEE/IEEE Frontiers in Education Conference F3A-1 (November 6–9, 2002, Boston, MA).

87. Oakes et al., "Service-Learning in Engineering," F3A-l.

88. See MIT Service Learning Classes and Seminars, Upcoming and Previous Courses, available at http://web.mit.edu/mitpsc/servlearn/students/classes.shtml, and at http://web.mit.edu/mitpsc/servlearn/students/pastclasses.shtml.

89. MIT Service Learning Classes.

90. Tsang et al., "Report on Service-Learning," 30.

91. ABET Accreditation Engineering Commission, "Criteria for Accrediting Engineering Programs."

92. José L. Cruz-Rivera, "Community Service Learning and K–12 Training and Enhancement: Creating a New Type of Engineer," in Proceedings, ASEE/IEEE Frontiers in Education Conference 12b9-3 (November 10–13, 1999, San Juan, Puerto Rico).

93. Cruz-Rivera, "Community Service Learning," 12b9-3.

94. Susan M. Lord, "Service-Learning in Introduction to Engineering at the University of San Diego: First Lessons, Proceedings ASEE/IEEE Frontiers in Education Conference 13b6-20 (November 10–13, 1999, San Juan, Puerto Rico).

95. Rosalyn S. Hobson, "The Changing Face of Classroom Instructional Methods: Service Learning and Design in a Robotics Course," in Proceedings, ASEE/IEEE Frontiers in Education Conference F3C-20 (October 18–21, 2000, Kansas City, MO).

96. Hobson, "Changing Face," 13b6-18; and Oakes et al., "Service-Learning in Engineering," F3A-1.

97. Cruz-Rivera, "Community Service Learning," 12b9-3.

98. Lord, "Service-Learning," 13b6-17.

99. Cruz-Rivera, "Community Service Learning," 12b9-3.

100. Lord, "Service-Learning," 13b6-20.

101. Tsang et al., "Report on Service-Learning," 36.

102. Tsang, "Use Assessment to Develop Service-Learning Reflection Course Materials," in Proceedings ASEE/IEEE Frontiers in Education Conference F2A-15 (November 6–9, 2002, Boston, MA); Lord, "Service-Learning," 1366–20.

103. David N. Rocheleau, "Habitat for Humanity Freshman Design and Build Experience," in Proceedings, ASEE/IEEE Frontiers in Education Conference T4G (1998).

104. John W. Martin and Mohammed E. Haque, "Service Learning Engineering Construction Science, and the Experiential Curriculum," in Proceedings, ASEE/IEEE Frontiers in Education Conference F3E-7 (October 10–13, 2001, Reno, NV).

105. Mark Sharfman, "Changing Institutional Roles: The Evolution of Corporate Philanthropy," 3 Business and Society 236 (1994).

106. Daniel A. Wren, "American Business Philanthropy and Higher Education in the Nineteenth Century," 57 Business History Review 321 (1983); Hutton v. West Cork Railway Co., 23 Law Reports 654 (Chancery Division, 1883).

107. Compare Steinway v. Steinway & Sons, 40 N.Y. Supp. 718 (1896) with Brinson Railroad v. Exchange Bank, 85 S.E. 634 (Ga. App. 1915).

108. Robert Hamilton Bremner, American Philanthropy 108 (1988); Washington Gladden, "Tainted Money," 52 Outlook 886 (1896).

109. Bremner, American Philanthropy, 117; Sharfman, "Changing Institutional Roles," 244.

110. Frank Emerson Andrews, Corporation Giving 30 (1952) (quoting Hughes).

111. Morrell Heald, The Social Responsibilities of Business, Company and Community 1900–1960 93 (1970).

112. Sharfman, "Changing Institutional Roles," 244–48. For examples, see Victor Brudney and Allen Ferrell, "Corporate Charitable Giving," 69 Chicago Law Review 1191 (2002).

113. A. P. Smith Manufacturing Company v. Barrow, 98 A.2d. 581, 586 (1953), appeal dismissed; 346 U.S. 861 (1953).

114. Peter S. Cohan, Value Leadership 238–39 (2003); Roper Starch Worldwide and Cone/Coughlin Communications, The Cone/Roper Study: A Benchmark Survey of Consumer Awareness and Attitudes Toward Cause-Related Marketing (1994); "PR Firms Find Value in Philanthropy," 52 Public Relations News 1 (1996).

115. Sharfman, "Changing Institutional Roles," 247.

116. Paul Ostergard, "Should Corporations Be Praised for Their Philanthropic Efforts? Yes: A Golden Age," 38 Across the Board (Conference Board, May–June 2001); Conference Board, Corporate Contributions: The View from 50 Years (2000).

117. Ostergard, "Should Corporations Be Praised," 44–45; Best Practices in Workplace Volunteering, Points of Light Foundation, available at http://www.pointsoflight.org/organizations/workplace_vol.cfm.

118. Corporate Employee Volunteering, Points of Light Foundation, available at http://www.pointsoflight.org/organizations/workplace_vol.cfm; Conference Board, Corporate Volunteer Programs: Benefits to Business 9, 11 (Report No. 1029, 1993); Shari Caudron, "Vounteerism and the Bottom Line," Industry Week, February 1994, 13–18; Craig Smith, "The New Corporate Philanthropy," 72 Harvard Business Review, May–June 1994, 105.

119. Points of Light Foundation, The Corporate Volunteer Program as a Strategic Resource: The Link Grows Stronger, available at http://www.pointsoflight.org/networks/business/; Mary Scott and Howard Rothman, Companies with a Conscience (1992); Jennifer Mullen, "Performance-Based Corporate Philanthropy: How 'Giving Smart' Can Further Corporate Goals," 42 Public Relations Quarterly 42, 44–48 (1997); Francoise L. Simon, "Global Corporate Philanthropy: A Strategic Framework," 12 International Marketing Review 20 (1995); Smith, "New Corporate Philanthropy," 108–11.

120. Ostergard, "Should Corporations Be Praised," 45; Timothy S. Mescon and Donn T. Tilson, "Corporate Philanthropy: A Strategic Approach to the Bottom Line," 29 California Management 49, 51–58 (1987); Conference Board, Corporate Contributions; Mullen, "Performance-Based Corporate Philanthropy"; Roper Starch Worldwide and Cone/Coughlin Communications, Cone/Roper Study; Cause Related Trends Report: The Evolution of Cause Branding (1999).

121. William J. Holstein, "The Snowball Effect of Volunteer Work," New York Times, November 21, 2004, E12; Bill Shaw and Frederick R. Post, "A Moral Basis for Corporate Philanthropy," 12 Journal of Business Ethics 745 (1993).

122. James W. Harvey and Kevin F. McCrohan, "Changing Conditions for Fund Rais-

ing and Philanthropy," in Critical Issues in American Philanthropy 59 (Jon V. Til and Assoc., eds., 1990); Brudney and Ferrell, "Corporate Charitable Giving," 1194; Stephen Garone, The Link Between Corporate Citizenship and Financial Performance 12 (Research Report No. 1234-99-RR, Conference Board, 1999); Nancy L. Knauer, "The Paradox of Corporate Giving: Tax Expenditures, the Nature of the Corporation, and the Social Construction of Charity," 44 DePaul Law Review 1, 57–60 (1994).

123.   Jennifer Mullen, "Performance-Based Corporate Philanthropy," 42 Public Relations Quarterly 42 1997; John A. Yankey, "Corporate Support of Nonprofit Organizations: Partnerships Across the Sectors," in Corporate Philanthropy at the Crossroads 7, 15 (Dwight F. Burlingame and Dennis R. Young, eds., 1996); Caudron, "Volunteerism," 14–18; Conference Board, Corporate Volunteer Programs, 15.

124.   Barbara R. Bartkus, Sara A. Morris, and Bruce Seifert, "Governance and Corporate Philanthropy: Restraining Robin Hood?," 41 Business and Society 319 (2002); Michelle Sinclair and Joseph Galaskiewicz, "Corporate Non Profit Partnerships: Varieties and Covariates," 41 New York Law School Law Review 1059, 1060 (1997); Nell Minow, "Corporate Charity: An Oxymoron?," 54 Business Lawyer 997, 999 (1999); Knauer, "Paradox of Corporate Giving," 83–85.

125.   "Caring in the Community," Management Today, March 1995, 19–20; Garone, Link Between Corporate Citizenship and Financial Performance, 8; Roper Starch Worldwide and Cone/Coughlin Communications, Cone/Roper Study; Yankey, "Corporate Support," 13.

126.   For employee loyalty and morale, see Caudron, "Volunteerism," 14; Smith, "New Corporate Philanthropy," 111; Bartkus, Morris, and Seifert, "Governance and Corporate Philanthropy"; Conference Board, Corporate Volunteer Programs, 20, 21; Garone, Link Between Corporate Citizenship and Financial Performance, 11. For performance, see Smith, "New Corporate Philanthropy"; Jan Larson, "Sweet Charity," Marketing Tools Magazine, May 1995, 69; Conference Board, Corporate Volunteer Programs.

127.   Brudney and Ferrell, "Corporate Charitable Giving." For discussion of the need for better research, see Mullen, "Performance-Based Corporate Philanthropy"; Garone, Link Between Corporate Citizenship and Financial Performance, 3.

128.   Michael Useem, The Inner Circle of Large Corporations and the Rise of Business Political Activity in the United States and the United Kingdom 121–26 (1984); Usha C. V. Haley, "Corporate Contributions as Managerial Masques: Reframing Corporate Contributions as Strategies to Influence Society," 28 Journal Management Studies 485, 494 (1991); Mary Lyn Stoll, "The Ethics of Marketing Good Corporate Conduct," 41 Journal of Business Ethics 121, 124 (2002); Neil J. Mitchell, The Generous Corporation: A Political Analysis of Economic Power (1989).

129.   Knauer, "Paradox of Corporate Giving," 55–97; Joseph Galaskiewwicz, "Corporate Contributions to Charity: Nothing More Than a Marketing Strategy?," in Philanthropic Giving: Studies in Varieties and Goals 246–52 (Richard Magat, ed., 1989).

130.   Donna J. Wood, Kimberley S. Davenport, Laquita C. Blockson, and Harry J. Van Buren III, "Corporate Involvement in Community Economic Development," 41 Business and Society 208, 222 (June 2002).

131.   Roper Starch Worldwide and Cone/Coughlin Communications, Cone/Roper Study.

132.   Bartkus, Morris, and Seifert, "Governance and Corporate Philanthropy."

133. William Damon, The Moral Advantage, 133–40 (2004); http://www.goodworkproject.org.

134. For discussion of some of these mechanisms, see Bartkus, Morris, and Seifert, "Governance and Corporate Philanthropy"; Minow, "Corporate Charity," 1005. For sample guidelines, see Points of Light Foundation, Principles of Excellence in Community Services: A Plan to Act (1992).

135. Mark Feinberg, "Starving for Good PR: Corporations Force-Feed the Poor," Business and Society Review, Summer 1989, 36. For other examples, see Knauer, "Paradox of Corporate Giving," 54–55.

136. For the role of earlier scandals in promoting ethics courses, see Lynnley Browning, "MBA Programs Now Screen for Integrity, Too," New York Times, September 15, 2002, B4. For the role of the organization that was formally titled the "American Assembly of Collegiate Schools of Business," see Wood et al., "Corporate Involvement," 226. See generally Edwin M. Epstein, "Business Ethics and Corporate Social Policy: Reflections on an Intellectual Journey, 1964–1996," 37 Business and Society 7 (1996).

137. The following business ethics textbooks were evaluated. Those that refer to community service have the percentage of pages covering the topic indicated in parentheses; only four texts include such references. Ronald R. Sims, Teaching Business Ethics for Effective Learning (2002); Leo V. Ryan et al., eds., Business Students Focus on Ethics, vol. 8 (2000); John R. Boatright, Ethics and the Conduct of Business (3d ed. 2000); Norman E. Bowie, Business Ethics: A Kantian Perspective (1999); Thomas Donaldson and Thomas W. Dunfee, Ties That Bind: A Social Contracts Approach to Business Ethics (1999) (0.04%); Rogene A. Buchholz and Sandra B. Rosenthal, Business Ethics: The Pragmatic Path Beyond Principles to Process (1998) (0.005%); Frederick Bruce Bird, The Muted Conscience: Moral Silence and the Practice of Ethics in Business (1996); Ken Smith and Phil Johnson, eds., Business Ethics and Business Behavior (1996) (0.003%); Thomas J. Donaldson and R. Edward Freeman, eds., Business as a Humanity (1994); James B. Wilbur, The Moral Foundation of Business Practice (1992); Edward Freeman, ed., Business Ethics: The State of the Art (1991); Gerald F. Cavanagh, American Business Values (1990); Clarence C. Walton, ed., Enriching Business Ethics (1990) (0.003%).

138. Institute of Business Ethics, available at http://www.ibe.org.uk.

139. Wood et al., "Corporate Involvement," 212.

140. Mahendra R. Gujarathi and Ralph J. McQuade, "Service Learning in Business Schools: A Case Study in an Intermediate Accounting Course," 77 Journal of Education for Business 144, 145 (January/February 2002); Bruce Macfarlane and Laura J. Spence, "Redefining the Scholarship of Business Ethics: An Editorial," 48 Journal of Business Ethics 1 (2003). See generally Timothy K. Stanton, "The Experience of Faculty Participants in an Instructional Development Seminar on Service-Learning," 1 Michigan Journal of Community Service Learning 7 (1994).

141. Macfarlane and Spence, "Redefining the Scholarship," 2; Thomas A. Kolenka, Gayle Porter, Walt Wheatley, and Marvelle Colby, "A Critique of Service Learning Projects in Management Education: Pedagogical Foundations, Barriers, and Guidelines," 15 Journal of Business Ethics 133, 137–38 (1996); Ann M. McCarthy and Mary L. Tucker, "Student Attitudes Toward Service-Learning: Implications for Implementation," 33 Journal of Management Education 554, 555 (1999).

142. Lyman W. Porter and Lawrence E. McKibben, Management Education and Development: Drift or Thrust into the 21st Century? 64 (1988).

143. Porter and McKibben, Management Education, 317; Edward Ziotkowski, "Opportunity for All: Linking Service-Learning and Business Education," 15 Journal of Business Ethics 1, 12 (1996).

144. McCarthy and Tucker, "Student Attitudes," 554; Kolenka et al., "Critique of Service Learning Projects," 138; John Kohls, "Student Experiences with Service Learning in a Business Ethics Course," 15 Journal of Business Ethics 45, 55 (1996).

145. "Stanford's Public-Management Program Emphasizes Social Responsibility," Chronicle of Philanthropy, available at http://philanthropy.com/free/articles/v16/i06/06002101.htm; Steven B. Kaufman, "The Talk of Academe—Stanford's Conscience," World Business, January/February 1996, 48.

146. "A Growing Presence," Harvard Business School, available at http://www.hbs.edu/socialenterprise/whatis.html; "What Is Social Enterprise at Harvard Business School?," Harvard Business School, available at http://www.hbs.edu/socialenterprise/whatis.html.

147. John Angelidis, Igor Tomic, and Nabil A. Ibrahim, "Service-Learning Projects Enhance Student Learning in Strategic Management Courses," Review of Business, Spring 2004, 32 (2004); Debbie Easterling and Fredrica Rudell, "Rationale, Benefits, and Methods of Service-Learning in Marketing Education," 73 Journal of Education for Business 58 (1997); Susan Hayes Godar, "Live Cases: Service-Learning Consulting Projects in Business Courses," 7 Michigan Journal of Community Service Learning 126 (2000); Wood et al., "Corporate Involvement." See generally Paul C. Godfrey, "Service-Learning and Management Education: A Call to Action," 8 Journal of Management Inquiry 363, 367 (1999).

148. Kohls, "Student Experiences," 47; Gujarathi and McQuade, "Service Learning," 146; Association to Advance College Schools of Business International, Eligibility Procedures and Accreditation Standards for Business Accreditation, Section 3: Participants' Standards 53 (revised January 1, 2004).

149. Kolenka et al., "Critique of Service Learning Projects," 134; Kohls, "Student Experiences," 52; Godfrey, "Service-Learning," 367; McCarthy and Tucker, "Student Attitudes," 555.

150. See Kolenka et al., "A Critique of Service Learning Projects," 140; McCarthy and Tucker, "Student Attitudes," 567–68; Wood et al., "Corporate Involvement," 228–30; Godar, "Live Cases," 131–32.

151. Compare the service rates noted in the text accompanying notes 24–26 in this chapter with notes 91–98 in Chapter 1.

CHAPTER FIVE

1. Mauro Cappelletti, James Gordley, and Earl Johnson, Toward Equal Justice: A Comparative Study of Legal Aid in Modern Societies 12 (1975); James A. Brundage, "Legal Aid for the Poor and the Professionalization of Law in the Middle Ages," 9 Journal of Legal History 169 (1988).

2. See Chapter 2; Cappelletti, Gordley, and Johnson, Toward Equal Justice, 12–14;

Michael Millemann, "Mandatory Pro Bono in Civil Cases: A Partial Answer to the Right Question," 49 Maryland Law Review 18, 75 (1990).

3. David Shapiro, "The Enigma of the Lawyer's Duty to Serve," 55 New York University Law Review 755, 786 (1980).

4. Cappelletti, Gordley, and Johnson, Toward Equal Justice, 19–24; League of Nations, Legal Aid for the Poor (1927).

5. Cappelletti, Gordley, and Johnson, Toward Equal Justice, 24–27 and 26 n. 81, p. 26; Report of the Committee on Legal Aid and Advice in England and Wales 45 (1945); Brian Abel-Smith and Robert Stevens, Lawyers and the Courts: A Sociological Study of the English Legal System 1750–1965, 136–64 (1967); Francis Regan, "Why Do Legal Aid Services Vary Between Societies? Re-examining the Impact of Welfare States and Legal Families," in The Transformation of Legal Aid: Comparative and Historical Studies 179–83 (Francis Regan et al., eds., 1999).

6. Abel-Smith and Stevens, Lawyers and the Courts, 136–64; Regan, "Why Do Legal Aid Services Vary," 179.

7. Regan, "Why Do Legal Aid Services Vary," 187; Francis Frances Regan and Aneurin Thomas, "Can Community Clinics Survive? A Comparative Study of Law Centres in Australia, Ontario, and England," in Regan et al., Transformation of Legal Aid 69, 68–70.

8. Committee of Ministers of the Council of Europe, Resolution (78) 8 on Legal Aid and Advice and Explanatory Memorandum 5–7 (1978). See generally Earl Johnson Jr., "Right to Counsel in Civil Cases: An International Perspective," 19 Loyola of Los Angeles Law Review 341, 352 (1985).

9. Mauro Cappelletti and Bryant Garth, "General Report," in Access to Justice: A World Survey (Mauro Cappelletti and Bryant Garth, eds., 1978); Deborah L. Rhode, "In the Interests of Justice: A Comparative Perspective on Access to Legal Services and Accountability of the Legal Profession," 56 Current Problems 93 (2003); Earl Johnson Jr., "Equal Access to Justice: Comparing Access to Justice in the United States and Other Industrial Democracies," 24 Fordham International Law Journal 183, 195 (2000); W. Kent Davis, The International View of Attorney Fees in Civil Suits: Why Is the United States the 'Odd Man Out' in How It Pays Its Lawyers?," 16 Arizona Journal of International and Comparative Law 361, 388 (1999); David Crerar, "A Cross-Jurisdictional Study of Legal Aid: Governance, Coverage, Eligibility, Financing, and Delivery in Canada, England and Wales, New Zealand, and the United States," 3 Report on the Ontario Legal Aid Review, A Blueprint for Publicly Funded Legal Services 1071 (1997).

10. Johnson, "Equal Access," 896; Rhode, "In the Interests of Justice," 103.

11. Francis Regan, "How and Why Pro Bono Is Flourishing: A Comparison of Recent Developments in Sweden and China," 19 Law in Context 148, 154 (2001); Victoria Rivkin, "Foreign Lawyers Seek Answers in New York to Pro Bono Woes," New York Law Journal, July 26, 1999, 1.

12. Deborah L. Rhode, Access to Justice (2004); Robert A. Kagan, Adversarial Legalism: The American Way of Law (2001).

13. Cappelletti and Garth, "General Report."

14. Deborah L. Rhode, Access to Justice; Deborah L. Rhode, In the Interests of Justice: Reforming the Legal Profession 136–37 (2000). See Mary C. Daly, "A Comparative Perspective on the Future of Multidisciplinary Partnerships in the United States, France,

Germany, and the United Kingdom after the Disintegration of Andersen Legal," 80 Washington University Law Quarterly 589, 627–31 (2002).

15. Thomas Burke, Lawyers, Lawsuits, and Legal Rights 7, 179 (2000); Kagan, Adversarial Legalism, 3–9, 11–16.

16. Burke, Lawyers, Lawsuits, 7, 179; Kagan, Adversarial Legalism, 46–58. For the relative scarcity of public interest legal organizations outside the United States, see Mary C. Daly, "The Structure of Legal Education and the Legal Profession: Multidisciplinary Practice, Competition, and Globalization," 52 Journal of Legal Education 489 (2002).

17. Scott L. Cummings, "The Politics of Pro Bono," 52 U.C.L.A. Law Review 1, 96–97 (2004); Regan and Thomas, "Can Community Clinics Survive?," 74–79; Regan, "Why Do Legal Aid Services Vary," 185–91.

18. Regan, "Why Do Legal Aid Services Vary," 188; Anne Owers, "Public Provision of Legal Services in the United Kingdom: A New Dawn?," 24 Fordham International Law Journal 143, 145–46 (2000).

19. Canadian Bar Association, The Legal Aid Crisis: Time for Action (2000).

20. Canadian Bar Association, Legal Aid Crisis, 45–48; Lisa Addario for the [Canadian] National Association of Women and the Law, Getting a Foot in the Door: Women Civil Legal Aid and Access to Justice (1998).

21. Regan, "Why Do Legal Aid Services Vary," 191–92; Jill Anderson and Gordon Renouf, "Legal Services 'For the Public Good,'" 28 Alternative Law Journal 13, 16 n. 18 (2003).

22. Jean-Luc Bédos, "Droits d'Urgence: Access of Citizens to Legal Information in France," 24 Fordham International Law Journal S1 (2000).

23. Cummings, "Politics of Pro Bono"; Terry Carter, "Exporting Compassion," ABA Journal, September 2002, 24; Nathan Koppol, "American Export," American Lawyer, September 2003, 92; Andrew Boon and Avis Whyte, Something for Nothing: The Provision of Legal Services Pro Bono Publico (2001).

24. Nathan Koppel, "The Globalization of Pro Bono Work," Legal Times, September 22, 2003, 18 (quoting Bédos).

25. Koppol, "American Export," 92.

26. Koppol, "American Export," 92; William J. Dean, "Pro Bono Conference in Chile," New York Law Journal, January 6, 2003, 3.

27. Koppol, "American Export," 92; Adrienne Sanders, "Pro Bono Goes Global," Recorder (San Francisco), May 13, 2004, 1; correspondence with Neta Ziv, University of Tel Aviv, August 12, 2004; Neta Ziv, "Combining Professionalism, Nation Building, and Public Service: The Professional Project of the Israeli Bar 1928–2002," 71 Fordham Law Review 1181 (2003).

28. Andrew Boon and Robert Abbey, "Moral Agendas? Pro Bono Publico in Large Law Firms in the United Kingdom," 60 Modern Law Review 630 (1997).

29. Andrew Boon and Abis Whyte, "'Charity and Beating Begins at Home': The Aetiology of the New Culture of Pro Bono Publico," Legal Ethics, Winter 1999, 169, 185.

30. Andrew Boon and Jennifer Levin, The Ethics and Conduct of Lawyers in England and Wales 234 (1999).

31. Joshua Rozenberg, "Why More of Our Leading Lawyers Are Doing It for Nothing," Daily Telegraph (London), June 5, 2003, 17.

32. Lisa Webley, "Pro Bono and Young Solicitors: Views from the Front Line," 3 Legal Ethics 152, 152–68 (2000).

33. The Law Society, "Fact Sheet 5: Changing Patterns of Legal Work Undertaken by Solicitors" (November 4, 2000), available at http://www.library.lawsociety.org.uk (citing Research and Policy Planning Unit Panel Study of Solicitors' Firms [1997]).

34. Webley, "Pro Bono and Young Solicitors," 162–63.

35. Webley, "Pro Bono and Young Solicitors," 158–61.

36. Webley, "Pro Bono and Young Solicitors," 168. See also Lisa Webley, "Comment: Pro Bono and the Young Profession: A View from England and Wales," 19 Law and Context 45, 49 (2001).

37. Boon and Abbey, "Moral Agendas," 640–52; Boon and Whyte, "Something for Nothing," 9–11.

38. Boon and Abbey, "Moral Agendas," 634; see also Boon and Levin, Ethics and Conduct, 235–36.

39. Boon and Abbey, "Moral Agendas," 634.

40. John Malpas, "Law Society Fails to Score on Pro Bono Target," Times (London), October 24, 2000.

41. Solicitors' Pro Bono Group Web site, available at http://www.probonogroup. org.uk/spbg/history.htm; Boon and Levin, Ethics and Conduct 240 (1996).

42. Boon and Levin, Ethics and Conduct, 240–41.

43. Bob Sherwood, "Caring Lawyers and the Case for Pro Bono Work," Financial Times, December 22, 2003, 12.

44. Sherwood, "Caring Lawyers," 12; Boon and Abbey, "Moral Agendas," 640.

45. "Clients Put Pressure on Firms to Undertake Pro Bono Work," Lawyer, March 15, 2004.

46. Boon and Levin, Ethics and Conduct, 152.

47. Boon and Levin, Ethics and Conduct, 152.

48. Boon and Levin, Ethics and Conduct, 156.

49. Boon and Levin, Ethics and Conduct, 156–57.

50. Lord Chancellor's Advisory Committee on Legal Education and Conduct, First Report on Legal Education and Training, 54 (1996), available at http://www.ukcle.ac.uk/resources/aclec.pdf; Frances Gibb, "Why Law for Free Is Not so Far-Fetched," Times (London), June 10, 2003.

51. Sara Browne, Solicitors' Pro Bono Group, "A Survey of Pro Bono at Law Schools and Universities," 3 (2000), available at http://www.students.probonogroup.org.uk/files/pro%20bono%20paper.pdf.

52. Solicitors' Pro Bono Group, Pro Bono Student Guide 2001/02, 12–13 (2001), available at http://www.students.probonogroup.org.uk/files/student%20guide.pdf; see also Solicitors' Pro Bono Group, Student Challenge Web site, available at http://www. students. probonogroup.org.uk/challenge/index.htm.

53. Augustina Akoto and Tobie Whitman, "Solicitors' Pro Bono Group: A Survey of Pro Bono at Law Schools and Universities," available at http://www.students.probonogroup. org.uk/files/Law%20Students%20and%20Paro%20Bono%20at%20University.pdf; Richard Grimes, "Law Schools and Pro Bono Work: The Public Service and Educational Potential—A Paper Presented to the Attorney General's Pro Bono Committee in February 2003" (2003), available at http://www.ukcle.ac.uk/resources/clinic.html.

54. Akoto and Whitman, "Solicitors' Pro Bono Group," 14–15.

55. Browne, "Survey," 25.

56. Akoto and Whitman, "Solicitors' Pro Bono Group," 19.

57. Akoto and Whitman, "Solicitors' Pro Bono Group," 18.

58. Akoto and Whitman, "Solicitors' Pro Bono Group," 5.

59. Akoto and Whitman, "Solicitors' Pro Bono Group," 5.

60. Akoto and Whitman, "Solicitors' Pro Bono Group," 12.

61. For service learning at the undergraduate level, see Chapter 3. For service learning in professional and business schools, see Chapter 4. For pro bono programs in law schools, see Chapter 6.

62. Christopher Arup, "Pro Bono in the Post-Professional Spectrum of Legal Services," 19 Law in Context 190, 198 (2001).

63. Mark Richardson and Steven Reynolds, "The Shrinking Purse: Civil Legal Aid in New South Wales, Australia," 5 Maryland Journal Contemporary Legal Issues, 349, 362 (1994).

64. John Lynch, "Early Australian Statutory Legal Aid Schemes and the Legal Profession," 19 Law and Context 138 (2001).

65. Richardson and Reynolds, "Shrinking Purse," 363.

66. Richardson and Reynolds, "Shrinking Purse," 365; Arup, "Pro Bono," 207.

67. Richardson and Reynolds, "Shrinking Purse," 366.

68. Richardson and Reynolds, "Shrinking Purse," 363.

69. Richardson and Reynolds, "Shrinking Purse," 363.

70. Rivkin, "Foreign Lawyers Seek Answers," 1; see also Public Interest Law Clearing House (PILCH) Web site, available at http://www.pilch.org.au/html/default.asp.

71. PILCH Annual Report 2001–2002 6 (2003), available at http://www.pilch.org.au/html/getFile.asp?/table=tbl_TCA Article Files&Field=image&id=80.

72. See [Australian] National Pro Bono Resource Centre, at http://www.national-probono.org.au; "Centering on Pro Bono," 77 Law Institute Journal 88 (2003).

73. Australian Bureau of Statistics, Legal Practices 2001–02, 8667.0, at 12 (2003).

74. Australian Bureau of Statistics, Legal Practices 2001–02, 12.

75. David Weisbrot, "Introduction to Report of the National Pro Bono Task Force and Recommended Action Plan," 19 Law in Context 214, 221 (2001).

76. Australian Bureau of Statistics, Legal Practices 2001–02, 12.

77. National Pro Bono Resource Centre, Submission to the Senate Legal and Constitutional References Committee, Inquiry into Legal Aid and Access to Justice 6 (October 2003), available at http://esvc000464.wic006u.server-web.com/publications/senateinquiry.pdf.

78. National Pro Bono Resource Centre, Submission, 6–9; see generally Elisabeth Wentworth, "Barriers to Pro Bono: Commercial Conflicts of Interest Reconsidered," 19 Law in Context 166 (2001).

79. National Pro Bono Resource Centre, Submission, 6–9; Marcus Priest, "Law Firms Wary About Pro Bono Work," Australian Financial Review, March 11, 2004, 3.

80. National Pro Bono Resource Centre, Submission, 9–10; Kath Walters, "Pro Bono Publico," Business Review Weekly, May 1, 2003.

81. "Equal Shares," 78 Law Institute Journal 84 (January 2004).

82. "Just Partners," 78 Law Institute Journal 93 (December 2003); "Government Releases Pro Bono Guidelines," 78 Law Institute Journal 22 (May 2003).

83. National Pro Bono Task Force, "Recommended Action Plan," 19 Law in Context 228, 232–34.

84. Weisbrot, "Introduction," 225.

85. Weisbrot, "Introduction," 226.

86. Arup, "Pro Bono," 190, 191.

87. Chris Dale, "The Blessings of Pro Bono," 78 Law Institute Journal 4 (April 1, 2004); "Under New Management," 78 Law Institute Journal 87 (March 1, 2004).

88. Les A. McCrimmon, "Law School Clinics Plus," 19 Law in Context 92, 94 (2001); Kingsford Legal Center, Guide to Clinical Legal Education (2000).

89. National Pro Bono Task Force, "Recommended Action Plan," 244.

90. Irene Styles and Archie Zariski, "Law Clinics and the Promotion of Public Interest Lawyering," 19 Law in Context 65 (2001).

91. Australian Law Reform Commission, Managing Justice: A Review of the Civil Justice System, Report No. 89 #5.20 (2000).

92. National Pro Bono Task Force, "Recommended Action Plan," 245–46.

93. "Under New Management," 87; "Heavy Medal," 78 Law Institute Journal 82 (April 2004); "Public Exposure," 77 Law Institute Journal 87 (August 2003).

94. Styles and Zariski, "Law Clinics," 65, 86.

95. Derk Bodde and Clarence Morris, Law in Imperial China 416–17 (1967).

96. Randall Peerenboom, China's Long March Toward Rule of Law 345 (2002); Jane J. Heller, "China's New Foreign Law Firm Regulations: A Step in the Wrong Direction," 12 Pacific Rim Law and Policy Journal 751, 754 (2003).

97. Benjamin L. Liebman, "Legal Aid and Public Interest Law in China," 34 Texas International Law Journal 211, 214–15 (1999).

98. Lawyers' Committee for Human Rights, Lawyers in China, 13–17; Randall Peerenboom, Lawyers in China: Obstacles to Independence and the Defense of Rights 12–13 (1998).

99. Lawyers' Committee for Human Rights, Lawyers in China, 13–14; Timothy A. Gelatt, "Lawyers in China: The Past Decade and Beyond," 23 New York University Journal of International Law and Policy 751, 752 (1991); Liebman, "Legal Aid," 216; Heller, "China's New Foreign Law Firm Regulations," 754.

100. Liebman, "Legal Aid," 216.

101. Liebman, "Legal Aid," 216.

102. Lawyers' Committee for Human Rights, Lawyers in China, 15; Jerome A. Cohen, The Criminal Process in the People's Republic of China, 1949–63 (1968).

103. Lawyers' Committee for Human Rights, Lawyers in China, 14–15; Peerenboom, Lawyers in China, 347; Laszlo Ladany, Law and Legality in China (1992).

104. Heller, "China's New Foreign Law Firm Regulations"; Stanley Lubman, "Bird in a Cage: Chinese Law Reform After Twenty Years," 20 Northwestern Journal of International Law and Business 383, 405–6 (2000).

105. Liebman, "Legal Aid," 218.

106. Liebman, "Legal Aid," 218.

107. Liebman, "Legal Aid," 219.

108. Gelatt, "Lawyers in China," 797.

109. Regan, "How and Why Pro Bono Is Flourishing," 148, 154.

110. Heller, "China's New Foreign Law Firm Regulations," 756.

111. Heller, "China's New Foreign Law Firm Regulations," 756.

112. Regan, "How and Why Pro Bono Is Flourishing" 155 (quoting Beijing, Legal Aid Centre, Ministry of Justice, "Basic Elements of Legal Aid System with Chinese Characteristics" [1999]).

113. Regan, "How and Why Pro Bono Is Flourishing," 154.

114. Lawyers' Law of the People's Republic of China, effective January 1, 1997.

115. Lawyers' Professional Morality and Professional Discipline Standards, in Handbook on the Use of China's Lawyers' Law, vol. 1, 499 (Tong Baogui, ed., 1996).

116. Liebman, "Legal Aid," 242–43; Regan, "How and Why Pro Bono Is Flourishing," 154. Eligible matters include family support, workplace injuries, and compensation from the state.

117. Liebman, "Legal Aid," 262.

118. Liebman, "Legal Aid," 230; Lawyers' Committee for Human Rights, Lawyers in China, 87.

119. Liebman, "Legal Aid," 231, 262.

120. Liebman, "Legal Aid," 266.

121. Regan, "How and Why Pro Bono Is Flourishing," 156–57.

122. Liebman, "Legal Aid," 263.

123. Liebman, "Legal Aid," 263.

124. Lawyers' Committee for Human Rights, Lawyers in China, 90.

125. Liebman, "Legal Aid," 263–64.

126. Liebman, "Legal Aid," 230.

127. Liebman, "Legal Aid," 276.

128. Liebman, "Legal Aid," 276.

129. Liebman, "Legal Aid," 277; Lawyers' Committee for Human Rights, Lawyers in China.

130. Liebman, "Legal Aid," 237–38.

131. Regan, "How and Why Pro Bono Is Flourishing"; Liebman, "Legal Aid," 257.

132. Liebman, "Legal Aid."

133. Liebman, "Legal Aid," 281; Lawyers' Committee for Human Rights, Lawyers in China, 52, 83–84.

134. Lawyers' Law of the People's Republic of China, Article 8.

135. Lawyers' Committee for Human Rights, Lawyers in China, 64–65.

136. Liebman, "Legal Aid," 233.

137. Liebman, "Legal Aid," 234.

138. Liebman, "Legal Aid," 236–37.

139. Liebman, "Legal Aid," 235.

140. For limitations on student practice and clinics, see Liebman, "Legal Aid," 236–37. For part-time law work, see Gelatt, "Lawyers in China," 767.

141. Lawyers' Committee for Human Rights, Lawyers in China, 52, 83–94.

142. Liebman, "Legal Aid," 267–68 (describing constraints on outside funds).

143. For Canada, see Tracey Tyler, "Crown Lawyers to Provide Legal Services for Free: Attorney General Creating Task Force, Wants to Improve Access to Justice," Toronto Star, May 7, 2004, A17. For Australia, see "Just Partners," 93; "Government Releases Pro Bono Guidelines," 22; and text accompanying notes 80 and 81. For the United States, see Chapter 1.

CHAPTER SIX

1. In 1987, Tulane Law School imposed the first requirement, which provided that students must perform 20 hours of law-related public service in their third year of law

school. See the discussion in Chapter 1 and Cynthia F. Adcock and Alison M. Keegan, A Handbook on Law School Pro Bono Programs: The Association of American Law Schools Pro Bono Project, 7 (2001); John Kramer, "Mandatory Pro Bono at Tulane Law School," in "Pro Bono at Law Schools, New Solutions to Old Problems," 7 NAPIL Connection (1990 supplement). By the end of 1991, several other schools, including the University of Pennsylvania School of Law, had instituted similar pro bono programs; Pennsylvania requires 70 hours of law-related service (Adcock and Keegan, Handbook, 7, 9).

2. Fordham Law School's Public Interest Resource Center has assisted a wide variety of student-run organizations providing pro bono services. See Deborah L. Rhode, "Cultures of Commitment: Pro Bono for Lawyers and Law Students," 67 Fordham Law Review 2415, 2437 (1999).

3. According to Cynthia Adcock, neither Chicago nor Northwestern had a formal pro bono program or pro bono coordinator, and neither had a member in the Association of American Law School (AALS) Section of Pro Bono and Public Service Opportunities. E-mail from Cynthia Adcock, Pro Bono Project Director, AALS (June 5, 2001).

4. In order to classify firms, research assistants calculated the average hours of pro bono work for the lawyers at the firms for the eight-year period. The firms were then ranked in descending order from the highest number of pro bono hours to the lowest number of pro bono hours and divided into three groups of contributors: high (50 hours or more), middle (between 35 and 50 hours), and low (fewer than 35 hours). Due to insufficient responses in each category, the ranking system dropped out of the analysis and the firms that completed the questionnaire were simply included in the overall analysis.

5. The surveys were mailed in three phases, beginning in spring 2001. The first two mailings sent a hard copy of the survey and an address to permit an online response. The third mailing sent only an electronic version. The entire sample received a questionnaire, a cover letter explaining the purposes of the survey, and a return stamped envelope. Participants could either fill out the survey by hand and mail it back or fill out the survey online. To ensure anonymity, to limit subsequent mailings to those who did not respond to earlier mailings, and to sort the results into the appropriate data sets, every survey had a code. The surveys that were returned by mail or online were only identifiable by code.

6. Catalyst, Women in Law: Making the Case (2001).

7. Of responding lawyers, 49% were women, 71% identified themselves as white, 6% as African American, 6% as Asian American, and 5% as Hispanic. Women constituted 38% of the targeted classes and 49% of the respondents. See American Bar Association (ABA) Official American Bar Association Guide to Approved Law Schools (1993 and 1997 eds.). At the time of the survey, women accounted for about 30% of the profession, and minorities accounted for about 10%. ABA, The Unfinished Agenda: Women and the Legal Profession 14 (report prepared by Deborah L. Rhode, 2001); Elizabeth Chambliss, Miles to Go 2000: Progress of Minorities in the Legal Profession (ABA Commission on Racial and Ethnic Diversity in the Profession, 2000).

8. Of the remainder, 15% were not currently practicing law, 12% were in solo practice, 11% were in government, and 7% were in-house corporate counsel. Because the questionnaire did not specifically list academia or the judiciary as response categories, some of those who classified themselves as not currently practicing law may be in those fields. In terms of employment status, 42% were associates, 18% were partners (15% nonequity,

3% equity), and 6% were staff attorneys. For the profession as a whole at the time of the survey, about 40% of lawyers in private practice were in firms, and a third were in solo practice. Of the lawyers in firms, about a third were associates. The remainder were either primarily partners or lawyers in firms with no associates. Of the lawyers not in private practice, about 10% were in government, and the remainder were in the judiciary (3%), academia (1%), and legal aid, public defender, or public interest offices (1%). Clara N. Carson, The Lawyer Statistical Report: The U.S. Legal Profession in 1995, 7, 9 (1999).

9. About a quarter of the sample (25%) reported an annual income below $70,000; a fifth of the sample (22%) between $70,000 and $150,000; a fifth (19%) between $150,000 and $200,000; and about one-sixth (14%) above $200,000. In terms of workload, 14% billed under 1800 hours, 20% billed between 1800 and 2000 hours, and 16% billed over 2400 hours. The remainder were in organizations that did not calculate billable hours or were not currently practicing law. In the profession generally, associates earned a median of $110,284 in 2001 and partners, $240,311 (2002 Survey of Law Firm Economics 143 [2002]). Associates billed a median of 1849 hours and nonequity partners billed 1756 (2002 Survey of Law Firm Economics, 110).

10. Responses were analyzed in several ways: percentage calculations, regression analysis (the R^2 test), a correlation test (the t-test), and a significance test (the F-test). Schuyler W. Huck, Reading Statistics and Research 585–88 (3d ed. 2000); William N. Venables and Brian D. Ripley, Modern Applied Statistics with S-Plus, 151–54 (3d ed. 1999).

11. Whether or not a regression result is "strong" is determined by the R^2 test. The R^2 statistic, or coefficient of determination, is the percentage of the total response variation explained by the independent variables. In this instance, it reveals how much of the difference in the amount of pro bono work is attributable to, or explained by, those variables. The R^2 coefficient is between 0 and 1, and the farther it lies from zero, the stronger the correlation between the dependent and independent variables. In social science research, a coefficient of 0.5 is considered to be a strong indication of significance. In studies like this one, involving relatively small data sets, 0.3 is considered somewhat significant. The p value falls between 0 and 1; the closer to 0, the more meaningful the results. Any p value 0.25 or less is generally considered suggestive, whereas a p value of 0.05 or less is generally considered highly significant. In the data tabulations here, p values that are greater than 0.25 are viewed as having no statistical significance. Fred L. Ramsey and Daniel W. Schafer, The Statistical Sleuth: A Course in Methods of Data Analysis 44–45 (1997).

In addition, the data were analyzed to determine whether the responses could be considered "applicable" for the entire population of lawyers and law firms that received questionnaires. Because those who responded were not expected to be an unbiased sample, the data were not expected to be applicable to the larger population. However, if certain factors ended up being statistically significant for the larger population, that fact indicated a particularly telling relationship to pro bono work. An F-test was used to determine such significance. In essence, each response category was analyzed through a calculation that took the sample size and variance into account. Whether or not results are "applicable" is determined by looking at the p value of the F-test. The p value is again a number that falls between 0 and 1; the closer the result is to 0, the more meaningful the results. A p value of 0.05 is generally considered "statistically significant," but p values up to 0.25 are still viewed as statistically meaningful. When findings are not applicable to the entire population, it means that the same results would not necessarily be seen in other samples from the same population, let alone the entire group from which the responses were drawn. Nonetheless, findings that cannot be applied to the population as a whole remain of interest because the results may reflect traits that led the respondents to participate in the survey in the first place. In this survey, findings that are not applicable to the population as a whole are still informative, because they indicate the views and characteristics of lawyers who are particularly likely to care about pro bono work.

12. Responses to each question were analyzed individually, rather than in multivariate format, because the number of answers that participants could select produced too much information for meaningful analysis. Initially, regression models for the individual questions were run against several different pro bono hour calculations: pro bono work performed in the last year; the typical number of pro bono hours performed per year; the number of hours of pro bono work performed for the poor in the last year; and the typical number of pro bono hours performed for the poor per year. In each case, the same patterns emerged because individuals almost never changed their answers for the different "pro bono hours" questions. It therefore made sense to average the hours and run the regression on the "conglomerate" count. It also was appropriate to analyze each of the data sets independently as well as collectively, because such a process could reveal relationships within individual groups that might not emerge if all of the participants were looked at together.

13. To determine whether a factor has a statistically significant relationship to pro bono work, a t-test was performed on the coefficient, and a p value was assigned based on the coefficient and the number of variables. For discussion of the t-test, see Jacob Cohen and Patricia Cohen, Applied Multiple Regression Correlation Analysis for the Behavioral Sciences 52 (2d ed. 1983); David W. Barnes and John M. Conley, Statistical Evidence in Litigation: Methodology, Procedure and Practice 106–7 (1986).

14. The p values were political commitment ($p = 0.03$) and employer encouragement ($p = 0.12$). Trial experience ($p = 0.23$) had a very weak correlation. The relationships were valid for the population beyond the sample (F-test $= 0.11$).

15. For individual attorney winners, only being female showed a relatively strong correlation ($p = 0.13$). No meaningful conclusions could be drawn concerning the demographic characteristics of those who filled out the questionnaire for firm award winners, not only because the numbers were small but also because those individuals may not have been the ones responsible for high levels of involvement.

The findings on race contrast with the only other recent empirical survey to date, which explored the career paths of University of Michigan graduates. It found that racial minorities admitted under affirmative action criteria were more likely to make pro bono contributions than white students admitted under standard criteria. Richard O. Lempert, David L. Chambers, and Terry K. Adams, "Michigan's Minority Graduates in Practice: The River Runs Through Law School," 25 Law and Social Inquiry 395, 401, 456 (2000).

16. In describing their motives, attorneys offered reasons such as "personal values," a "desire for public service," a "sense of justice," an "affinity to help the disadvantaged," and a "general commitment to public service [and] liberal ideas." See Matthew Rice, Establishing Empathy: Strategies for Encouraging Pro Bono and Public Interest Lawyering 6 (unpublished student paper, August, 2001, on file with author) (noting that the majority of pro bono award winners wanted to do pro bono or public interest work by the time they entered or completed law school); Jessica Haspel, Dissecting the Public Service Experience: An Analysis of Differential Responses from Private and Public Sector Lawyers

9–10 (unpublished student paper, August 2001, on file with author) (describing social justice commitment of award winners).

17. Representative explanations included "experiences growing up without a lot of money"; family members who fostered an "ethic of public service"; "upbringing—family, church, etc."; and the experience of "living in a small minority community where violations of civil rights . . . occur daily."

18. For discussion of law school experiences, see Chapter 7.

19. Another attorney who found pro bono experiences not "satisfying or rewarding" preferred "charitable activities [that] are non-legal."

20. See American Bar Association Commission on Billable Hours Report 52 (2002), available at http://www.abanet.org/careeercounsel/billlable/toolkit/bhcomplete.pdf. In an American Lawyer survey, only 28% of respondents' firms credited time on pro bono activities toward minimum billable hour requirements. "Commission AmLaw 100 and Law Firm Questionnaires," American Lawyer, August 2002, 52.

21. Far less dissatisfaction was reported in another recent study that followed some 5000 lawyers for 10 years; in that sample, less than a fifth wanted more pro bono opportunities. See Bryant G. Garth, After the J.D. (2004), summarized in 15 Researching Law 1 (Newsletter of the American Bar Research Foundation, Summer 2004).

22. Among individual winners, the most common sources of opportunities after employer committees or coordinators were bar association programs (21%), clients (16%), and supervising attorneys (11%). Among firm winners, more work came from friends (23%) and legal service providers (12%).

CHAPTER SEVEN

1. Cynthia F. Adcock and Alison M. Keegan, A Handbook on Law School Pro Bono Programs: The AALS Pro Bono Project 7 (2001).

2. Data were not collected from firms because those who filled out the questionnaire would not necessarily have personally performed exceptional amounts of pro bono work (unlike individual award winners) and might not have had a law school experience comparable to that of the other graduates represented in the survey.

3. See Chapter 2, discussing surveys at Tulane, Columbia, and Louisville Law Schools; John Kramer, "Mandatory Pro Bono at Tulane Law School," National Association for Public Interest Law, Connection Closeup Newsletter, September 30, 1991, 1–2; Committee on Legal Assistance, "Mandatory Law School Pro Bono Programs: Preparing Students to Meet Their Ethical Obligations," 50 Record 170, 176 (1995); Association of American Law Schools (AALS) Focus Group Interviews, discussed in AALS, Commission on Pro Bono and Public Service Opportunity in Law Schools, Learning to Serve: The Findings and Proposals of the AALS Commission on Pro Bono and Public Service Opportunities in Law Schools (1999).

CHAPTER EIGHT

1. Richard W. Painter, "Rules Lawyers Play By," 76 New York University Law Review 665, 728 (2001).

2. Judith L. Maute, "Pro Bono Publico in Oklahoma: Time for Change," 53 Okla-

homa Law Review 527 (2000) (noting the effects of pro bono amendments in 22 states and the District of Columbia); Florida Bar Standing Committee, Report to the Supreme Court of Florida, 3; American Bar Association (ABA) Standing Committee on Pro Bono and Public Service, State Pro Bono Reporting: A Guide for Bar Leaders and Others Considering Strategies for Expanding Pro Bono, August 1999, available at http://www.abanet.org/legalservices/probono/pbreportingguide.html; Kellie Isbell and Sarah Sawle, "Pro Bono Publico: Voluntary Service and Mandatory Reporting," 15 Georgetown Journal of Legal Ethics 845, 860–61 (2002).

3. For examples, see Lawyers for One America, Bar None: Report to the President of the United States on the Status of People of Color and Pro Bono Services in the Legal Profession 30–31, 45–46 (2000); Elizabeth Chambliss, Miles to Go 2000: Progress of Minorities in the Legal Profession, ix (2004); Bar Association of San Francisco, Goals and Timetables for Minority Hiring and Advancement (2000).

4. Corporate Pro Bono.Org survey available at http://corporateprobono.org.

5. For efforts by the Solicitors' Pro Bono Group in Great Britain, see Chapter 5 and "Clients Put Pressure on Firms to Undertake Pro Bono Work," Lawyer, March 15, 2004.

6. 2001 California Statutes Chapter 880, Section 3 (AB 913) (amending Section 6072 of the California Business and Professions Code, effective January 1, 2003). The minimum number of hours are "equal to the lesser of 30 multiplied by the number of full time attorneys in the firm's offices in the state, with the number of hours prorated on an actual day basis for any contract period of less than a full year or 10% of its contract with the state." If the firm fails to provide the required hours, the factors to be considered in determining its good-faith efforts include the number of hours provided; the firm's efforts to obtain pro bono work; the firm's history of providing pro bono services; and the types of pro bono services provided.

7. Shannon Lafferty, "Santa Clara to Require Pro Bono from Firms," San Francisco Recorder, April 11, 2002, 2.

8. See the discussion of the Victoria government requirement in Chapter 5 and "Government Releases Pro Bono Guidelines," 78 Law Institute Journal 22 (May 2003).

9. "The A List," American Lawyer, September 2003, 84 (basing list on profitability, diversity, associate satisfaction, and pro bono work).

10. For example, Professors Dennis Curtis and Stephen Wizner have offered a course at Yale Law School on Professionalism in the Public Interest that requires students to develop a five-year plan to meet their public service goals after graduation. Students then negotiate with prospective employers willing to accommodate such plans. Stephen Wizner, "Can Law Schools Teach Students to Do Good? Legal Education and the Future of Legal Services for the Poor," 3 New York City Law Review 259 (2000).

11. Lauren Hallinan, "What Judges Can Do to Increase Equal Access to the Courts," Judges Journal, Winter 2001, 6.

12. Susan J. Curry, "Meeting the Need: Minnesota's Collaborative Model to Deliver Law Student Public Service," 28 William Mitchell Law Review 347 (2001).

13. Equal Justice Works, Pro Bono Legal Corps Program, available at http://www.equaljusticeworks.org.

14. See Deborah L. Rhode, "Pro Bono in Times of Crisis: Looking Forward by Looking Back," 31 Fordham Urban Law Journal 1011 (2004); Thomas Adcock, "Terrorist Attack Upstages Legal Services Initiatives but Provides Greater Urgency for It," New York Law

Journal, August 6, 2002, 1; "Record Number of Lawyers Answer the Call to Take on Pro Bono," New York Law Journal, July 11, 2002.

15. David Hechler, "9/11 Response Was Largest Pro Bono Project in History," National Law Journal, July 7, 2004, A1.

16. Russell Engler, "Normalcy After 9/11: Public Service as the Crisis Fades," Fordham Urban Law Journal (2004); Judith L. Maute and Cheryl Lynn Wofford Hill, "Delivery Systems Under Construction," 72 University of Missouri at Kansas City Law Review 377, 391 (2003).

17. "Access to Justice: Does It Exist in Civil Cases? Symposium Transcript," comments of Esther Lardent, 17 Georgetown Journal of Legal Ethics 455, 481 (2004).

18. For examples, see Thomas H. Morsch, "Discovering Transactional Pro Bono," 72 University of Missouri at Kansas City Law Review 423 (2003); Karen Hall, "Corporate Crusaders," American Lawyer, December 2000, 74; Sean Delany, "Biz Law Is Future of Pro Bono Growth," National Law Journal, August 28, 2000, C18; Laurie A. Morin, "Legal Services Attorneys as Partners in Community Economic Development: Creating Wealth for Poor Communities Through Cooperative Economics," 50 University of the District of Columbia Law Review 125, 158 (2000); Janet Spragens and Nina E. Olson, "Tax Clinics: The New Face of Legal Services," ABA Committee on Pro Bono and Public Service, Dialogue Newsletter, Winter 2001, 11–12; Lisa Finnegan, "A Brand New World: Pro Bono Goes Corporate," Washington Lawyer, May/June, 1999, 25; Tatiana Boncompagni, "Rebuilding a Reputation," American Lawyer, December 2002, 85, 86; Laurie A. Morin, "Mapping a Labyrinth to Justice: Lessons and Insights from Innovative Legal Service Delivery Methodologies Implemented in the District of Columbia," 50 University of the District of Columbia Law Review 91 (2000).

19. James Feroli, "When Pro Bono Work Is a Crime: The Government Lawyer and 18 USC §205," ABA Government and Public Sector Lawyers Division Newsletter, Public Lawyer, Winter 2001, 2. For an example, see the description of the United States Department of Justice Pro Bono Program in Lawyers for One America, Bar None, 64–65.

20. Marc Galanter, "'Old and in the Way': The Coming Demographic Transformation of the Legal Profession and Its Implications for the Provision of Legal Services," 1999 Wisconsin Law Review 1081 (2000); Morin, "Mapping a Labyrinth," 91–92.

21. David B. Ball, "Interfaith Legal Services: Taking Stock of a Faith-Based Pro Bono Initiative," 72 University of Missouri at Kansas City Law Review 301 (2003).

22. Beth Slater, "A New Firm Niche: Part-Time Pro Bono," National Law Journal, August 2, 1999, A13.

23. Terry Carter, "Taking Up the Slack," ABA Journal, October 2001, 22 (describing Bay Area programs).

24. Kristin Glen, "Thinking Out of the Bar Exam Box: A Challenge and Proposal for Change," 102 Columbia Law Review 1696 (2002).

25. Glen, "Thinking Out of the Bar Exam Box"; Robert E. McBeth, "Judicial Activism," Judges Journal, Winter 2001, 12. For a critique of bar exams, see Deborah L. Rhode, In the Interests of Justice: Reforming the Legal Profession 150–52 (2000).

26. For examples, see Scott L. Cummings, "The Politics of Pro Bono," 52 U.C.L.A. Law Review 1, 64–68 (2004); probono.net, at http://www.probono.net; Elizabeth Amon, "Corporate Pro Bono Gets Boost: In House Counsel Group Uses Web in Outreach to

Members," National Law Journal, September 11, 2000, A1; Morsch, "Discovering Transactional Pro Bono," 426; Maute and Hill, "Delivery Systems," 421–22.

27. For the problems that arise when such efforts are lacking, see the discussion in Chapters 2 and 6.

28. Hallinan, "What Judges Can Do," 9.

29. Margaret Graham Tebo, "New Approaches to Pro Bono," ABA Journal, December 2001, 24 (discussing rural poor); Scott L. Cummings, "The Politics of Pro Bono," 52 U.C.L.A. Law Review 1, 94 (2004) (describing the challenges of meeting rural needs); Linda F. Smith, "The Potential of Pro Bono," 72 University of Missouri at Kansas City Law Review 452 (2003) (describing practitioners' lack of interest in matters such as public benefits); Deborah L. Rhode, Access to Justice 139 (2004) (describing lack of competent pro bono counsel for death penalty cases).

30. Margaret Graham Tebo, "Full-Service Assistance," ABA Journal, December 2001, 26.

31. Tebo, "Full-Service Assistance," 26.

32. Edgar S. Cahn, "Coproducing Justice: The New Imperative," 5 University of District of Columbia Law Review 105 (2000).

33. Rhode, "Pro Bono in Times of Crisis."

34. ABA Standing Committee on Pro Bono and Public Service, Standards for Programs Providing Civil Pro Bono Legal Services to Persons of Limited Means (1996).

35. Thomas Adcock, "Plan for Statewide Pro Bono System on Drawing Board," New York Law Journal, August 6, 2002, 1 (quoting William J. Dean); Cummings, "Politics of Pro Bono," 143.

36. See A. J. Noble, "Greenberg's Pro Bono Patrol," American Lawyer, March 1999, 20; Erik Cummins, "Novel Proposal Would Privatize Legal Services for Poor," San Francisco Daily Journal, August 22, 2001, 1, 16 (describing proposal for 2% contribution of gross revenues by largest firms to support legal services); Kenneth L. Jacobs, "How to Institutionalize Pro Bono at Your Office," Michigan Bar Journal, January/February 1999, 52, 56 (noting that "[a]ny lawyer can afford $300 a year," which works out to "82 cents per day, far less than most lawyers spend on their daily coffee").

37. William Carlsen, "San Francisco Lawyer Proposes a Tax on Lawyers," San Francisco Chronicle, February 7, 1989, A7 (describing proposal for 6% tax on fees by law firms taking in more than $500,000).

38. Martin Luther King Jr., Strength to Love 24 (1963).

39. Sean Groom, "Courthouse Pro Bono," Washington Lawyer, June, 2004, 21; Crystal Nix Hines, "Without a Lawyer," New York Times, July 31, 2001, C1, C16; Russell Engler, "And Justice for All—Including the Unrepresented Poor: Revisiting the Roles of the Judges, Mediators, and Clerks," 67 Fordham Law Review 1987 (1999); Jona Goldschmidt, "How Are Courts Handling Pro Se Litigants?," 82 Judicature 13, 20–22 (July/August 1998); Robert E. Yegge, "Divorce Litigants Without Lawyers," 28 Family Law Quarterly 407, 413–17 (1994).

40. See Goldschmidt, "How Are Courts Handling Pro Se Litigants?," 20.

41. Rhode, Access to Justice, 83–85.

42. For an example of such an approach, see the description of the Haight Ashbury Free Clinic and Homeless Advocacy Project partnership in Robert Lennan, "The Big Picture," American Lawyer, December 2002, 87–88.

43. For bar prohibitions, see Model Rule 5.4, DR 3-102(A), ABA House of Delegates Resolution 10F (2002). For a critical view of the bar's rejection of reform proposals, see Deborah L. Rhode and Geoffrey Hazard Jr., *Professional Responsibilities and Regulation* 183–88 (2002); Rhode, *Access to Justice*, 91–93.

44. I have discussed this issue at length for the last quarter century. See Rhode, *In the Interests of Justice*, 135–36; Rhode, *Access to Justice*, 87–91; Deborah L. Rhode, "Why the ABA Bothers: A Functional Perspective on Professional Codes," 59 *Texas Law Review* 704–6 (1981); Deborah L. Rhode, "Professionalism in Perspective: Alternative Approaches to the Delivery of Legal Services by Nonlawyers," 22 *New York University Review of Law and Social Change* 706 (1996).

45. See sources cited in Rhode, *In the Interests of Justice*, 135–36; Herbert Kritzer, *Legal Advocacy*, 193–203 (1998). In the one reported survey of consumer satisfaction, non-lawyers rated higher than lawyers. See Rhode, "Delivery of Legal Services," 209, 230–31; Yegge, "Divorce Litigants," 418.

46. For examples of such proposals, see sources cited in Rhode, "Professionalism," 715 n. 57.

47. At the ABA's 2000 midyear meeting, the House of Delegates voted to strengthen enforcement of unauthorized practice prohibitions. Patricia Manson, "Target Unauthorized Practice, ABA Urges," *Chicago Daily Law Bulletin*, February 14, 2000, 1. For a similar state bar recommendation, see "Illinois Lawyers Protect Their Monopoly," HALT Newsletter, Legal Reformer, Fall 2000, 3 (describing Illinois task force on unauthorized practice enforcement); State Bar of Arizona, at http://www.azbar.org (describing recommendations of the consumer protection committee of the Arizona bar to combat non-lawyer practice).

48. Cummings, "Politics of Pro Bono," 149.

49. Cartoon by P. Byrnes, *New Yorker*, January 3, 2005, 29.

50. Findings from the Association of the Bar of the City of New York Survey Report, *Public Service in a Time of Crisis*, quoted in Rhode, "Pro Bono in Times of Crisis," 1021.

Index

Page numbers in *italic* type refer to tables.